ORGANIZATIONAL CHANGE

Organizational change is a reality of 21st-century working life, but what psychological effects does it have on individual workers, and what coping strategies can be used to mediate its impact? In today's turbulent work and career environment, employees are required not only to accept changes as passive recipients, but to proactively initiate changes and demonstrate attitudes, behaviors and skills valued by current employers. As a result, organizational psychologists, both researchers and practitioners, have had to acknowledge and understand the myriad of challenges faced by employees as a result of organizational change.

In this important new book, an international range of prominent scholars examine the key psychological issues around organizational change at the individual level, including:

- health and well-being
- stress and emotional regulation
- performance and leadership
- attitudes and implications for the psychological contract.

Analyzing and presenting the impact of organizational change, and possible coping strategies to successfully manage change, the volume is ideal for students and researchers of work and organizational psychology, business and management and HRM.

Maria Vakola (PhD) is an organizational psychologist and associate professor at the Athens University of Economics and Business, Greece. Maria has published three books, and articles in a number of prestigious academic journals. She teaches undergraduate and postgraduate courses in change management and organizational psychology. She is the co-founder of the International Forum for the Psychology of Organizational Change, and the co-founder of an award winning nonprofit organization called job-pairs.gr which enhances youth employability.

Paraskevas Petrou (PhD) is an assistant professor at the Erasmus University Rotterdam, The Netherlands. He is a member of the European Association of Work and Organizational Psychologists and holds a BPS certificate (Levels A and B) on psychological testing. He has published in several international academic journals on topics including organizational change, self-regulation, job crafting and leisure behavior. He teaches undergraduate and postgraduate courses of organizational psychology.

Current Issues in Work and Organizational Psychology

Series Editor: Arnold B. Bakker

Current Issues in Work and Organizational Psychology is a series of edited books that reflect the state-of-the-art areas of current and emerging interest in the psychological study of employees, workplaces and organizations.

Each volume is tightly focused on a particular topic and consists of seven to ten chapters contributed by international experts. The editors of individual volumes are leading figures in their areas and provide an introductory overview.

Example topics include: digital media at work, work and the family, workaholism, modern job design, positive occupational health and individualised deals.

Organizational Change: Psychological effects and strategies for coping
Edited by Maria Vakola and Paraskevas Petrou

A Day in the Life of a Happy Worker
Edited by Arnold B. Bakker and Kevin Daniels

The Psychology of Digital Media at Work
Edited by Daantje Derks and Arnold B. Bakker

New Frontiers in Work and Family Research
Edited by Joseph G. Grzywacz and Evangelia Demerouti

Time and Work, Volume 1: How time impacts individuals
Edited by Abbie J. Shipp and Yitzhak Fried

Time and Work, Volume 2: How time impacts groups, organizations and methodological choices
Edited by Abbie J. Shipp and Yitzhak Fried

ORGANIZATIONAL CHANGE

Psychological Effects and Strategies for Coping

Edited by
Maria Vakola and Paraskevas Petrou

LONDON AND NEW YORK

First published 2018
by Routledge
2 Park Square, Milton Park, Abingdon, Oxon OX14 4RN

and by Routledge
711 Third Avenue, New York, NY 10017

Routledge is an imprint of the Taylor & Francis Group, an informa business

© 2018 selection and editorial matter, Maria Vakola and Paraskevas Petrou; individual chapters, the contributors

The right of Maria Vakola and Paraskevas Petrou to be identified as the author of the editorial material, and of the authors for their individual chapters, has been asserted in accordance with sections 77 and 78 of the Copyright, Designs and Patents Act 1988.

All rights reserved. No part of this book may be reprinted or reproduced or utilised in any form or by any electronic, mechanical, or other means, now known or hereafter invented, including photocopying and recording, or in any information storage or retrieval system, without permission in writing from the publishers.

Trademark notice: Product or corporate names may be trademarks or registered trademarks, and are used only for identification and explanation without intent to infringe.

British Library Cataloguing-in-Publication Data
A catalogue record for this book is available from the British Library

Library of Congress Cataloging-in-Publication Data
A catalog record for this book has been requested

ISBN: 978-1-138-23037-8
ISBN: 978-1-138-23038-5
ISBN: 978-1-315-38610-2

Typeset in Bembo
by Apex CoVantage, LLC

CONTENTS

List of contributors	*vii*

1 An overview of the impact of organizational
   change on individuals and organizations:
   an introductory note   1
   Maria Vakola and Paraskevas Petrou

PART I
Resources as change facilitators   **13**

2 Organizational change and employee functioning:
   investigating boundary conditions   15
   Victoria Bellou, Despoina Xanthopoulou and
   Panagiotis Gkorezis

3 Change consultation during organizational restructuring:
   buffering and exacerbating effects in the context
   of role demands   27
   Nerina L. Jimmieson and Michelle K. Tucker

4 Individual and external coping resources as predictors of
   employees' change attitudes   47
   Alannah E. Rafferty and Nerina L. Jimmieson

vi Contents

PART II
Emotions and cognitions and change outcomes 65

5 Feelings about change: the role of emotions and emotion
regulation for employee adaptation to organizational change 67
Karen van Dam

6 How workers' appraisals of change influence
employee outcomes 78
Karina Nielsen

7 Dynamics of trust and fairness during organizational
change: implications for job crafting and work engagement 90
Janne Kaltiainen, Jukka Lipponen and Paraskevas Petrou

8 Organizational change: implications for
the psychological contract 102
Maria Tomprou and Samantha D. Hansen

9 Measuring change recipients' reactions: the development
and psychometric evaluation of the CRRE scale 114
Ioannis Tsaousis and Maria Vakola

PART III
Organizational-level and team-level
facilitators of change 129

10 Destructive uncertainty: the toxic triangle, implicit
theories and leadership identity during organizational change 131
Pedro Neves and Birgit Schyns

11 Organizational change and health: the specific role
of job insecurity 142
Birgit Thomson and Alexandra Michel

12 Improving our understanding of collective attitudes
towards change formation 163
Gavin Schwarz and Dave Bouckenooghe

Index 177

CONTRIBUTORS

Victoria Bellou is Associate Professor of Management in the Department of Economics, University of Thessaly. She holds a doctoral degree (PhD) in Business Administration from the University of Piraeus, a postgraduate degree (MBA) from the University of Macedonia and an undergraduate degree from the University of New Haven, USA. The most important journals she has published research in include *Journal of Occupational and Organizational Psychology*, *Journal of Business Research*, *International Journal of Human Resource Management* and *Career Development International*. Her main research interests include change management, leadership, employee performance and service quality.

Dave Bouckenooghe's research focuses on the pivotal role of employees in organizations. He is especially interested in how people and collectives are impacted by change, and how they make sense of and respond to change. Dr. Bouckenooghe's work appears or is forthcoming in leading management and I&O psychology journals such as *Journal of Management*, *Journal of Business Ethics*, *Applied Psychology: An International Review* and *European Journal of Work and Organizational Psychology*, among others. Dr. Bouckenooghe also reviews for a variety of other leading scholarly journals, including *Journal of Management Studies*, *Technovation* and *Journal of Applied Psychology*.

Panagiotis Gkorezis is Assistant Professor at the Aristotle University of Thessaloniki. He holds a PhD in Human Resource Management and Organizational Behavior. His main research interests include high-performance work practices, leadership, psychological empowerment, nonverbal communication, overqualification and workplace humor. His articles have been published in several journals, such as *Journal of Occupational and Organizational Psychology*, *Human Performance*, *The International Journal of Human Resource Management*, *Management Decision* and

viii Contributors

Leadership and Organization Development Journal. He is also Senior Editor of Europe's *Journal of Psychology*.

Samantha D. Hansen is Associate Professor of OBHRM at the University of Toronto Scarborough and the Rotman School of Management. She holds a PhD in Industrial-Organizational Psychology (University of Waterloo). Samantha's primary research interests concern the employee-employer relationship, including what each party promises, expects and is obligated to give to the other. She studies the dynamics and consequences (e.g., emotions, attitudes and behaviors) of resource exchange among these parties over time with the aim of helping organizations enhance/repair their relationships with employees. Samantha's work has been published in outlets including the *Journal of Applied Psychology* and the *Journal of Organizational Behavior*.

Nerina L. Jimmieson holds an appointment at the School of Management, Queensland University of Technology. She conducts a program of both basic and applied research on occupational stress and employee health and organizational change management designed to improve workplace effectiveness at the individual, group and organizational levels. Across both of these research agendas, she employs multiple methodologies, including laboratory-based task simulations, organizational surveys, diary studies and interviews. Her research is well supported by competitive national grants and funding from industry partners in the field of workplace health and safety regulation.

Janne Kaltiainen (M.Soc.Sc.) is currently finalizing his doctoral dissertation in Social Psychology at the University of Helsinki. His dissertation investigates the dynamics of employees' experiences and psychological processes as they develop via reinforcing relationships throughout unfolding organizational change events. His key findings have shed light on the longitudinal and reciprocal relationships between employees' fairness perceptions and trust in management and between cognitive appraisals of change and work engagement across pre- and post-change phases of significant organizational change events.

Jukka Lipponen is currently Senior Lecturer in Social Psychology at the University of Helsinki. His research focuses on organizational justice, organizational identification, leadership, trust, personal values, work engagement and intergroup relations in the context of organizational changes.

Alexandra Michel is Scientific Director at the Federal Institute for Occupational Safety and Health and Associate Professor for Work and Organizational Psychology at the University of Heidelberg, Germany. Besides being an academic, she is a practitioner with experience as a Human Resources and Change Manager as well as a coach. She is co-editor of the book *The Psychology of Organizational Change: Viewing Change From the Employee's Perspective* and has published her research in several peer-reviewed journals including *Journal of Applied Psychology*, *Journal of Organizational Behavior*, *Journal of Organizational and Occupational Psychology* and *European Journal of Work and Organizational Psychology*, among others. Her primary research interests refer to resource-oriented interventions at work, organizational change, coaching and occupational health.

Pedro Neves is Associate Professor at Nova School of Business and Economics and is currently the Director of the PhD in the Management program. He has published in journals such as *Journal of Applied Psychology*, *Journal of Occupational and Organizational Psychology* and *The Leadership Quarterly*, and has (co)authored/edited six books. His research interests focus on leadership and interpersonal relationships in the workplace, change management and entrepreneurship. He serves on the editorial board of *The Leadership Quarterly* and *Journal of Change Management*.

Karina Nielsen holds a Chair of Work Psychology and is Director of the Institute of Work Psychology, Sheffield University Management School at the University of Sheffield, UK. She is a research affiliate at the CPH-NEW, USA, and Karolinska Institutet, Sweden. Her research interests lie within changing organizations. She is currently on the editorial boards of *Human Relations*, *The Leadership Quarterly* and *Journal of Business and Psychology*, and she is an associate editor of *Work & Stress*. She has published her work in journals such as *Human Relations*, *Work & Stress*, *The Leadership Quarterly* and *Journal of Occupational Health Psychology*.

Paraskevas Petrou (PhD) is Assistant Professor of Organizational Psychology at the Erasmus University Rotterdam, The Netherlands. He is a member of the European Association of Work and Organizational Psychologists (EAWOP) and the Dutch Society of Work and Organizational Psychology Researchers (WAOP), and he holds a British Psychological Society certificate (Levels A and B) on psychological testing. His research activity concerns a wide range of topics such as self-regulation, job crafting, leisure behavior adaptation and creativity.

Alannah E. Rafferty is Associate Professor in the Department of Employment Relations and Human Resources at Griffith University. Alannah's research interests include organizational change and development, readiness for change, change attitudes, transformational leadership and abusive supervision. Alannah has extensive experience in the development, administration and use of surveys to inform leadership development and strategic change and within a range of private and public-sector organizations.

Gavin Schwarz (PhD, University of Queensland) is Associate Professor in the School of Management, at UNSW Business School, University of New South Wales. His research and work interests include organizational change and organizational inertia, with a particular focus in better understanding how organizations fail when changing, and developing applied strategies for dealing with failure to

x Contributors

change. He is also interested in exploring how knowledge develops in organizational and change theory.

Birgit Schyns joined Neoma Business School as Professor in Organisational Behaviour in 2017, after 11 years in the UK, first as Reader at University of Portsmouth and then at Durham University, and later as full Professor at Durham University. Her research focus is leadership, particularly the follower side of leadership and the dark side of leadership. Birgit has edited several special issues and four books. She was Associate Editor for *European Journal of Work and Organizational Psychology* and *British Journal of Management*, and is currently Associate Editor for *Applied Psychology: An International Review*. Birgit serves on several editorial boards.

Birgit Thomson (PhD) is a senior researcher at the German Federal Institute of Occupational Safety and Health (BAuA). She has a background in economics and work/organizational psychology. Since 2002 she is concerned with various research issues around the well-being and health impact of major organizational change, job insecurity and the role of leadership in this process. Moreover she is involved in teaching at various German universities and has extensive contact with both the national and international scientific community.

Maria Tomprou is Research Scientist at Human-Computer Interaction Institute, School of Computer Science at Carnegie Mellon University. Her research focuses on managing employment relationships such as psychological contracts, social exchanges and i-deals. She has also been involved in research projects that bridge organizational psychology with human-computer interaction and machine learning to promote interventions in employees' work and careers. Her work is published in *Journal of Organizational Behavior* and the *Proceedings of Computer-Supported Cooperative Work and Social Computing* (CSCW) among other outlets.

Ioannis Tsaousis is Associate Professor in Psychometrics at the University of Crete, Department of Psychology. His research interests include psychometric theory, test development and theoretical as well as empirical measurement of individual differences (i.e., personality and intelligence). The corollary of this research activity is the development and standardization of more than 20 psychometric instruments in Greek and English. He is author and co-author of numerous scientific papers in the field of psychometrics and individual differences, and he serves as a reviewer and member of the editorial board of numerous scientific peer-reviewed journals in the field of psychometrics.

Michelle K. Tucker is a registered psychologist (PhD Organisational Psychology). She works as a researcher in the School of Management, Queensland University of Technology, and her primary research interests include occupational health, leadership, group processes and employee well-being.

Maria Vakola (PhD) is an organizational psychologist and Associate Professor at the Athens University of Economics and Business, Greece. Maria has published three books and several articles in a number of academic journals such as the *Journal of Applied Psychology* and *European Journal of Work and Organizational Psychology*, among others. She teaches undergraduate and postgraduate courses in Change Management and Organizational Psychology. She is the co-founder of the International Forum for the Psychology of Organizational Change and the co-founder of an award-winning nonprofit organization called job-pairs.gr which enhances youth employability.

Karen van Dam is Professor of Work and Organizational Psychology at the Open University, The Netherlands. She received her PhD from the University of Amsterdam and has taught across the full spectrum of Organizational Behavior and Human Resource Management topics. Her research focuses on how employees adapt to changes at work; topics include individual adaptability, resistance, emotion regulation, appraisal processes, workplace learning, employability and career management. She has published in journals such as the *Journal of Applied Psychology*, *Journal of Vocational Behavior*, *Journal of Occupational and Organizational Psychology*, *Journal of Management* and *Personality and Individual Differences*.

Despoina Xanthopoulou is Assistant Professor of Organizational Psychology at the School of Psychology, Aristotle University of Thessaloniki, Greece. Her research interests include job (re)design, personal resources, employee well-being, recovery, crossover and spillover processes, and diary studies. Her research has been published in peer-reviewed journals such as the *Journal of Applied Psychology*, *Human Relations* and *Journal of Organizational Behavior*. She is Associate Editor of *European Journal of Work and Organizational Psychology*, and she serves on the editorial boards of *Journal of Occupational Health Psychology*, *Journal of Personnel Psychology*, *Occupational Health Science* and *Stress & Health*.

1

AN OVERVIEW OF THE IMPACT OF ORGANIZATIONAL CHANGE ON INDIVIDUALS AND ORGANIZATIONS

An introductory note

Maria Vakola and Paraskevas Petrou

Introduction

Organizational change is seen as an integral part of organizational life and as a critical driver of organizational success (Beer & Nohria, 2000). Recent studies reveal that there is a high rate of failure of organizational change (Beer & Nohria, 2000) which in some cases reaches the pessimistic 80% to 90% (Burnes, 2011; Cartwright & Schoenberg, 2006). The potential impact of change on both organizations and individuals is significant. On the positive side, change can challenge the status quo and provide opportunities for growth, learning and development; but, on the negative side, it can create major problems in organizational life with impact on how people think, feel and behave (Cartwright & Cooper, 1993; Kotter, 2007).

More specifically, change has both work-related and personal consequences. According to a systematic review by Oreg, Vakola, and Armenakis (2011), the most frequently considered consequence of organizational change is organizational commitment (e.g., Fedor, Caldwell, & Herold, 2006; Oreg, 2006) which focuses on employees' perceptions of their alignment with or attachment to their entire organization (Meyer & Allen, 1991). Change planning and implementation can impact organizational commitment as change challenges individuals' alignment with the organization (Hui & Lee, 2000; Judge, Thoresen, Pucik, & Welbourne, 1999). Apart from organizational commitment, many authors have established the relationship between the effect of change implementation and career outcomes or work attitudes such as job satisfaction (Amiot, Terry, Jimmieson, & Callan, 2006; Axtell et al., 2002; Judge et al., 1999). Other related constructs that are affected by organizational change are intentions to leave the organization, organizational citizenship behavior, motivation and morale (Ashford, 1988; Fedor et al., 2006).

Apart from work-related consequences as a result of the change, there are important personal consequences to consider. Oreg et al. (2011) reviewed evidence on the impact of change on change recipients' psychological well-being, mental health and somatic health complaints (Cartwright & Cooper, 1993; Näswall, Sverke, & Hellgren, 2005), psychological withdrawal (Fried, Tiegs, Naughton, & Ashforth, 1996), work-related irritation (Wanberg & Banas, 2000), leisure satisfaction (Pierce & Dunham, 1992), emotional exhaustion (Paulsen et al., 2005), anxiety (Axtell et al., 2002) and stress or strain (Bordia, Jone, Gallois, Callan, & Difonzo, 2006).

This chapter aims at setting up the scene to understand the dark and bright side of organizational change. Examining the impact of change on individuals and organizations may reveal important contingencies that can explain how positive organizational outcomes during times of change can be stimulated. Another aim of this introductory note is to discuss potential resources and strategies of coping with organizational change through the lenses of the contributing authors. That means that a synthesis of results coming from each chapter will be discussed here offering insights regarding the impact of organizational change and effective ways of dealing with aspects of this impact (Figure 1.1).

The dark and bright side of organizational change

The high failure rate of organizational change may explain why research very often focuses on the dark side of organizational change. Following a systematic analysis conducted by Fedor et al. (2006) and Oreg et al. (2011), the negative impact of organizational change on individuals is found in research considering the following:

- increased workload and job complexity; role conflicts, increased work demands (Spector, 2002; Axtell et al., 2002);
- fears and uncertainties; job insecurity, career uncertainties, a loss of control, uncertainty for the employees about their future with the organization and fear of failure as they face new job demands (Armstrong-Stassen, 1998; Cunningham et al., 2002; Fried et al., 1996; Näswall et al., 2005; Paulsen et al., 2005);
- threats to individual sense making (Ledford, Mohrman, Mohrman, & Lawler, 1990);
- perceptions of distributive justice and anticipated negative outcomes (Armenakis, Bernerth, Pitts, & Walker, 2007; Paterson & Cary, 2002).

According to Fedor et al. (2006) the bulk of the research evidence seems to suggest that increasing amounts of change are associated with negative individual outcomes and reactions. They also pointed out that even in cases that change can ultimately be positive for some individuals, most of the existing literature seems to indicate that change tends to be disturbing for employees (e.g., Oreg, 2003) at least for a short term until change can be finalized (Fedor et al., 2006).

Although most evidence on organizational change focuses on its negative consequences, there are studies revealing that organizational change does not always

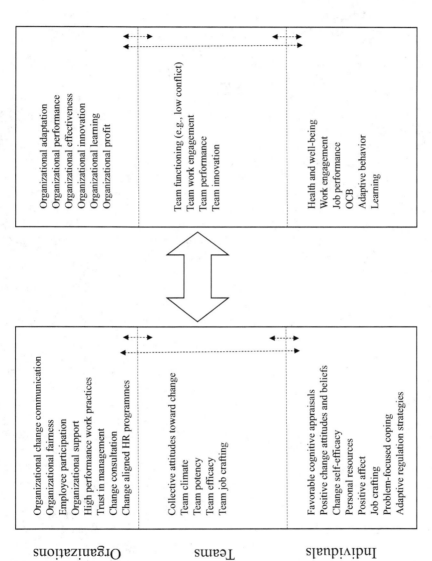

FIGURE 1.1 Success change factors and positive change outcomes

have to be negative or detrimental. The analysis of the positive impact of organizational change can be found in research that considers anticipated positive outcomes such as more interesting and challenging work, increased personal development or improved employability, and increased pay (Bartunek, Rousseau, Rudolph, & DePalma, 2006) and outcome favorability (Daly, 1995; Coyle-Shapiro, 2002). Furthermore, studies have shown that anticipating positive outcomes is related to positive attitudes toward change, such as greater readiness and acceptance of the change and higher commitment and willingness to participate in it (e.g., Van Dam, 2005). Perceived positive outcomes from change are also found to be related with change recipients' post-change job attitudes, such that there was a positive relationship with organizational commitment and job satisfaction and a negative one with turnover intentions (Fedor et al., 2006; Herold, Fedor, & Caldwell, 2007; Rafferty & Griffin, 2006; Wanberg & Banas, 2000). In addition, research on positive organizational change showed that employees' and leaders' positive psychological and social resources and behaviors are key factors to deal with dysfunctional attitudes and behaviors related to organizational change and can lead to positive organizational change (Avey, Wernsing, & Luthans, 2008).

Taken together, the evidence above regarding the negative and positive side of organizational change suggests that rather than treating change as good or bad, researchers should focus on the factors that highlight the negative or positive potential of change. In other words, literature identifies factors on the organizational, team and individual level that can make organizational change a success or failure. This is also the perspective that the present book takes. As organizational changes of increasing frequency and severity become the norm, improving our understanding of success factors and their underlying relationships becomes increasingly important. As a result, the discussion is not about the positive or negative impact of change but has to focus on exploring the factors that contribute to it.

The content of this book

In Chapter 2, Bellou, Xanthopoulou and Gkorezis discuss the direct assessment of organizational change (i.e., the frequency of change implementation, the extent of the change or its impact on daily work), its immediate consequences and most importantly, potential moderators that may buffer its unfavorable effects on employee functioning (i.e., well-being, attitudes and performance). They suggest that organizational changes may be particularly unfavorable for employees when resources at the organizational, the team and the individual level of analysis are scarce. In contrast, the availability of resources is likely to shield change recipients against the negative implications of organizational change. The authors conclude that organizational-level resources (i.e., resources that are allocated through the way work in managed, organized and designed) such as high performance work practices, justice, trust and communication, buffer unfavorable change consequences and increase commitment during change. In similar vein, team-level resources (residing within the team context; e.g., leader-member exchange, team climate

An overview **5**

strength) and individual resources (employee's characteristics or actions; e.g., optimism, meaning-making and proactive behavior) may buffer the negative impact of organizational changes on employee functioning and in turn facilitate employee adaptation to change.

In Chapter 3, Jimmieson and Tucker analyze change consultation in the form of information and participation that fulfill various motivational and cognitive functions. While change consultation is recognized as a vital step in change planning, there is a lack of research examining its role as a job resource, protecting against employee strain in the face of specific role demands. Sample 1 comprises 191 employees of a government agency undergoing restructuring and redundancies, in addition to the announcement of a relocation of all employees to another geographical location. The authors explain that change consultation moderates the effect of role conflict on cognitive weariness, physical fatigue and intentions to change jobs within the organization. However, the assumed stress-buffering effect of change consultation is not found. Rather, the positive association between role conflict and employee strain is more marked for those perceiving high, compared to low, change consultation. Employee strain is at its lowest when role conflict is low and change consultation was high. Overall, this pattern of results suggests that the effectiveness of change consultation is dependent on other demands placed on employees. In Sample 2 (1,100 employees from an energy company experiencing prolonged restructuring for two years), the authors replicate the effect among a group of redeployed employees through a multi-group comparison. Specifically, role ambiguity is more stressful when change consultation is high. However, the effect is evident only for those who are still in their original position. The authors suggest that change consultation is not effective when role stressors are high.

In Chapter 4, Rafferty and Jimmieson identify three internal resources (generalized self-efficacy, dispositional resistance to change and trait positive affectivity) and two external resources (information about change and participation in change) as antecedents of the dimensions of change readiness, in a cross-sectional survey conducted within an Australian provider of community and residential aged care. In line with Bellou, Xanthopoulou and Gkorezis (Chapter 2), the authors conclude that both internal and external resources are important in predicting the change readiness dimensions. More specifically, of the three internal resources examined, dispositional resistance to change and trait positive affectivity are most influential as reflected in their significant relationships with most of the dimensions of change readiness. As a result, organizations may need to consider providing additional support such as coaching or mentoring employees so that they take a positive perspective on change. Rafferty and Jimmieson conclude that the relationships between the external resources and the change readiness dimensions are slightly stronger than the relationships with the internal resources. They suggest that even if one does not have a dispositional profile of internal resources to promote change readiness, if organizations introduce the right change processes, then they may still be able to build change readiness.

In Chapter 5, van Dam suggests that organizational change often serves as an affective event that can elicit different emotions in employees ranging from negative emotions, such as worry, anxiety and anger, to positive ones, such as excitement and enthusiasm. Change research has shown that negative emotions can serve as antecedents of employees' change attitudes and behaviors and are indicative of employees' resistance to the change. It is important to note that while emotions are often seen as irrational or problematic during change implementation, they are inherently motivational and could be valuable, signifying employees' perceptions, concerns, sense making and adaptation to the change. Van Dam calls for more attention to how employees regulate their emotions which has an impact on employee behavior and well-being at work. Employees will adjust to the change more easily when they apply adaptive regulation strategies such as positive reappraisal and distraction.

In Chapter 6, Nielsen explores the impact of cognitive appraisal on the well-being of employees experiencing organizational change. Cognitive appraisal theory suggests that the positive, neutral or negative appraisals of events influence well-being. The existing literature on cognitive appraisals of organizational change has found that appraisals of a better or a worsened standing/position in the organization after the change have severe well-being consequences. She suggests that employees are not just passive recipients of organizational change but actively appraise whether the change is good or bad for them and whether the change process itself is problematic or positive. Positive appraisals of the change process and the way it is handled by management are related to better well-being and less fears of losing one's job. As a result, Nielsen recommends to organizations to ensure that employees appraise the change and the changes processes in a positive light as these appraisals influence employees' well-being. More specifically, she recommends effective communication of the change vision, employee involvement in the change process during and after change implementation, active leadership role, increased trust and fairness perceptions, managers' training and continuous monitoring of the change.

In Chapter 7, Kaltiainen, Lipponen and Petrou suggest that trust and fairness have the potential to boost employee work engagement via appraisals of the change, and by enhancing proactive employee behaviors targeted at improving one's work environment (i.e., job crafting). On basis of the literature they review, they suggest that changing organizations should follow a holistic approach, recognizing that both trust and fairness could be and should be built both at the supervisor and at the top management level. To enhance trust and fairness perceptions, it is important that leaders and managers are perceived to share common values with the employees, demonstrate consistency in their actions and decisions over time and across people, aim for common good, are competent and effective, provide opportunities for employees to express their opinions, treat others with respect and are ready to trust others. Within this context, it is more likely that employees will appraise change as a challenge and less as a threat. Challenge appraisals will empower employees to engage in expansive forms of job crafting that will help them learn and grow, even in the face of organizational changes.

In Chapter 8, Tomprou and Hansen suggest that psychological contract obligations may become particularly challenging to manage during change interventions. Change is likely to interfere with the organization's ability to fulfill its obligations to employees which can cause psychological contract breach (for example, budget cuts may mean that flexible scheduling or bonuses can no longer be guaranteed). Perceptions of breach are associated with negative employee affect (e.g., feelings of violation), attitudes and behavior all of which damage effective organizational functioning and can interfere with the success of the change intervention. The authors explain that recent developments in psychological contract (PC) theory suggest that some organizational change efforts, although still disruptive to the PC, may lead to positive outcomes. For example, the organizational change initiative may satisfy personal goals and lead to obligation fulfillment through the delivery of valued inducements or provide an opportunity for employees to request customized work arrangements. Thus, whether the change is perceived as positive or negative, disruption of the PC is likely to have significant implications for the success of the change effort. In accordance with Nielsen (Chapter 6), Thomson and Michel (Chapter 11) and Kaltiainen, Lipponen and Petrou (Chapter 7), the authors recommend two-way communication and trust in management to deal with negative disruptions because of the change. The authors also recommend activation of social networks (i.e., structures of social ties in the workplace) which are an important source of information during organizational change. Tomprou and Hansen explain that employees can become active agents and work with their employer toward revising their employment relationship examining the resources available for negotiation by individuals and their organization.

In Chapter 9, Tsaousis and Vakola offer a scale to measure change recipients' attitudes to a specific change following the tridimensional nature of attitudes – namely, cognitive, affective and behavioral. The existing literature has frequently overlooked the possibility that change recipients may distinguish between change attitudes in general and attitudes toward a specific change. The authors report four studies related to the development of the Change Recipients' Reactions (CRRE) scale. The first study involves initial item development, examination and revision, with piloting carried out in a primarily employee sample. The second study aims at refining and confirming the factor structure of the developed scale. The third study examines the reliability of the scale and the fourth one presents details regarding the convergent, divergent and incremental validity of the scale. The results of these four studies provide sufficient evidence regarding the psychometric properties of the CRRE which could be a particularly valuable measure for both researchers and practitioners aiming at understanding and dealing with recipients' reactions to the changes at hand.

In Chapter 10, Neves and Schyns suggest that the failure of change efforts is a result of the lack of understanding of the dynamics of individual and collective resistance to change. While they agree that leadership for effective and successful change management is one of the most important factors, they propose a fuller understanding of individual and collective reactions to change, particularly the interplay between leaders, followers and context. Specifically, they suggest that change efforts fail faster and more abruptly when there is a combination of factors: leaders enacting destructive behaviors, followers demonstrating a susceptible stance and the environment facilitating such behaviors, which creates a "toxic triangle". In order to break this toxic triangle, organizations should invest in modeling implicit theories or explicit roles related to how they expect leaders and followers to behave in a change event. Organizations should also highlight the motivational rewards for engaging in the adoption of positive leadership roles as well as engaged follower roles during change. Within this context, leadership during change can serve as a boundary condition that inhibits the toxic relational process from spiraling and might even transform it into a virtuous process, which should help increase commitment to change.

In Chapter 11, Thomson and Michel explain, based on the healthy organizational change model (HOC-M), that drastic and abrupt organizational change such as restructuring can potentially damage employee mental and physical health, well-being, career prospects, future salary development and work quality. They systematically review 223 mostly cross-sectional studies published between 2000 and 2014 and they conclude that change results in work stressors such as job insecurity which is consistently and significantly related to health (mental and physical) related outcomes. In accordance with Nielsen's recommendations in Chapter 6, Thomson and Michel suggest that organizations need to pay attention to (1) broad acceptance of the change vision; (2) sufficient and well-structured communication regarding the urgency of change, change-related training, change objectives and the change measures; (3) employee participation; (4) change-aligned HR programs; and (5) control of success as regards change measures.

In Chapter 12, Schwarz and Bouckenooghe respond to a call for more attention to be directed toward considering multilevel organizational analysis that incorporates the collective nature of change attitudes. The authors argue that change attitudes formed collectively do not necessarily emerge from a linear aggregation of individual-level experiences or observations but they reflect interactions between sets of individuals which produce higher level group attitudes. Specifically, in justifying aggregation of individual attitudes at the collective level values of .70 have been used (e.g., for r_{wg}) as the traditional cut-off point denoting high versus low values of within-group agreement. Applied to a measure of collective change attitudes, proposing such a definitive boundary is tantamount to drawing a line in the sand for change researchers. Very often in studies when individual attitudes towards change at the collective level do not meet this criterion, a lack of agreement at the collective level leads to discarding this data further for multilevel analysis. Yet disagreement and further analysis of these 'discarded' data may offer valuable insights on how the collective attitude is in the process of coming together. They also suggest that to establish attitude as a shared unit construct (rather than one of consensus or based on universal principles) researchers should re-evaluate having a definitive measurement criterion cut off. They conclude that a more predictable collective shared attitude will emerge when the team members are strongly connected.

Members with weaker ties may be more useful to plant a seed in the collective mindset that challenges existing routines and beliefs.

Concluding notes

All the contributors to this book recognize that organizational change may have negative impact on both organizations and individuals. If organizations introduce the right processes, change can be adopted and promoted by teams and individuals. Our analysis of each chapter led us to conclude that coping strategies and facilitators of change can be found at three distinct levels, namely, organizational, team and individual. Therefore, the content of most chapters can be synthesized in the following three levels of facilitators of organizational change:

At the organizational level, change is facilitated via resources that are allocated through the way work is managed, such as high performance work practices, justice, trust and communication. It is important for organizations to ensure that employees appraise the change in a positive light through the effective communication of the change vision, broad acceptance of this vision, employee involvement in the change process, active leadership role, increased trust and fairness perceptions, managers' training and continuous monitoring of the change. A fuller understanding of the interplay between leaders' potentially destructive behaviors, followers' attitudes and the context that tolerates such behaviors will help organizations articulate what behavior is acceptable or not during change and reward early adoption of acceptable behaviors. Other ways of coping with the impact of change is activation of social networks (i.e., structures of social ties in the workplace) which are an important source of information during organizational change.

At the team level, resources that reside within the team context such as leader-member exchange and team climate strength also buffer the negative impact of change. Changing organizations should be aware that a holistic approach is needed to deal with the impact of change which means that strategies such as building trust need to be included in both team and organizational processes. One way to enhance trust and fairness is through supervisors and managers who share common values with the employees, demonstrate consistency in their actions and decisions over time and across people, aim for common good, are competent and effective, provide opportunities for employees to express their opinions and treat others with respect.

At the individual level, personal resources such as employees' optimism, meaning-making, generalized self-efficacy, dispositional resistance to change, trait positive affectivity and proactive behaviors can also facilitate employees' adaptation to change. In addition, the elicitation of different emotions such as worry or anger during change should not be seen as irrational or problematic but as a potentially valuable factor that signifies employees' perceptions, concerns, sense making and adaptation to the change. Apart from affect, employees' cognitions play an important role in buffering negative processes or creating successful changes. Employees' positive change appraisals are related to better well-being and adaptation to change.

Furthermore, resources may lead employees to appraise changes in a positive way and, thereby, display proactive behaviors (e.g., job crafting) that can help them make the most of change.

In conclusion, some employees may enter an organization predisposed to be less ready for change compared to others. As a result, organizations need to create those conditions to help employees take a positive perspective on change. Organizational and team-level resources such as information about the change and participation in change, mentoring, communication of common vision, consistency between words and actions and leader-member exchange will help employees to appraise change in a positive light and align their efforts in effectively dealing with change.

References

Amiot, C., Terry, D., Jimmieson, N., & Callan, V. (2006). A longitudinal investigation of coping processes during a merger: Implications for job satisfaction and organizational identification. *Journal of Management, 32*, 552–574.

Armenakis, A. A., Bernerth, J. B., Pitts, J. P., & Walker, H. J. (2007). Organizational change recipients' beliefs scale: Development of an assessment instrument. *Journal of Applied Behavioral Science, 43*, 495–505.

Armstrong-Stassen, M. (1998). The effect of gender and organizational level on how survivors appraise and cope with organizational downsizing. *Journal of Applied Behavioral Science, 34*, 125–142.

Ashford, S. J. (1988). Individual strategies for coping with stress during organizational transitions. *Journal of Applied Behavioral Science, 24*, 19–36.

Avey, J. B., Wernsing, T. S., & Luthans, F. (2008). Can positive employees help positive organizational change? Impact of psychological capital and emotions on relevant attitudes and behaviors. *The Journal of Applied Behavioral Science, 44*, 48–70.

Axtell, C., Wall, T., Stride, C., Pepper, K., Clegg, C., Gardner, P., & Bolden, R. (2002). Familiarity breeds content: The impact of exposure to change on employee openness and well-being. *Journal of Occupational and Organizational Psychology, 75*, 217–231.

Bartunek, J. M., Rousseau, D. M., Rudolph, J. W., & DePalma, J. A. (2006). On the receiving end: Sensemaking, emotion, and assessments of an organizational change initiated by others. *Journal of Applied Behavioral Science, 42*, 182–206.

Beer, M., & Nohria, N. (2000). Cracking the code of change. *Harvard Business Review, 78*, 133–141.

Bordia, P., Jones, E., Gallois, C., Callan, V. J., & Difonzo, N. (2006). Management are aliens! Rumors and stress during organizational change. *Group and Organization Management, 31*, 601–621.

Burnes, B. (2011). Introduction: Why does change fail, and what can we do about it? *Journal of Change Management, 11*, 445–450.

Cartwright, S., & Cooper, C. L. (1993). The psychological impact of merger and acquisition on the individual: A study of building society managers. *Human Relations, 46*, 327–347.

Cartwright, S., & Schoenberg, R. (2006). Thirty years of mergers and acquisitions research: Recent advances and future opportunities. *British Journal of Management, 17*, S1–S5.

Coyle-Shapiro, J. A. (2002). Changing employee attitudes: the independent effects of TQM and profit sharing on continuous improvement orientation. *The Journal of Applied Behavioral Science, 38*, 57–77.

Cunningham, C. E., Woodward, C. A., Shannon, H. S., MacIntosh, J., Lendrum, B., Rosenbloom, D., & Brown, J. (2002). Readiness for organizational change: A longitudinal study of workplace, psychological and behavioural correlates. *Journal of Occupational and Organizational Psychology, 75*, 377–392.

Daly, J. P. (1995). Explaining changes to employees: The influence of justification and change outcomes on employees' fairness judgments. *Journal of Applied Behavioral Science, 31*, 415–428.

Fedor, D. B., Caldwell, S., & Herold, D. M. (2006). The effects of organizational changes on employee commitment: A multilevel investigation. *Personnel Psychology, 59*, 1–29.

Fried, Y., Tiegs, R. B., Naughton, T. J., & Ashforth, B. E. (1996). Managers' reactions to a corporate acquisition: A test of an integrative model. *Journal of Organizational Behavior, 17*, 401–427.

Herold, D. M., Fedor, D. B., & Caldwell, S. D. (2007). Beyond change management: A multilevel investigation of contextual and personal influences on employees' commitment to change. *Journal of Applied Psychology, 92*, 942–951.

Hui, C., & Lee, C. (2000). Moderating effects of organization-based self-esteem on organizational uncertainty: Employee response relationships. *Journal of Management, 26*, 215–232.

Judge, T. A., Thoresen, C. J., Pucik, V., & Welbourne, T. M. (1999). Managerial coping with organizational change: A dispositional perspective. *Journal of Applied Psychology, 84*, 107.

Kotter, J. P. (2007). Leading change. *Harvard Business Review, 85*, 96–103.

Ledford, G. E., Jr, Mohrman, S. A., Mohrman, A. M., & Lawler, E. E. (1990). The phenomenon of large-scale organizational change. In A. M. Mohrman et al. (Eds.), *Large scale organizational change* (pp. 1–31). San Francisco, CA: Jossey-Bass.

Meyer, J. P., & Allen, N. J. (1991). A three-component conceptualization of organizational commitment. *Human Resource Management Review, 1*, 61–89.

Näswall, K., Sverke, M., & Hellgren, J. (2005). The moderating role of personality characteristics on the relationship between job insecurity and strain. *Work & Stress, 19*(1), 37–49.

Oreg, S. (2003). Resistance to change: Developing an individual differences measure. *Journal of Applied Psychology, 88*, 680–693.

Oreg, S. (2006). Personality, context, and resistance to organizational change. *European Journal of Work and Organizational Psychology, 15*, 73–101.

Oreg, S., Vakola, M., & Armenakis, A. (2011). Change recipients' reactions to organizational change: A 60-year review of quantitative studies. *The Journal of Applied Behavioral Science, 47*, 461–524.

Paterson, J. M., & Cary, J. (2002). Organizational justice, change anxiety, and acceptance of downsizing: Preliminary tests of an AET-based model. *Motivation and Emotion, 26*, 83–103.

Paulsen, N., Callan, V. J., Grice, T. A., Rooney, D., Gallois, C., Jones, E., . . . Bordia, P. (2005). Job uncertainty and personal control during downsizing: A comparison of survivors and victims. *Human Relations, 58*, 463–496.

Pierce, J. L., & Dunham, R. B. (1992). The 12-hour work day: A 48 hour, eight-day week. *Academy of Management Journal, 35*, 1086–1098.

Rafferty, A. E., & Griffin, M. A. (2006). Perceptions of organizational change: A stress and coping perspective. *Journal of Applied Psychology, 91*, 1154–1162.

Spector, P. E. (2002). Employee control and occupational stress. *American Psychological Society, 11*, 153–156.

Van Dam, K. (2005). Employee attitudes toward job changes: An application and extension of Rusbult and Farrell's investment model. *Journal of Occupational and Organizational Psychology, 78*, 253–272.

Wanberg, C. R., & Banas, J. T. (2000). Predictors and outcomes of openness to changes in a reorganizing workplace. *Journal of Applied Psychology, 85*, 132–142.

PART I

Resources as change facilitators

2

ORGANIZATIONAL CHANGE AND EMPLOYEE FUNCTIONING

Investigating boundary conditions

Victoria Bellou, Despoina Xanthopoulou and Panagiotis Gkorezis

Organizational change is systematically associated with poor employee functioning, expressed through negative reactions, such as feelings of uncertainty (Rafferty & Griffin, 2006), reduced morale (Gilmore, Shea, & Useem, 1997), frustration (Ashford, 1988), and impaired well-being (e.g., Petrou, Demerouti, & Schaufeli, 2015), as well as counterproductive attitudes and behaviors (for a review, Oreg, Vakola, & Armenakis, 2011). Previous studies are important because they shed light on how individuals experience organizational changes, how they react to these and which are the outcomes of these reactions. However, their main shortcoming is that they do not assess change directly, with the exceptions being few. For example, Petrou et al. (2015) assessed the degree to which change influenced employees' daily work, Xanthopoulou, Gkorezis, Bellou and Petridou (2016a) examined the degree to which employees faced changes at work, while Fedor, Caldwell and Herold (2006) tested the extent of change occurring at the work-unit level.

In this chapter, we argue that the direct assessment of organizational change (i.e., the frequency of change implementation, the extent of the change or its impact on daily work) is important because it allows not only examining its immediate consequences but, most importantly, potential moderators that may buffer its unfavorable effects on employee functioning. By functioning we refer to all those indicators (i.e., well-being, attitudes and performance) that designate employees' ability to function properly during change implementation. Specifying the factors that mitigate the unfavorable change outcomes has important practical implications as well, because it indicates what needs to be considered during change design and implementation.

We use the job demands-resources (JD-R) theory (Bakker & Demerouti, 2014) and conservation of resources (COR) theory (Hobfoll, 1989) as our theoretical frameworks. We limit our investigation to resources at the organizational, the team and the individual level of analysis that are argued to buffer the effect of demanding

16 Victoria Bellou et al.

and stressful environmental conditions. Our purpose is not to provide a systematic review of all empirical studies that support the moderating role of specific resources on the relationship between organizational changes and employee functioning. Rather, we aim at highlighting specific resources from different levels of analysis that have been linked to successful adaptation in changing organizations and whose role as buffers can be theoretically justified (even if it has not yet received empirical support). Based on this inquiry, the ultimate aim is to put together a theoretical model that can be used as a guide for future research.

Theoretical framework

The main assumptions of the JD-R theory (Bakker & Demerouti, 2014) in combination with the central tenets of COR theory (Hobfoll, 1989) allow explaining how and why resources at the organizational, the team and the individual level of analysis may function as boundary conditions that buffer the impact of organizational changes on employee functioning. According to the JD-R theory, the characteristics of each work environment can be distinguished in two categories: job demands and job resources. Job demands refer to those aspects of the job that require sustained physical and/or psychological effort and are, therefore, associated with certain costs. Job resources are the characteristics of the work environment that facilitate goal achievement, and stimulate personal growth and development. Also, job resources help employees deal with the threatening aspects of the job demands, thus buffering their negative outcomes. In line with the JD-R theory, organizational change can be defined as a job demand because when employees face frequent or extensive changes or changes that have a significant impact on their daily work, they are required to invest energy. Therefore, the degree to which resources (e.g., support, coaching) are available at different levels of the work environment (e.g., organizational, team or job level) will determine whether changes will harm employees or not. According to the buffer hypothesis of the JD-R model, organizational changes are expected to be particularly detrimental when resources are absent or limited, while the availability of resources buffers the negative effect of changes on employee functioning.

COR theory (Hobfoll, 1989) also emphasizes the role of resources as factors that may determine whether the adaptation to threatening environments, such as the context of change, will be unfavorable or not. COR theory complements the JD-R theory (Bakker & Demerouti, 2014) in that it provides a broader definition of resources. Accordingly, resources are "those entities that are either centrally valued in their own right, or act as means to obtain centrally valued ends" (Hobfoll, 2002, p. 307). Hobfoll (1989) proposes that people strive to protect, conserve and enrich their resources (i.e., objects, conditions, personal characteristics and energies) in order to adapt in their environment and that problems arise when resources are scarce, lost or difficult to be replaced. On the basis of this more general definition, we propose that resources inherent in the work environment but also in change

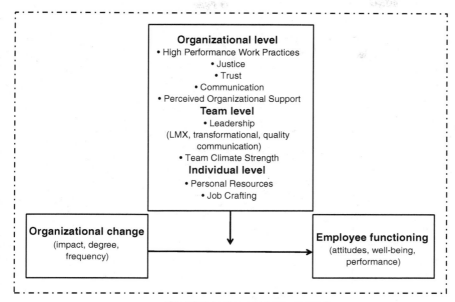

FIGURE 2.1 The hypothesized model

recipients may act as boundary conditions that determine the outcomes of organizational changes on employee functioning.

Based on the buffer hypothesis of the JD-R theory (Bakker & Demerouti, 2014) and the main tenets of COR theory (Hobfoll, 1989) we argue that, when employees possess adequate resources, they can better cope with the demanding changes, thus preventing unfavorable outcomes. Following the classification of resources proposed by Nielsen et al. (2017), we analyze the buffering role of organizational-level resources (i.e., resources that are allocated through the way work is managed, organized, and designed), team-level resources (that reside within the team context) and individual resources that refer to employee's characteristics or actions. Figure 2.1 summarizes our central propositions.

Resources at the organizational level

Organizational-level resources concern resources that originate from the way work is managed, organized and designed (Nielsen et al., 2017). In order to cover these different facets of organizational-level resources, we focus on high performance work practices, justice, trust, communication and support. **High performance work practices** (or high performance work systems and high involvement work practices) are regarded as those human resource management practices that have a synergistic effect on organizational effectiveness and performance (Posthuma,

18 Victoria Bellou et al.

Campion, Masimova, & Campion, 2013). Although not restricted to change contexts, such practices may serve as resources that buffer the unfavorable consequences of change (Combs, Liu, Hall, & Ketchen, 2006). Since HPWP enhance participation in decision-making, learning and motives to engage in extra role behavior (White, Hill, McGovern, Mills & Smeaton, 2003), they equip change recipients with the means that are necessary to deal with the change and can thus reduce its negative impact. In changing contexts, Sharif and Scandura (2014) found that low employee involvement in the change process diminished the positive relationship between ethical leadership and change recipients' performance (both in-role and extra-role). Similarly, Wanberg and Banas (2000) revealed that the relationship between resilience and job satisfaction was negative when participation was low (vs. high). These findings indicate that lack of participation buffers the potential facilitating effects of other resources (e.g., ethical leadership or resilience) on employee functioning. Although these studies did not directly assess the role of high performance work practices as buffers on the relationship between change and employee functioning, the supportive evidence is in line with our main theoretical assumption.

Organizational justice has also been conceptualized as a buffer against job demands, such as organizational change (Proost, Verboon, & van Ruysseveldt, 2015; Wang, Lu, & Siu, 2015). Given that uncertainty and subsequent ambiguity about the precise nature of change and its implications are inherent in change initiatives (Schweiger & DeNisi, 1991), researchers have argued that fairness is a resource, providing individuals a means to cope with uncertainty (Wang et al., 2015). Xanthopoulou et al. (2016a) hypothesized that both procedural and distributive justice buffer the negative relationship between organizational changes and change recipients' work engagement in a study among Greek employees. The hypothesis was supported for distributive but not procedural justice since the relationship was negative for low levels of distributive justice and positive for high levels of distributive justice. Although the buffering role of procedural justice was not found in this study, the importance of following fair procedures during times of change should not be undermined.

A concept related to justice is trust since employees are more likely to trust fair organizations. Although **organizational trust** has long been recognized as a key resource for managing change-related demands (Oreg, 2006), it is only recently that Bouckenooghe (2012) verified its buffering role on the relationship between organizational politics and commitment to change. Findings indicated that organizational politics related negatively to normative and affective commitment only when trust was low. In a similar vein, Jiang and Probst (2016) investigated employees at a university which underwent budget cuts and found that high (vs. low) organizational trust reduced the positive effect of job insecurity on burnout, while Fryxell, Dooley, and Li (2004) found that managerial trustworthiness reduced the negative impact of job-related uncertainties on commitment during organizational restructuring. Since change initiatives are inevitably followed by uncertainty about the future, distrust in the organization is likely to strengthen the unfavorable consequences of uncertainty for employee well-being and performance. In contrast, change recipients who trust the organization are likely to be more tolerant toward the uncertainty that changes cause, thus buffering its negative effects. This is because organizational trust is indicative of consistency, integrity and concern for the employees (Morgan & Zeffane, 2003).

Communication has been viewed as a key organizational resource during changes, due to change recipients' increased need for information to deal with the uncertainty that goes together with change (Milliken, 1987). In line with the JD-R theory (Bakker & Demerouti, 2014), Bouckenooghe (2012) proposed that communication offered formally by the organization is a resource during times of change that helps employees deal with the increased job demands that accompany uncertainty, preventing negative attitudes towards change. Given that individuals tend to search for information that explain negative and unexpected events that are likely to influence them (Wong & Weiner, 1981) and that changes include an array of unclear and confusing messages (Kotter, 1995), formal communication can be considered as a means for helping individuals cope with uncertainty-related stress. Along this line of thinking, Kiefer, Hartley, Conway and Briner (2015) emphasized the need to investigate the moderating role of communication approaches and internal communications on employee responses during change initiatives.

Finally, **perceived organizational support** (POS) has been already conceptualized as a resource that buffers the effects of the demands aspects at work (Bakker & Demerouti, 2014). In the context of change, Self, Armenakis and Schraeder (2007) showed that POS moderated the relationship between the impact of change and change justification. Specifically, this relationship was positive for change recipients who experienced high levels of POS and negative for those experiencing low POS, as the greater the POS the more likely it is for change recipients to be and feel able to successfully manage the increased job demands that arise from the change initiative.

Resources at the team level

With team-level resources we refer to resources that are inherent in the leader and the team. Various leadership aspects are argued to play a vital role in the processes of change. For example, scholars suggested that transformational and change leadership (Herold, Fedor, Caldwell, & Liu, 2008; van der Voet, Groeneveld, & Kuipers, 2014), as well as high-quality leader-member exchanges (van den Heuvel, Demerouti, & Bakker, 2014) are likely to promote functioning during organizational changes.

Drawing on COR theory, a recent study by Tanner and Otto (2016) proposed that **high-quality superior-subordinate communication** may buffer the negative effect of low management support of the change on work-related irritation. They posited that when resources are lost, gaining new resources is of utmost importance. In this sense, when management support is lacking, qualitative communication between superiors and subordinates may compensate for this loss and mitigate the negative relationship between low support for the change and employees' work-related irritation. Similarly, Self et al. (2007) hypothesized that **leader–member exchange** (LMX) moderates the relationship between the impact of change and its justification, as LMX offers resources that enable the acceptance of the new reality. Although these moderating effects were not supported empirically, the buffering role of both high-quality superior-subordinate communication and LMX is theoretically justified. We may also argue that transformational leaders - who inspire, motivate, and support their subordinates while guiding them through change (Bass & Avolio, 1990) - may help their subordinates deal effectively with the change thus mitigating the negative effects on their functioning.

Rafferty and Jimmieson (2010) examined how team change climate, described as teams' shared perceptions regarding change processes, influence team well-being. They encompassed two dimensions of change climate, namely change information and change participation, and tested their negative relation with distress. Moreover, they argued that **team change climate strength** may moderate this relationship. Based on the work of Mischel (1973) on situational strength, the authors argued that strong team climates, where team members share views over the situation and behave as one, are more resourceful than weak team climates, where behavior in ambiguous situations is more likely to be determined by individual differences rather than by team beliefs. However, contrary to expectations, their findings showed no statistical interaction between team change climate and team change climate strength in accounting for team well-being.

Resources at the individual level

Next to the resources at the organizational and the team level of analysis, the way employees are, feel, think and behave may also determine the degree and the way in which they are affected by and react to organizational changes. Systematic evidence shows that personality traits (e.g., locus of control, self-efficacy or trait affect), coping styles (e.g., problem-solving or defense mechanisms), psychological needs (e.g., need for achievement or growth, autonomy or mastery), as well as demographic variables (e.g., tenure or educational level) may impede or facilitate employee functioning in times of change (Oreg et al., 2011). However, most studies view change recipients' characteristics as antecedents of functioning during changes, thus neglecting their potential buffering role. Based on the limited evidence on the moderating role of change recipients' characteristics, as well as on the factors that emerge as relevant from recent research, we focus on employees' personal resources, and proactive behaviors (i.e., job crafting) towards adaptation to organizational change. Although job crafting is not a resource *per se*, it falls under the definition of resources proposed by COR theory (Hobfoll, 2002) since it acts as a means to obtain centrally valued resources at the job-level of analysis.

Personal resources are those aspects of the self that concern individuals' sense of their ability to control their environment successfully (Hobfoll, Johnson, Ennis, & Jackson, 2003). In congruence with COR theory (Hobfoll, 1989), it may be argued that all individual characteristics that fall under the definition of personal resources help employees deal with the threatening aspects of change, thus buffering their unfavorable effects on employee functioning. In support of this proposition, Walter and Cole (2011) found that leaders' cynicism about organizational change associated negatively with transformational leadership behaviors during times of change but this effect was valid only for leaders low (vs. high) in optimism. In other words, high optimism was found to buffer cynical attitudes towards changes on productive leadership behaviors. Also, Bellou and Chatzinikou (2015) tested whether personal computer literacy (i.e., a specific type of self-efficacy) moderates the relationship between overall job satisfaction and burnout during episodic organizational changes. Results revealed that the negative relationship between job satisfaction and burnout was less strong for less literate employees.

Another personal resource that may function as a buffer is meaning-making. Meaning-making is defined as individuals' ability to link work meaning to meaning in life in order to evaluate and reflect on work meaning in light of personal values and goals. Van den Heuvel, Demerouti, Schreurs, Bakker and Schaufeli (2009) have emphasized the beneficial role of meaning-making for employee functioning in times of organizational change, positing that reflecting on one's personal values to find meaning in a change situation enhancing coping with it. Indeed, their results showed that meaning-making related positively to employees' willingness to change over and above other valuable personal resources such as optimism, self-efficacy, mastery, coping and meaning in life. Although there is no evidence supporting the buffering role of meaning-making on the relationship between change and employee functioning, this moderating effect can be justified on the basis of COR theory (Hobfoll, 1989). Namely, employees who try to find meaning in the changes introduced in their work environment that is in line with their life values and goals are more likely to deal effectively with change, thus weakening its negative consequences.

Just like meaning-making, **proactive behaviors** that are initiated by employees and aim at creating a meaningful, healthy and motivating work environment for themselves have been found to facilitate adaptation during times of organizational change, by helping achieve a better person-job fit (Ghitulescu, 2013). Job crafting is such a proactive behavior and can be defined as employees' attempts to seek for more resources and challenges and reduce the threatening job demands in their work environment (Petrou, Demerouti, Peeters, Schaufeli, & Hetland, 2012). Empirical evidence supports the beneficial role of job crafting for adaptation to organizational change. Specifically, Petrou et al. (2015) found seeking resources and challenges to relate positively to employee task performance during the implementation of organizational changes, while reducing demands was found to relate negatively to performance. Based on the JD-R theory (Bakker & Demerouti, 2014) it may be argued that employees who try to look actively for resources or challenges in their changing environment are better able to cope with organizational change, thus mitigating its negative effects on their functioning.

Lawrence and Callan (2011) explored how employees mobilize their social support to cope during a large-scale change and downsizing. They found that support mobilization mediates the negative relationship between change-related stress and job satisfaction. However, this effect was dependent on the perceived levels of supervision, colleague and non-work support. Their results showed that change-related stress activated employees to mobilize their resources particularly when support from the supervisor (but not from colleagues) was absent, while support mobilization was beneficial for job satisfaction only when colleague support was lacking. Although this study does not test the buffering hypothesis directly, it implies that proactive behaviors like seeking resources in the change environment may prevent or reduce negative outcomes, particularly when other resources are lacking.

Concluding remarks

In this chapter, our aim was to understand under which specific conditions organizational changes are particularly detrimental for employee functioning. To this end, we used the JD-R theory (Bakker & Demerouti, 2014) and COR theory (Hobfoll, 1989) as our guiding frameworks, and looked for resources at the organizational, the team and the individual level of analysis that may buffer the negative impact of organizational changes on employee functioning and in turn facilitate employee adaptation to changing work environments.

As shown in Figure 2.1, we have focused on resources (e.g., justice, positive team climate or personal resources), as well as on energies (i.e., proactive, job crafting behaviors) that may act as means to achieve valuable resources (e.g., job resources). According to the buffering hypothesis of the JD-R theory (Bakker & Demerouti, 2014), we argued that organizational changes may be particularly unfavorable for employees when resources at the organizational, the team, and the individual level of analysis are scarce. In contrast, the availability of resources is likely to shield change recipients against the negative implications of organizational change. This theoretical argument has important implications because it helps unravel the conditions that make organizational change particularly detrimental for employee functioning. Furthermore, our literature review provides supportive evidence for the idea of resource substitution (Hobfoll & Lieberman, 1987), as, for instance, lacking resources at the organizational or the team level of analysis may be substituted by available resources at the individual level of analysis.

Although not resulted from our review of relevant studies, in our proposed model (see Figure 2.1), we also recognize the broader socioeconomic context (e.g., financial, social) that organizations operate within, as this could act as a boundary condition that moderates the effects of change. For instance, in times of economic recession, the increased unemployment rates are likely to suppress employees' negative reactions to change, in fear of losing their job. To this end, Petrou, Demerouti and Xanthopoulou (2017) tested the relationships between job crafting strategies on exhaustion and work engagement by considering two different change contexts: (1) general changes aiming at organizational development in a country with a stable economy (i.e., The Netherlands), and (2) austerity-led changes in a country that has been severely affected by the global financial crisis (i.e., Greece). Results revealed

Employee functioning **23**

some differences across contexts as to which job crafting strategies are favorable for employee functioning in changing times, underlying the role of the broader socio-economic context in the study of organizational change.

Our proposed model has significant implications for practice too, suggesting that when senior management decides to implement changes it should make sure that change recipients have access to valuable resources of different types. To do so, it is necessary that they invest time, effort and/or money prior, during and after the implementation of the initiative, in order to supply change recipients with the proposed resources. Furthermore, our model suggests that change recipients should have a certain level of autonomy to adopt proactive behaviors such as job crafting, when changes are implemented, since these strategies allow resource replenishment.

Although our model includes a significant number of resources at different levels of analysis that may determine when organizational changes will be particularly harmful for employees, it is not an extensive analysis neither of all the potential factors that may act as buffers nor of all the mechanisms in which resources may interact with organizational changes in explaining employee functioning. As concerns the former issue, we only refer to resources at the job level of analysis indirectly, as we explain how these may be formed via job crafting, even though this type of resources has been found to mitigate the effect of demands on organizational outcomes (Bakker & Demerouti, 2014). Furthermore, for many of the resources we propose as potential buffers on the relationship between change and its outcomes, we found indirect and not direct empirical support.

As concerns the latter issue, this chapter solely focuses on the buffering role of resources. However, according to the coping or boosting hypothesis of the JD-R theory (Bakker & Demerouti, 2014) resources are particularly salient for employee functioning in conditions that are highly demanding (i.e., when organizational changes are implemented). This means that resources do not only buffer the negative effect of changes on employee functioning but also exhibit their full potential when employees are confronted with challenging demands. Empirical evidence provides support for this boosting hypothesis. For instance, Xanthopoulou, Petrou, Demerouti, Kalogeropoulou and Kostas (2016b) showed that daily resources seeking behaviors related positively to work engagement particularly for employees who reported that the implemented changes had a significant impact on their daily work. This evidence suggests that both the buffering and the boosting hypothesis should be considered in order to understand under which conditions changes are favorable, unfavorable or irrelevant for employees. However, and despite these limitations, we do hope that our propositions will inspire and guide researchers in the – relatively unexplored – role of boundary conditions under which organizational changes are particularly damaging for employee functioning.

References

Ashford, S. J. (1988). Individual strategies for coping with stress during organizational transitions. *Journal of Applied Behavioral Science*, *24*, 19–36.

Bakker, A. B., & Demerouti, E. (2014). Job demands-resources theory. In P.Y. Chen & C. L. Cooper (Eds.), *Work and wellbeing: Wellbeing: A complete reference guide* (Vol. III, pp. 37–64). Chichester: Wiley-Blackwell.

Bass, B. M., & Avolio, B. J. (1990). *Improving organizational effectiveness through transformational leadership.* Thousand Oaks, CA: SAGE Publications.

Bellou, V., & Chatzinikou, I. (2015). Preventing employee burnout during episodic organizational changes. *Journal of Organizational Change Management, 28,* 673–688.

Bouckenooghe, D. (2012). The role of organizational politics, contextual resources, and formal communication on change recipients' commitment to change: A multilevel study. *European Journal of Work and Organizational Psychology, 21,* 575–602.

Combs, J., Liu, Y., Hall, A., & Ketchen, D. (2006). How much do high-performance work practices matter? A meta-analysis of their effects on organizational performance. *Personnel Psychology, 59,* 501–528.

Fedor, D. B., Caldwell, S., & Herold, D. M. (2006). The effects of organizational changes on employee commitment: A multilevel investigation. *Personnel Psychology, 59,* 1–29.

Fryxell, G. E., Dooley, R. S., & Li, W. (2004). The role of trustworthiness in maintaining employee commitment during restructuring in China. *Asia Pacific Journal of Management, 21,* 515–533.

Ghitulescu, B. E. (2013). Making change happen the impact of work context on adaptive and proactive behaviors. *The Journal of Applied Behavioral Science, 49,* 206–245.

Gilmore, T. N., Shea, G. P., & Useem, M. (1997). Side effects of corporate cultural transformations. *The Journal of Applied Behavioral Science, 33,* 174–189.

Herold, D. M., Fedor, D. B., Caldwell, S., & Liu, Y. (2008). The effects of transformational and change leadership on employees' commitment to a change: A multilevel study. *Journal of Applied Psychology, 93,* 346.

Hobfoll, S. E. (1989). Conservation of resources: A new attempt at conceptualizing stress. *American Psychologist, 44,* 513–524.

Hobfoll, S. E. (2002). Social and psychological resources and adaptation. *Review of General Psychology, 6,* 307–324.

Hobfoll, S. E., Johnson, R. J., Ennis, N., & Jackson, A. P. (2003). Resource loss, resource gain, and emotional outcomes among inner city women. *Journal of Personality and Social Psychology, 84,* 632–643.

Hobfoll, S. E., & Lieberman, J. R. (1987). Personality and social resources in immediate and continued stress resistance among women. *Journal of Personality and Social Psychology, 52,* 18–26.

Jiang, L., & Probst, T. M. (2016). The moderating effect of trust in management on consequences of job insecurity. *Economic and Industrial Democracy,* 1–25

Kiefer, T., Hartley, J., Conway, N., & Briner, R. B. (2015). Feeling the squeeze: Public employees' experiences of cutback- and innovation-related organizational changes following a national announcement of budget reductions. *Journal of Public Administration Research and Theory, 25,* 1279–1305.

Kotter, J. P. (1995, May/April). Leading change: Why transformation efforts fail. *Harvard Business Review,* 59–67.

Lawrence, S. A., & Callan, V. J. (2011). The role of social support in coping during the anticipatory stage of organizational change: A test of an integrative model. *British Journal of Management, 22,* 567–585.

Milliken, F. J. (1987). Three types of perceived uncertainty about the environment: State, effect, and response uncertainty. *Academy of Management Review, 12,* 133–143.

Mischel, W. (1973). Toward a cognitive social learning reconceptualization of personality. *Psychological Review, 80,* 252.

Morgan, D., & Zeffane, R. (2003). Employee involvement, organizational change and trust in management. *International Journal of Human Resource Management, 14*, 55–75.

Nielsen, K., Nielsen, M. B., Ogbonnaya, C., Känsälä, M., Saari, E., & Isaksson, K. (2017). Workplace resources to improve both employee well-being and performance: A systematic review and meta-analysis. *Work & Stress, 31*(2), 101–120.

Oreg, S. (2006). Personality, context, and resistance to organizational change. *European Journal of Work and Organizational Psychology, 15*, 73–101.

Oreg, S., Vakola, M., & Armenakis, A. (2011). Change recipients' reactions to organizational change: A 60-year review of quantitative studies. *The Journal of Applied Behavioral Science, 47*, 461–524.

Petrou, P., Demerouti, E., Peeters, M. C., Schaufeli, W. B., & Hetland, J. (2012). Crafting a job on a daily basis: Contextual correlates and the link to work engagement. *Journal of Organizational Behavior, 33*, 1120–1141.

Petrou, P., Demerouti, E., & Schaufeli, W. B. (2015). Job crafting in changing organizations: Antecedents and implications for exhaustion and performance. *Journal of Occupational Health Psychology, 20*, 470–481.

Petrou, P., Demerouti, E., & Xanthopoulou, D. (2017). Regular versus cut-back related change: The role of employee job crafting in organizational change contexts of different nature. *International Journal of Stress Management, 24*, 62–84.

Posthuma, R. A., Campion, M. C., Masimova, M., & Campion, M. A. (2013). A high performance work practices taxonomy: Integrating the literature and directing future research. *Journal of Management, 39*, 1184–1220.

Proost, K., Verboon, P., & Van Ruysseveldt, J. (2015). Organizational justice as buffer against stressful job demands. *Journal of Managerial Psychology, 30*, 487–499.

Rafferty, A. E., & Griffin, M. A. (2006). Perceptions of organizational change: A stress and coping perspective. *Journal of Applied Psychology, 91*, 1154–1162.

Rafferty, A. E., & Jimmieson, N. L. (2010). Team change climate: A group-level analysis of the relationships among change information and change participation, role stressors, and well-being. *European Journal of Work and Organizational Psychology, 19*, 551–586.

Schweiger, D. M., & Denisi, A. S. (1991). Communication with employees following a merger: A longitudinal field experiment. *Academy of Management Journal, 34*, 110–135.

Self, D. R., Armenakis, A. A., & Schraeder, M. (2007). Organizational change content, process, and context: A simultaneous analysis of employee reactions. *Journal of Change Management, 7*, 211–229.

Sharif, M. M., & Scandura, T. A. (2014). Do perceptions of ethical conduct matter during organizational change? Ethical leadership and employee involvement. *Journal of Business Ethics, 124*, 185–196.

Tanner, G., & Otto, K. (2016). Superior-subordinate communication during organizational change: Under which conditions does high-quality communication become important? *International Journal of Human Resource Management, 27*, 2183–2201.

Van den Heuvel, M., Demerouti, E., & Bakker, A. B. (2014). How psychological resources facilitate adaptation to organizational change. *European Journal of Work and Organizational Psychology, 23*, 847–858.

Van den Heuvel, M., Demerouti, E., Schreurs, B. H. J., Bakker, A. B., & Schaufeli, W. B. (2009). Does meaning-making help during organizational change? Development and validation of a new scale. *Career Development International, 14*, 508–533.

Van der Voet, J., Groeneveld, S., & Kuipers, B. S. (2014). Talking the talk or walking the walk? The leadership of planned and emergent change in a public organization. *Journal of Change Management, 14*, 171–191.

26 Victoria Bellou et al.

Walter, F., & Cole, M. S. (2011, August). Change cynicism, transformational leadership, and the buffering role of dispositional optimism. *Paper Presented at the 71st Annual Meeting of the Academy of Management*, San Antonio, TX.

Wanberg, C. R., & Banas, J. T. (2000). Predictors and outcomes of openness to changes in a reorganizing workplace. *Journal of Applied Psychology*, *85*, 132–142.

Wang, H. J., Lu, C. Q., & Siu, O. L. (2015). Job insecurity and job performance: The moderating role of organizational justice and the mediating role of work engagement. *Journal of Applied Psychology*, *100*, 1249–1258.

White, M., Hill, S., McGovern, P., Mills, C., & Smeaton, D. (2003). 'High-performance' management practices, working hours and work–life balance. *British Journal of Industrial Relations*, *41*, 175–195.

Wong, P. T., & Weiner, B. (1981). When people ask "why" questions, and the heuristics of attributional search. *Journal of Personality and Social Psychology*, *40*, 650–663.

Xanthopoulou, D., Gkorezis, P., Bellou, V., & Petridou, E. (2016a, April). Organizational justice matters for employee functioning in changing environments: A study of Greek organizations in times of financial recession. *Paper Presented at the 12th European Academy of Occupational Health Psychology Conference*, Athens, Greece.

Xanthopoulou, D., Petrou, P., Demerouti, E., Kalogeropoulou, E-L., & Kostas, S. (2016b, April). When daily crafting matters more for employee functioning? The moderating role of organizational changes. *Paper Presented at the 12th European Academy of Occupational Health Psychology Conference*, Athens, Greece.

3

CHANGE CONSULTATION DURING ORGANIZATIONAL RESTRUCTURING

Buffering and exacerbating effects in the context of role demands

Nerina L. Jimmieson and Michelle K. Tucker

Change is ever-present in organizations and, although change can offer future opportunities, organizational change, especially involving mergers, acquisitions, restructuring and downsizing, is often appraised as stressful (Pahkin, Mattila-Holappa, Nielsen, Widerszal-Bazyl, & Wiezer, 2014; Seo & Hill, 2005). Employee strain during change can manifest in a range of physical and psychological ill-health indicators (Lippel & Quinlan, 2011). Poor communication and lack of participation in the change process are primary reasons change efforts fail (Barrett, 2002; Klein, 1996; Kotter, 1995, 1999). Change consultation in the forms of information and participation fulfills various motivational and cognitive functions, but of particular importance, it allows employees to maintain prediction, understanding and control in the midst of uncertainty (Sutton & Kahn, 1986). While change consultation is recognized as a vital step in change planning, there is a lack of research examining its role as a job resource, protecting against employee strain in the face of specific role demands.

In this chapter, we present two studies with employees in the midst of prolonged organization-wide change. Sample 1 was employees of a state government department undergoing restructuring and redundancies. Sample 2 was employees from an energy provider that had been experiencing corporatization, restructuring and downsizing for the last two years. For Sample 2, a distinction was made between those designated as redeployees versus those who had not. In both studies, the extent to which change consultation acts as a valuable job resource that alleviates the negative consequences of three specific role demands (overload, conflict and ambiguity) on employee strain is considered.

Heightened role demands during change

Psychosocial working conditions are often eroded as a result of change and thus have immediate and long-term negative effects on employees, leading to a range of illnesses (Lippel & Quinlan, 2011). However, studies on change exposure do not typically look at what stressors the change context trigger. J. B. Shaw, Fields, Thacker and Fisher (1993) argued that role demands are bound to be salient due to the inherent uncertainty associated with change. Employees may experience role overload because there are fewer people to do the job or when new job duties go beyond employees' current knowledge, skills and abilities. Indeed, Kubicek, Paskvan and Korunka (2015) have discussed how accelerated change in organizations leads to work intensification, a phenomena that goes hand in hand with time pressure. Role conflict also may become prevalent, given that expectations are in flux and may be in direct contrast to the expectations of the old organization. Role ambiguity may occur when the expectations applicable to the old organization have not been replaced with clear expectations set by the new organization.

Several qualitative studies examining sources of change stress speak to the salience of role demands. Interviews with six female medical secretaries over three time points during structural changes in the Swedish health care system found that too much work was the most profound stress-producer (Hertting, Nilsson, Theorell, & Satterlund-Larsson, 2003). Interviews with 27 government employees undergoing transformational change revealed that increased workload was the most common stressor cited, because of the extra time and effort required of them, especially the need to implement changes on top of current responsibilities with fewer resources (Robinson & Griffiths, 2005). Not knowing how one's role would change was the second most prevalent stressor. Boyd, Tuckey and Winefield (2014) conducted a case-centered narrative analysis with four individuals who had witnessed downsizing in their respective workplaces, also revealing implications for increased role overload and time pressure, as well as role conflict that came from juggling service and non-service demands. Smollan (2015) interviewed 31 employees of a NZ public health organization and showed that increased workload was most salient before, and then again after, the change event, whereas unclear role expectations emerged as a stressor during the change event. Rowlands and Rees (2015) interviewed 25 UK academics in their fourth year of restructuring and redundancies and found that increased workload was a major theme, very much intertwined with the issue of role conflict in which increased teaching loads were incompatible with current and also new expectations around research activities.

Change consultation

Successful change management is reliant on the social exchange between decision-makers and employees being well-received, and this requires extensive communication, dialog and discussion (Rowlands & Rees, 2015). Change management is the framework and associated practices followed by senior leaders, managers and change agents to inform, motivate and support employees through the process of change implementation. Change consultation refers to the degree to which employees are provided with information about organizational changes and provided with the opportunity to participate in decisions that affect their work (Cousins et al., 2004). Indeed, in the context of restructuring, Pahkin et al. (2014) included good communication from top management and supervisors and employee participation during planning and implementation as critical principles underlying what they refer to as a "sound change process".

As a change management practice, employee change consultation is critical for educating and informing employees in an accurate and opportune manner that allows one to anticipate and make sense of and interpret change. It empowers employees, providing them with a sense of personal control, confidence to deal with stressors and better coping options. It also provides opportunities for voice, input and influence, fosters procedural fairness, builds trust and, as reviewed below, protects employees' health. There is a vast empirical literature showing that communication and participation influences personal (health) and work (job satisfaction and organizational commitment) outcomes for employees (see Oreg, Vakola, & Armenakis, 2011, for a 60-year review of quantitative studies).

Cross-sectional studies using the UK's HSE Management Standards Indicator Tool (Cousins et al., 2004) have provided consistent empirical support for change consultation as protective for employees (Bevan et al., 2010; Guidi et al., 2012; Kerr et al., 2009; Marcatto et al., 2014; Ravalier, McVicar, & Munn-Giddings, 2013). In a four-year time-lagged investigation of 9,913 Northern Ireland Civil Service employees, Houdmont, Kerr and Addley (2012) showed that change consultation at Time 1 predicted absence ascribed to work-related stress at Time 2. Also using a time-ordered design, Jimmieson, Hobman, Tucker and Bordia (2016) showed that employees with constant low and constant moderate change consultation reported greater psychological distress, emotional exhaustion and job dissatisfaction (compared to those with constant high change consultation). Employees with constant low change consultation expressed stronger intent to take stress-remedial actions. Employees with constant moderate change consultation reported more gastrointestinal upsets. A decrease in change consultation over time was associated with more psychological distress, emotional exhaustion, sleep disturbance, job dissatisfaction and stress-remedial intentions. In contrast to expectations, however, employees who experienced an increase in change consultation over time reported increased psychological distress compared with employees who had high change consultation at both points in time. This finding was attributed to a third variable of a stressful nature, such as exposure to a change event occurring at some point in time between baseline and follow-up.

Change consultation as a coping resource

Despite establishing itself as valuable in practice, there is a lack of empirical research exploring whether change consultation as a job resource buffers against the detrimental impacts of role demands on employee strain. This assertion is consistent with established theories of stress and coping that suggest that individuals are particularly prone to negative stress reactions when they lack resources to cope with the respective stressor (Lazarus & Folkman, 1984). In the work context, both the Job Demand-Control Model (Karasek, 1979) and the Job Demands-Resources Model (Demerouti, Bakker, Nachreiner, & Schaufeli, 2001) include predictions that role demands and job resources interact to create a number of potential job conditions. Both models acknowledge that there are times when high job demands cannot be minimized due to the nature of the role or organizational context, which is likely to be the case during times of change. However, according to the stress-buffering hypothesis, job resources should help to protect employees from the negative effects of high job demands. Given the positive psychological states and behaviors that arise from increasing employee knowledge of changes and participation in decision-making, our aim is to provide an empirical test of change consultation as a moderator of role demands for employees in organizations undergoing significant change. When employees feel consulted about change, they will appraise the situation as one in which they feel efficacious in their ability to cope, such that it provides a protective mechanism for employees experiencing high levels of role demands. Thus, it was hypothesized that high change consultation would be stress-buffering and, in contrast, low change consultation would be stress-exacerbating.

Study 1

Method

Participants were from an Australian workplace health and safety regulator. At the time of data collection, the organization was in its sixth month of an organization-wide restructure, accompanied by significant redundancies. A second round of restructuring was impending and there also had been a recent announcement that all operations would move from a major inner city to another municipality, requiring an extra hour of travel. We distributed 1,319 surveys online to all 19 departments, and 249 employees responded (response rate = 18.88%). Response rates across departments were variable, ranging from 2% to 56% and an average response rate per department of 22%. Due to missing data, 44 cases were deleted, leaving 205 as the useable sample. This sample comprised 113 women (55%) and 88 men (43%). Age ranged from 23 to 67 years ($M = 43.32$, $SD = 10.53$). Organizational tenure ranged from 3 months to 28 years ($M = 7.69$, $SD = 6.28$).

Role overload and role ambiguity were measured with four items (Cousins et al., 2004). Role conflict was measured with four items (Haynes, Wall, Bolden, Stride, & Rick, 1999). Change consultation was measured using four items capturing being consulted, informed and voice opportunities (two items from Cousins et al. and two items from Jimmieson, Peach, & White, 2008). In terms of employee strain, cognitive weariness, considered to be the mental exhaustion component of job burnout, was measured using five items (e.g., I feel I'm not focused in my thinking) from Shirom and Melamed (2006), sleep disturbance was measured with four items (sleep latency, sleep maintenance, early morning awakening and trouble getting back to sleep) from Levine et al. (2003) and intention to transfer jobs within the organization was measured with a single item.

Results

Descriptive statistics are in Table 3.1 and hierarchical regressions are in Table 3.2. All role demands had significant positive associations with employee strain. Higher change consultation was associated with lower cognitive weariness and sleep disturbance, regardless of which role demand was in the model. Significant two-way interactions between role conflict and change consultation were found on cognitive weariness (β = .16, t = 2.49, p = .014), and intention to transfer jobs (β = .17, t = 2.60, p = .010). In addition, a significant two-way interaction was found between role ambiguity and change consultation on intention to transfer jobs (β = .20, t = 2.76, p = .006).

Figure 3.1 shows, as expected, that the positive association between role conflict and cognitive weariness was significant for employees with low change consultation. However, in contrast with initial expectations, high change consultation did not act as a stress-buffer and in fact had a stronger stress-exacerbating effect on

TABLE 3.1 Descriptive data and correlations for Study 1 (n = 205)

Variables	M	SD	α	1	2	3	4	5	6	7
1. Role Overload	3.03	1.45	.91	—						
2. Role Conflict	3.43	1.59	.93	.610***	—					
3. Role Ambiguity	2.32	1.21	.90	.354***	.533***	—				
4. Change Consultation	3.90	1.61	.88	−.474***	−.524***	−.438***	—			
5. Cognitive Weariness	2.97	1.51	.98	.406***	.443***	.530***	−.340***	—		
6. Sleep Disturbance	2.46	1.07	.81	.330***	.337***	.292***	−.341***	.445***	—	
7. Intention to Transfer Jobs	2.52	1.98	—	.337***	.359***	.294***	−.191**	.394***	.201**	—

Notes: *p < .05; **p < .01; ***p < .001; Role demands rated on a scale of 1 (never) to 7 (always); Change consultation rated on a scale of 1 (strongly disagree) to 7 (strongly agree); Cognitive weariness rated on a scale of 1 (never or almost never) to 7 (always or almost always); Sleep disturbance rated on a scale of 1 (no, not in the past 4 weeks) to 5 (yes, 5 or more times a week); Intentions to transfer jobs rated on a scale of 1 (extremely unlikely) to 7 (extremely likely).

32 Nerina L. Jimmieson and Michelle K. Tucker

TABLE 3.2 Hierarchical regression analyses for Study 1

	Cognitive Weariness β	Sleep Disturbance β	Intention to Transfer Jobs β
Step 1 – Predictors			
Role Overload (RO)	.317***	.217**	.318***
Change Consultation (CC)	−.192**	−.239**	−.041
R^2	.194***	.153***	.115***
F	24.075***	17.930***	13.125***
Step 2 – Two-Way Interactions			
RO x CC	.039	−.017	.085
ΔR^2	.001	.000	.006
ΔF	0.342	0.064	1.481
Step 1 – Predictors			
Role Conflict (RC)	.364***	.219**	.356***
Change Consultation (CC)	−.151*	−.226**	−.005
R^2	.212***	.151***	.129***
F	26.966***	17.711***	14.921***
Step 2 – Two-Way Interactions			
RC x CC	.158*	.001	.173*
ΔR^2	.024*	.000	.028*
ΔF	6.190*	0.000	6.758*
Step 1 – Predictors			
Role Ambiguity (RA)	.471***	.174*	.260**
Change Consultation (CC)	−.132*	−.263***	−.077
R^2	.294***	.140***	.091***
F	41.742***	16.244***	10.124***
Step 2 – Two-Way Interactions			
RA x CC	.062	−.083	.200**
ΔR^2	.003	.006	.033**
ΔF	0.899	1.329	7.600**

Notes: *$p < .05$; **$p < .01$; ***$p < .001$; n varies from 202 to 205 across regression models due to listwise deletion; Beta coefficients reported at step at which they were entered; Results did not change when gender, age and tenure were controlled for in an initial step, nor did these demographic characteristics interact with the predictors.

cognitive weariness (than low change consultation). While change consultation was beneficial when role conflict was low, when this stressor was high, cognitive weariness was as high as for employees with low change consultation. Overall, this pattern of findings demonstrates a diminishing benefit of change consultation at high role conflict (compared to low role conflict) and that employees with and without change consultation are no better off than each other at high role conflict, both having high cognitive weariness.

In regards to intentions to transfer to a different job in the organization (Figures 3.2 & 3.3), both role conflict and role ambiguity had significant positive effects for employees lacking in change consultation, such that this behavioral

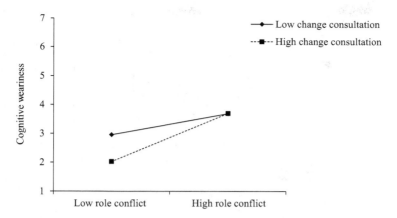

FIGURE 3.1 Role conflict on cognitive weariness at low ($b = .23, t = 2.77, p = .006$) and high ($b = .53, t = 5.26, p < .001$) levels of change consultation (Study 1)

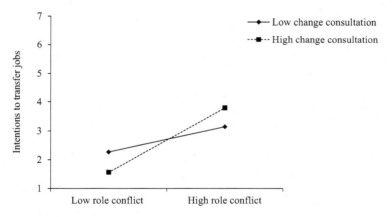

FIGURE 3.2 Role conflict on intentions to transfer jobs at low ($b = .28, t = 2.43, p = .016$) and high ($b = .70, t = 5.12, p < .001$) levels of change consultation (Study 1)

intention was heightened. Again, however, high change consultation was not protective and exacerbated the positive effects of these role demands on job transfer intentions. As observed above, change consultation was beneficial at low levels of conflict and ambiguity. Interestingly, when these role demands were high, high change consultation caused job transfer intentions to surpass employees with low change consultation. This somewhat different pattern to that observed in the prediction of cognitive weariness may be due to the fact that having plans to move to a different job is a proactive attempt to deal with the changes underway. The employees most motivated to change jobs are those stressed by their role but with sufficient consultation to inform such a decision.

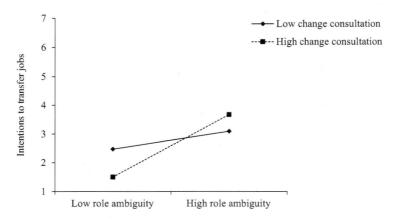

FIGURE 3.3 Role ambiguity on intentions to transfer jobs at low ($b = .26, t = 1.92, p = .057$) and high ($b = .89, t = 4.29, p < .001$) levels of change consultation (Study 1)

Discussion

Employees who perceived high change consultation reported lower employee strain in terms of less cognitive weariness and sleep disturbance. It is of interest to note that the pattern of correlations suggested that high change consultation was associated with lower experiences of role demands, also demonstrating its protective function. Furthermore, the benefits of high change consultation were evident when role conflict and role ambiguity were low, and a lack of change consultation increased the positive effect of these two role demands on cognitive weariness and intentions to transfer to a different job in the organization. However, quite inconsistent with expectations, there was a more marked positive association between these two role demands and employee strain for employees with high change consultation. Thus, while change consultation is viewed as imperative in practice, there appears to be caveats to its application as a change management practice when employees are dealing with role demands.

Indeed, there are studies examining either the main or stress-buffering effects of communication and participation in the context of organizational change that show it can be ineffectual or capable of generating unintended negative consequences. Jimmieson, Terry and Callan (2004) tested for a stress-buffering effect of information provision in a restructuring context and found no evidence it buffered against quantitative workload and role ambiguity in the prediction of employee strain. As noted earlier, Jimmieson et al. (2016) found that employees who experienced an increase in change consultation over time reported increased psychological distress compared with employees who had high change consultation at both points in time.

In addition, a systematic review of participative decision-making by Egan et al. (2007) concluded that, when such interventions were implemented alongside restructuring and downsizing, results tended to suggest benign or adverse health effects. In a review of the participative decision-making literature both in general and specific to educational settings, Somech (2010) cautioned against the intuitive appeal of participative methods in light of the modest empirical evidence in regards to job satisfaction and much more limited and even counter-intuitive results for strain.

Several theoretical perspectives help to make sense of these findings. Both information provision and control opportunities in the context of a stressor is thought to exacerbate strain under certain circumstances, particularly if the outcome is considered to be aversive and those aversive features are made salient and predictable (Averill, 1973; Burger, 1989; Miller, 1980; Thompson, 1981). In addition, Brasher's (2001) theory of uncertainty management states that not knowing may provide a sense of hope or optimism regarding the impending outcome rather than the guarantee of a negative outcome. Oreg (2006) found that information about the change event predicted an increase in both cognitive and behavioral resistance for 177 defense employees undergoing an organizational restructure, which he said is possible when there is something to be lost. Axtell et al. (2002) also concluded that one would not expect positive reactions to change consultation when the change is threatening in light of the results of their change consultation intervention with distribution workers.

Our results suggest that change consultation is not stress-buffering during change and is even harmful to the well-being of individuals but only when they are under high role demands. Information-based and participation-based change strategies require a significant investment from employees in terms of time and cognitive and emotional resources. Consistent with Conservation of Resources (Hobfoll, 1989), employees experiencing significant stress due to the loss of important resources that organizational change typically incurs mean that they are vulnerable to depleted resources that, along with high levels of role demands, lead to a spiral of resource loss. Thus, employees are not able to take advantage of the information and participation opportunities afforded to them because they cannot make further cognitive and emotional investments. Rather, these resources come at a cost in terms of cognitive load (as it did on cognitive weariness) and well-being. Somech (2010) raised the idea that participation opportunities will be stressful when employees perceive that their ability to adapt is constrained by time pressure and workload (p. 185). As an example that points to this explanation, O'Connor, Jimmieson and White (in press) showed that the extent to which information and participation predicted job behaviors to support a building relocation (through positive attitudes, normative pressure and personal control) was diminished when time pressure was high.

Redeployees and personal impact

Kozlowski, Chao, Smith and Hedlund (1993) argued that employees exposed to downsizing will have stronger reactions when the downsizing has significant personal implications, and this level of impact would not be expected to be the same for all employees. One discriminating feature of the level of impact is the practice of redeployment, common in downsizing organizations, where an employee's position is declared redundant or "surplus" and the employee is left to find another position in the organization within a specified time period or be laid off (Armstrong-Stassen, 1997, 2002). Being a redeployee is bound to be one of great disempowerment. Indeed, Kanter's (1977, 1993) structural theories of power and behavior in organizations state that one's position in the organization is critical to the empowerment of employees, more so than traits and individual factors. Power originates from structural opportunities that allow for professional growth and three power supplies: resources to do one's job; access to information and communication; and support and feedback. If these three channels are blocked, one is unconnected from the mission of the organization and is rendered powerless.

In a small comparative analysis of managers designated redundant versus managers who were not, Armstrong-Stassen (1997) found that redeployed managers used less adaptive coping at Time 1 and reported more tension and burnout six months later. Armstrong-Stassen (2002) found that redundant employees reported a significant decline in trust and commitment compared to those not being made redundant. Armstrong-Stassen, Cameron and Horsburgh (2001) compared job transferees (due to being displaced/redundant) to the rest of the organization during a hospital merger/downsizing and found that the transferees perceived less co-worker support and organizational commitment than those less impacted by the change but both groups did not fare well on various other Time 1–2 morale indicators.

Wisse and Sleebos (2016) also argued that change is not as equally stressful to all employees. For Dutch employees going through a restructure, Wisse and Sleebos showed that emotional exhaustion was highest for employees perceiving that the restructure had significant personal consequences for them combined with a high sense of personal self-construal. Studies are yet to provide an explicit test of the extent to which employees who have the most to lose find change consultation non-protective or even detrimental in the context of the stressor-strain relationship compared to employees less impacted by the change. Thus, in Study 2, we compared redeployees to the rest of the organization. Based on the theories and studies just reviewed, we expect the stress-exacerbating effects of high change consultation to be more evident for redeployees compared to the rest of the organization.

Study 2

Method

Participants were from an Australian energy provider that had been corporatized. At the time of data collection, the organization was in the midst of a prolonged two-year period of restructuring and associated redundancies, following a number of mergers with other energy companies. The changes also involved redeployment in which some employees had had their position made redundant but still remained

Change consultation **37**

employed. Although all employees were impacted by the change, redeployees were considered to be the most proximal to the adverse changes taking place.

We distributed 4,179 surveys online, and 1,252 employees responded (response rate = 30%). Fifty-one were redeployees (response rate = 35%) and 1,201 employees were from the rest of the organization (response rate = 25%). For the redeployee group, 34 were women (67%) and 17 were men (33%). Age ranged from 20 to 71 years (M = 47.71, SD = 11.05). Organizational tenure ranged from 13 months to 30 years (M = 11.42, SD = 6.11). Due to missing data in the rest of the organization sample, 122 cases were deleted, leaving 1,079 as the useable sample. For this group, 749 were men (69%), 295 were women (27%) and 35 did not report their gender (3%). Age ranged from 21 to 69 years (M = 45.34, SD = 9.61). Organizational tenure ranged from 3 months to 56 years (M = 14.21, SD = 9.37).

Role demands, change consultation, cognitive weariness and sleep disturbance all were measured with the same scales as used in Study 1. As an additional indicator of employee strain, six anxiety/depression items from the GHQ-12 (Goldberg, 1972) were used.

Results

Descriptive statistics for both samples are in Table 3.3. A series of t-tests indicated that redeployees perceived lower role overload and role conflict compared to the rest of the organization. This is interpretable in light of the fact that redeployees had no set job position, were acting in seconded low-level positions considered to be deskilling, a theme also borne out in the qualitative comments provided as part of the surveying process: *"I am sitting around all day doing nothing"; "I am not performing any real role"; "I am not permitted to do meaningful work"*. Redeployees were exposed to more role ambiguity. Redeployees felt less consulted about the change and were higher on anxiety/depression, job burnout and cognitive weariness. The two groups did not differ on sleep disturbance. Overall, the change experience was quite different for the redeployees compared to the rest of the organization.

As shown in Table 3.4, hierarchical regressions revealed that role overload and role conflict had positive associations with all three of the employee stress reactions, for both redeployees and the rest of the organization. Role ambiguity was consistently related to employee strain in the rest of the organization, but not for the redeployees. Regardless of which role demand variable was in the model, change consultation had negative associations with employee strain for the rest of the organization but was of no consequence for redeployee strain.

Two significant two-way interactions were found for redeployees: role ambiguity x change consultation on anxiety/depression (β = .42, t = 2.49, p = .016; Figure 3.4) and sleep disturbance (β = .36, t = 2.07, p = .045; Figure 3.5). As anticipated, when change consultation was high, role ambiguity had a significant positive effect on anxiety/depression and sleep disturbance, suggesting a stress-exacerbating

TABLE 3.3 Descriptive data and correlations for Study 2 for redeployees (n = 51) and rest of organization (n = 1,079)

Variables	Redeployees			Rest of Organization			1	2	3	4	5	6	7
	M	SD	α	M	SD	α							
1. Role Overload	2.65^t	1.51	.92	3.17	1.34	.87	—	.641***	.295*	−.170	.373**	.412**	.370**
2. Role Conflict	2.86^t	1.46	.92	3.40	1.42	.90	.606***	—	.098	−.145	.334*	.326*	.422**
3. Role Ambiguity	3.11^t	1.71	.92	2.11	1.01	.87	.299***	.405***	—	−.618***	.232	.299*	.042
4. Change Consultation	2.85^t	1.64	.94	3.88	1.44	.90	−.227**	−.319***	−.443***	—	−.176	−.194	.057
5. Anxiety/Depression	3.63^t	1.66	.91	3.08	1.25	.90	.451***	.442***	.368***	−.362***	—	.773***	.553***
6. Cognitive Weariness	3.82^t	1.89	.98	3.10	1.35	.96	.331***	.367***	.384***	−.321***	.680***	—	.363**
7. Sleep Disturbance	2.78	1.23	.86	2.76	1.09	.82	.263***	.256***	.169***	−.243***	.543***	.436***	—

Notes: *p < .05; **p < .01; ***p < .001; Correlations for Redeployees presented above diagonal and correlations for Rest of Organization presented below diagonal; Role demands rated on a scale of 1 (never) to 7 (always); Change consultation rated on a scale of 1 (strongly disagree) to 7 (strongly agree); Anxiety/depression rated on a scale of 1 (never) to 7 (always); Cognitive weariness rated on a scale of 1 (never or almost never) to 7 (always or almost always); Sleep disturbance rated on a scale of 1 (no, not in the past 4 weeks) to 5 (yes, 5 or more times a week); t = t-tests demonstrated means for Redeployees versus Rest of Organization statistically different.

TABLE 3.4 Hierarchical regression analyses for Study 2

	Anxiety/Depression		Cognitive Weariness		Sleep Disturbance	
	β		β		β	
	Redeployees	Rest of Organization	Redeployees	Rest of Organization	Redeployees	Rest of Organization
Step 1 – Predictors						
Role Overload (RO)	.353*	.388***	.389**	.270***	.391**	.218***
Change Consultation (CC)	−.116	−.272***	−.116	−.257***	.124	−.191***
R^2	.152*	.274***	.183**	.172***	.152*	.104***
F	4.298*	201.652***	5.264**	110.627***	4.300*	61.431***
Step 2 – Two-Way Interactions						
RO x CC	−.141	−.011	−.094	.021	.168	−.037
ΔR^2	.014	.000	.006	.000	.020	.001
ΔF	0.772	0.179	0.364	0.574	1.108	1.552
Step 1 – Predictors						
Role Conflict (RC)	.315*	.364***	.301*	.294***	.439**	.198***
Change Consultation (CC)	−.130	−.246***	−.140	−.225***	.121	−.178***
R^2	.128*	.251***	.125*	.180***	.192**	.094***
F	3.521*	178.877***	3.361*	116.954***	5.709**	55.081***
Step 2 – Two-Way Interactions						
RC x CC	−.071	.003	.019	.012	−.067	−.038
ΔR^2	.004	.000	.000	.000	.004	.001
ΔF	0.215	0.013	0.016	0.183	0.212	1.624
Step 1 – Predictors						
Role Ambiguity (RA)	.200	.259***	.287	.301***	.125	.075*
Change Consultation (CC)	−.052	−.247***	−.020	−.186***	.135	−.209***
R^2	.056	.185***	.090	.175***	.013	.063***
F	1.416	121.498***	2.321	113.036***	0.316	35.840***
Step 2 – Two-Way Interactions						
RA x CC	.416*	.013	.145	.070*	.359*	.027
ΔR^2	.110*	.000	.014	.004*	.082*	.001
ΔF	6.205*	0.175	0.696	5.308*	4.263*	0.699

Notes: *$p < .05$; **$p < .01$; ***$p < .001$; n varies from 50 to 51 for Redeployees and from 1,063 to 1,074 for Rest of Organization across regression models due to listwise deletion; Beta coefficients reported at step at which they were entered; Results for Redeployees and Rest of Organization did not change when gender, age and tenure were controlled for in an initial step, nor did these demographic characteristics interact with the predictors; For Redeployees, diagnostics revealed one case that was a univariate and multivariate outlier (for the role overload analyses across all dependent variables) but removal of this outlier did not change the results.

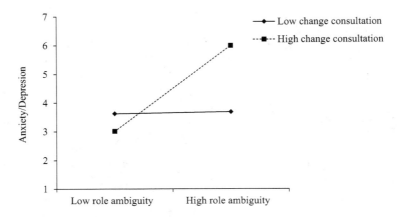

FIGURE 3.4 Role ambiguity on anxiety/depression at low ($b = .02, t = 0.09, p = .925$) and high ($b = .87, t = 2.74, p = .009$) levels of change consultation for redeployees (Study 2)

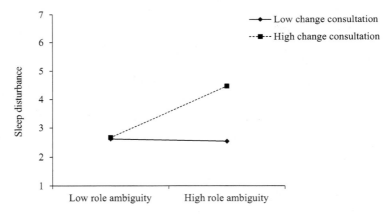

FIGURE 3.5 Role ambiguity on sleep disturbance at low ($b = -.02, t = -0.02, p = .864$) and high ($b = .53, t = 2.14, p = .038$) levels of change consultation for redeployees (Study 2)

effect. However, when change consultation was low, the simple slopes were not significant for anxiety/depression and sleep disturbance, suggesting a stress-buffering effect. Thus, consistent with Study 1 and subsequent expectations, redeployees found high change consultation aversive when dealing with an ambiguous job situation. It was expected that low change consultation would, to a lesser extent, also be stress-exacerbating but it had a stress-buffering effect.

The latter finding is in line with Olson and Tetrick's (1988) argument that some categories of employees, such as low-level employees with less control over the change, might want to distance themselves from the change. It also is consistent with the monitoring and blunting hypothesis proposed by Miller (1981, 1989, 1990, 1992) which states that, under conditions of threat, people have different information-seeking preferences that varies along two dimensions: (1) the extent to which individuals prefer to seek out (high monitors) or avoid (low monitors) threat-relevant information and (2) the extent to individuals prefer to distract themselves (high blunters) or attend to (low blunters) threat-relevant information. It is possible that redeployees were managing their negative arousal in the face of threat by distracting themselves from informational cues.

The role ambiguity x change consultation interaction on cognitive weariness was significant for the rest of the organization ($\beta = .07$, $t = 2.30$, $p = .021$) and demonstrated a similar pattern of results to those observed in Study 1 (Figure 3.6). The relationship between role ambiguity and cognitive weariness was significant and positive at both low and high change consultation, with the steepness of the slope more marked for high change consultation. Again, the benefits of change consultation appeared to have diminishing benefits as a function of role demands, such that neither group differed in terms of their cognitive weariness at high role stressors.

General discussion

Results of these two studies showed that change consultation was not effective when role demands were high, a pattern of effects that was replicated when examining redeployees versus the rest of the organization. Further, redeployees were buffered against role demands in terms of their mental health and sleep when change consultation was low. Nevertheless, change consultation worked as predicted when

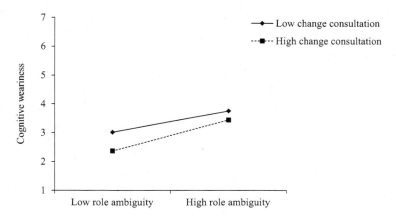

FIGURE 3.6 Role ambiguity on cognitive weariness at low ($b = .37$, $t = 8.20$, $p < .001$) and high ($b = .54$, $t = 7.62$, $p < .001$) levels of change consultation for rest of the organization (Study 2)

role demands were low. Theoretical implications point to the need for stress and resource theories to isolate the conditions under which change consultation will be beneficial or not to the stress and coping process for employees. Conservation of resources appears to be very relevant in the context of change, as there will be some employees who need to conserve resources and thus not benefit from well-intended but resource-intensive change management practices. Practical implications point to the need for change managers and agents to pay attention to role demands when leading and implementing change and also need to devise tailored interventions for employees with the most to lose from the change.

Limitations of our change consultation measure were that different sources (top management versus supervisors) were not identified and the items confounded both downward communication and upward opportunities to have input and voice. It is acknowledged that it is possible there were other categories of employees experiencing the change with different ramifications that we were not able to capture. Indeed, studies have shown that hierarchical level (Martin, Jones, & Callan, 2006; Hill, Seo, Kang, & Taylor, 2012) and occupation type (Falkenberg, Näswall, Sverke, & Sjoberg, 2009; Martin et al., 2006) determines the way in which different employee groups appraise and react to change. For example, Martin et al., showed that upper-level employees and managers perceive more change control and Hill et al. showed that perceived effectiveness of change communication deteriorated the further employees were from the top management team in terms of hierarchical distance. Future research also could include a subjective assessment of the personal impact of the change (see Wisse & Sleebos, 2016).

Several other methodological limitations need to be noted, such as the small sample size of just 51 for the redeployees. There was the potential for sampling bias due to low response rates, variable response rates across departmental groupings and missing data that further reduced the sample size. Nevertheless, the obtained gender profile matched the overall workforce for both organizations (Study 1 female-dominated and Study 2 male-dominated) and a full range was captured for age, tenure and occupation, and all departmental or service groupings were captured. The cross-sectional research design also is problematic for causal inferences and does not allow us conclude if the role demands were heightened by the change event or an inherent part of the job. Thus, future research should incorporate the stage of the change event into the research design. Indeed, Smollan's (2015) interviews with change recipients revealed that different stressors varied in salience before, during, and after the restructure. Shumacher, Schreurs, Van Emmerik and De Witte (2016) also showed that the exhaustion process was more prominent for employees in the midst of change, compared to employees in the early and late stages of change.

As synthesized by Armenakis and Bedeian (1999), organizational change happens in the context of a complex set of variables related to change content, context and process. Somech (2010), in a review of participation, also noted that, although participation is a fundamental practice in response to the challenges of a changing environment, there is still much to learn in terms of mediating motivators and cognitions and moderators at multiple levels of analysis. Mediating mechanisms requiring future research include the extent to which change consultation shapes primary appraisals of threat (and even challenge) and secondary appraisals that reveal the extent to which change consultation is effective in reducing uncertainty and increasing control, and also the types of coping strategies triggered. Contextual moderating variables and when it will yield positive or negative effects include the type of participative opportunities provided, message type (excuses versus justifications; see J. C. Shaw, Wild, & Colquitt, 2003), the extent to which the situation will lead to undesirable personal outcomes and, at the broadest level, the type of organizational event. Individual differences of theoretical relevance to change consultation (information processing style, desire for control, proactivity and openness to change) also need more investigation.

In conclusion, change consultation, although considered an essential tool and ethical imperative in any change management intervention, should not be applied across an organization's internal stakeholders in a universal manner. Our results shed light on some of the past counter-intuitive findings in regards to information and participation on change reactions by showing that, across employees, it is beneficial at low role demands and detrimental at high role demands. However, for employees with the most to lose because of organizational change (such as redeployees), low change consultation was stress-buffering. Overall, these findings suggest that change consultation is not the simple solution for protecting employees from generally poor working conditions. The change environment is a complex one that operates in a broader psychosocial climate and change management practices will not suffice and even backfire when there are job design deficiencies. Furthermore, change implementation must cater for employees who are the most impacted by change because change consultation may not be what they are seeking in order to maintain their well-being unless other coping resources also are in place, a direction that holds much promise for future research.

References

Armenakis, A. A., & Bedeian, A. G. (1999). Organizational change: A review of theory and research in the 1990s. *Journal of Management, 25*, 293–315.

Armstrong-Stassen, M. (1997). The effect of repeated management downsizing and surplus designation on remaining managers: An exploratory study. *Anxiety, Stress, and Coping, 10*, 377–384.

Armstrong-Stassen, M. (2002). Designated redundant but escaping lay-off: A special group of lay-off survivors. *Journal of Occupational and Organizational Psychology, 75*, 1–13.

Armstrong-Stassen, M., Cameron, S. J., & Horsburgh, M. E. (2001). Downsizing-initiated job transfer of hospital nurses: How do the job transferees fare? *Journal of Health and Human Services Administration, 23*, 470–489.

Averill, J. R. (1973). Personal control over aversive stimuli and its relationship to stress. *Psychological Bulletin, 80*, 286–303.

Axtell, C., Wall, T., Stride, C., Pepper, K., Clegg, C., Gardner, P., & Bolden, R. (2002). Familiarity breeds content: The impact of exposure to change on employee openness and well-being. *Journal of Occupational and Organizational Psychology, 75*, 217–231.

Barrett, D. J. (2002). Change communication: Using strategic employee communication to facilitate major change. *Corporate Communications, 7*, 219–231.

Bevan, A., Houdmont, J., & Menear, N. (2010). The management standards indicator tool and the estimation of risk. *Occupational Medicine*, *60*, 525–531.

Boyd, C. M., Tuckey, M. R., & Winefield, A. H. (2014). Perceived effects of organizational downsizing and staff cuts on the stress experience: The role of resources. *Stress and Health*, *30*, 53–64.

Brashers, D. E. (2001). Communication and uncertainty management. *Journal of Communication*, 477–497.

Burger, J. M. (1989). Negative reactions to increases in perceived personal control. *Journal of Personality and Social Psychology*, *56*, 246–256.

Cousins, R., Mackay, C. J., Clarke, S. D., Kelly, C., Kelly, P. J., & McCaig, R. H. (2004). Management standards' and work-related stress in the UK: Practical development. *Work and Stress*, *18*, 113–136.

Demerouti, E., Bakker, A. B., Nachreiner, F., & Schaufeli, W. B. (2001). The job demands-resources model of burnout. *Journal of Applied Psychology*, *86*, 499–512.

Egan, M., Bambra, C., Thomas, S., Petticrew, M., Whitehead, M., & Thomson, H. (2007). The psychosocial and health effects of workplace reorganization: A systematic review of organizational-level interventions that aim to increase employee control. *Journal of Epidemiology and Community Health*, *61*, 945–954.

Falkenberg, H., Näswall, K., Sverke, M., & Sjoberg, A. (2009). How are employees at different levels affected by privatization? A longitudinal study of two Swedish hospitals. *Journal of Occupational and Organizational Psychology*, *82*, 45–65.

Goldberg, D. P. (1972). *The detection of psychiatric illness by questionnaire*. London: Oxford University Press.

Guidi, S., Barnara, S., & Fichera, G. P. (2012). The HSE indicator tool, psychological distress, and work ability. *Occupational Medicine*, *62*, 203–209.

Haynes, C. E., Wall, T. D., Bolden, R. I., Stride, C., & Rick, J. E. (1999). Measures of perceived work characteristics for health services research: Test of a measurement model and normative data. *British Journal of Health Psychology*, *4*, 257–275.

Hertting, A., Nilssson, K., Theorell, T., & Satterlund-Larsson, U. (2003). Personnel reductions and structural changes in healthcare: Work-life experiences of medical secretaries. *Journal of Psychosomatic Research*, *54*, 161–170.

Hill, N. S., Seo, M. G., Kang, J. H., & Taylor, M. S. (2012). Building employee commitment to change across organizational levels: The influence of hierarchical distance and direct managers' transformational leadership. *Organization Science*, *23*, 758–777.

Hobfoll, S. E. (1989). Conservation of resources: A new attempt at conceptualizing stress. *American Psychologist*, *44*, 513–524.

Houdmont, J., Kerr, R., & Addley, K. (2012). Psychosocial factors and economic recession: The Stormont Study. *Occupational Medicine*, *62*, 98–104.

Jimmieson, N. L., Hobman, E. V., Tucker, M. K., & Bordia, P. (2016). Change in psychosocial work factors predicts follow-up employee strain: An examination of Australian employees. *Journal of Occupational and Environmental Medicine*, *58*, 1002–1013.

Jimmieson, N. L., Peach, M., & White, K. M. (2008). Utilizing the theory of planned behavior to inform change management: An investigation of employee intentions to support organizational change. *Journal of Applied Behavioral Science*, *44*, 237–262.

Jimmieson, N. L., Terry, D. J., & Callan, V. J. (2004). A longitudinal study of employee adaptation to organizational change: The role of change-related information and change-related self-efficacy. *Journal of Occupational Health Psychology*, *9*, 11–27.

Kanter, R. M. (1977, 1993). *Men and women in the corporation*. New York: Basic Books.

Karasek, R. A. (1979). Job demands, job decision latitude, and mental strain: Implications for job redesign. *Administrative Science Quarterly*, *24*, 285–308.

Kerr, R., McHugh, M., & McCrory, M. (2009). HSE management standards and stress-related work outcomes. *Occupational Medicine, 59*, 574–579.

Klein, S. M. (1996). A management communication strategy for change. *Journal of Organizational Change Management, 9*, 32–46.

Kotter, J. P. (1995). Leading change: Why transformational efforts fail. *Harvard Business Review, 73*, 59–67.

Kotter, J. P. (1999). Leading change: The eight steps to transformation. In J. A. Conger, G. M. Spreitzer, & E. E. Lawler (Eds.), *The leader's change handbook: An essential guide to setting direction and taking action* (pp. 87–99). San Francisco, CA: Jossey-Bass.

Kozlowski, S. W. J., Chao, G. T., Smith, E. M., & Hedlund, J. (1993). Organizational downsizing: Strategies, interventions, and research implications. In C. L. Cooper & I. T. Robertson (Eds.), *International review of industrial and organizational psychology* (pp. 263–332). New York: John Wiley & Sons.

Kubicek, B., Paskvan, M., & Korunka, C. (2015). Development and validation of an instrument for assessing job demands arising from accelerated change: The Intensification of Job Demands Scale (IDS). *European Journal of Work and Organizational Psychology, 24*, 898–913.

Lazarus, R. S., & Folkman, S. (1984). *Stress, appraisal, and coping.* New York: Springer.

Levine, D. W., Kripke, D. F., Kaplan, R. M., Lewis, M. A., Naughton, M. J., Bowen, D. J., & Shumaker, S. A. (2003). Reliability and validity of women's health initiative insomnia rating scale. *Psychological Assessment, 15*, 137–148.

Lippel, K., & Quinlan, M. (2011). Regulation of psychosocial risk factors at work: An international review. *Safety Science, 49*, 543–546.

Marcatto, F., Colautti, L., Filon, F. L., Luis, O., & Ferrante, D. (2014). The HSE management standards indicator tool: Concurrent and construct validity. *Occupational Medicine, 64*, 365–371.

Martin, A. J., Jones, E. S., & Callan, V. J. (2006). Status differences in employee adjustment during organizational change. *Journal of Managerial Psychology, 21*, 145–162.

Miller, S. M. (1980). Why having control reduces strain: If I can stop the roller coaster, I don't want to get off. In J. Garber & M. E. P. Seligman (Eds.), *Human helplessness: Theory and applications* (pp. 71–95). New York: Academic Press.

Miller, S. M. (1981). Predictability and human stress: Towards a clarification of evidence and theory. In L. Berkowitz (Ed.), *Advances in experimental social psychology* (pp. 203–256). New York: Academic Press.

Miller, S. M. (1989). Cognitive informational styles in the process of coping with threat and frustration. *Advances in Behavior Research and Therapy, 11*, 223–234.

Miller, S. M. (1990). To see or not to see: Cognitive informational styles in the coping process. In M. Rosenbaum (Ed.), *Learned resourcefulness: On coping skills, self-control, and adaptive behavior* (pp. 95–126). New York: Springer Press.

Miller, S. M. (1992). Individual differences in the coping process: What to know and when to know it. In B. N. Carpenter (Ed.), *Personal coping: Theory, research, and application* (pp. 77–91). West Port, CT: Praeger.

O'Connor, P. J., Jimmieson, N. L., & White, K. M. (in press). Too busy to change: High job demands reduce the beneficial effects of information and participation on employee support. *Journal of Business and Psychology.*

Olsen, D. A., & Tetrick, L. E. (1988). Organizational restructuring: The impact on role perceptions, work relationships, and satisfaction. *Group and Organization Studies, 13*, 374–388.

Oreg, S. (2006). Personality, context, and resistance to organizational change. *European Journal of Work and Organizational Psychology, 15*, 73–101.

Oreg, S., Vakola, M., & Armenakis, A. A. (2011). Change recipients' reactions to organizational change: A 60-year review of quantitative studies. *Journal of Applied Behavioral Science, 47*, 461–524.

Pahkin, K., Mattila-Holappa, P., Nielsen, K., Widerszal-Bazyl, M., & Wiezer, N. (2014). A sound change: Ways to support employees' well-being during organizational restructuring. In S. Leka & R. R. Sinclair (Eds.), *Contemporary occupational health psychology: Global perspectives on research and practice* (pp. 165–180). Chichester: John Wiley & Sons.

Ravalier, J. M., McVicar, A., & Munn-Giddings, C. (2013). The management standards indicator tool and evaluation of burnout. *Occupational Medicine, 63*, 145–147.

Robinson, O., & Griffiths, A. (2005). Coping with the stress of transformational change in a government department. *Journal of Applied Behavioral Science, 41*, 204–221.

Rowlands, K. E., & Rees, C. J. (2015). Organizational change and workplace stress in teaching and learning settings: Case study evidence from a public sector university in the UK. In F. E. P. Dievernich, K. O. Tokarski, & J. Gong (Eds.), *Change management and the human factor* (pp. 167–178). Switzerland: Springer.

Schumacher, D., Schreurs, B., Van Emmerik, H., & De Witte, H. (2016). Explaining the relation between job insecurity and employee outcomes during organizational change: A multiple group comparison. *Human Resource Management, 55*, 809–827.

Seo, M. G., & Hill, N. S. (2005). Understanding the human side of merger and acquisition: An integrative framework. *Journal of Applied Behavioural Science, 41*, 422–443.

Shaw, J. B., Fields, M. W., Thacker, J. W., & Fisher, C. D. (1993). The availability of personal and external coping resources: Their impact on job stress and employee attitudes during organizational restructuring. *Work and Stress, 7*, 229–246.

Shaw, J. C., Wild, E., & Colquitt, J. A. (2003). To justify or excuse? A meta-analytic review of the effects of explanations. *Journal of Applied Psychology, 88*, 444–458.

Shirom, A., & Melamed, S. (2006). A comparison of the construct validity of two burnout measures in two groups of professionals. *International Journal of Stress Management, 13*, 176–200.

Smollan, R. K. (2015). Causes of stress before, during, and after organizational change: A qualitative study. *Journal of Organizational Change Management, 28*, 301–314.

Somech, A. (2010). Participative decision making in schools: A mediating-moderating analytical framework for understanding school and teacher outcomes. *Educational Administration Quarterly, 46*, 174–209.

Sutton, R. I., & Kahn, R. L. (1986). Prediction, understanding, and control as antidotes to organizational stress. In J. Lorsch (Ed.), *Handbook of organizational behavior* (pp. 272–285). Englewood Cliffs, CA: Prentice Hall.

Thompson, S. C. (1981). Will it hurt less if I can control it? A complex answer to a simple question. *Psychological Bulletin, 90*, 89–101.

Wisse, B., & Sleebos, E. (2016). When change causes stress: Effects of self-construal and change consequences. *Journal of Business and Psychology, 31*, 249–264.

4

INDIVIDUAL AND EXTERNAL COPING RESOURCES AS PREDICTORS OF EMPLOYEES' CHANGE ATTITUDES

Alannah E. Rafferty and Nerina L. Jimmieson

Researchers have identified change attitudes as critical to the success of organizational change efforts (Armenakis & Harris, 2002; Miller, Johnson, & Grau, 1994; Rafferty, Jimmieson, & Armenakis, 2013). Indeed, Miller et al. argued that, although the failure to successfully implement planned change may be attributed to many factors, employees' attitudes toward change are especially influential. Two change attitudes have received the majority of theoretical attention – change readiness and resistance to change (Bouckenooghe, 2010). Despite this, surprisingly little empirical attention has focused on the construct of change readiness and its antecedents. In this study, we identify three internal resources (generalized self-efficacy, dispositional resistance to change and trait positive affectivity) and two external resources (change information and change participation) as antecedents of change readiness.

The most comprehensive theoretical framework of change readiness was developed by Armenakis and his colleagues (Armenakis & Harris, 2002; Armenakis, Harris, & Mossholder, 1993). Initially, Armenakis et al. (1993) identified two beliefs as components of change readiness including the belief that change is needed (i.e., the *discrepancy* belief) and the belief that the individual and organization has the capacity to undertake change (i.e., *change self-efficacy*). Armenakis and his colleagues (Armenakis & Harris, 2002; Armenakis, Harris, & Feild, 1999) expanded this analysis and identified an additional three components of change readiness including: (1) the belief that change is *appropriate*, (2) the belief that change will have positive outcomes (the *valence* of change) and (3) the belief that there is organizational support for change (*principal support*) such that the organization and its members will provide tangible support for change. More recently, Rafferty et al. (2013) have argued that approaches to the study of change readiness have been overly focused on cognitions and have thus ignored affective elements of change readiness. In particular, these authors argued that employees' positive emotional responses to change are an important but ignored component of change readiness. *Affect* consists of discrete, qualitatively different *emotions* such as love, hate, sadness, happiness, excitement, boredom, anger, acceptance, joy and sorrow (Crites, Fabringar, & Petty, 1994). Rafferty et al. proposed that individual's *positive* emotional responses to change are an important component of change readiness. To date, though, researchers have not yet empirically examined positive affective responses to change as a component of change readiness.

Resources

A range of theoretical perspectives have emphasized the importance of individuals' possessing and building resources in the workplace. For example, Hobfoll's (1989, p. 516) Conservation of Resources (COR) theory argues that people "strive to retain, protect, and build resources and what is most threatening to them is the potential or actual loss of these valued resources". Hobfoll (2001, p. 339) defined resources as "those objects, personal characteristics, conditions, or energies that are valued in their own right, or that are valued because they act as conduits to the achievement or protection of valued resources". In the context of organizational change, Ashford (1988) identified feelings of control (internal versus external locus of control), self-efficacy, self-esteem and tolerance of ambiguity as coping resources.

Shaw, Fields, Thacker and Fisher (1993) distinguished personal or internal resources (e.g., self-efficacy, personal control, self-esteem, tolerance for ambiguity) from external coping resources such as socio-emotional support, information, structural mechanisms within an organization or other forms of tangible, external aid that affect the perception of stressors in the work environment or the actual strain experienced by an employee. These authors argued that external coping resources provide employees with a vicarious sense of control in stressful situations and may indirectly reduce stressors and lessen strain by increasing an individual's perceived personal coping resources. For example, social support is likely to be positively associated with an employee's sense of self-esteem. We focus on three internal resources – generalized self-efficacy (GSE), dispositional resistance to change (DRC) and trait positive affectivity (TPA) – as key internal resources during change. We also identify two external resources (change information and change participation) as antecedents of the dimensions of change readiness.

Coping resources and change readiness dimensions

Generalized self-efficacy

Chen, Gully and Eden (2001, p. 63) defined GSE as "one's belief in one's overall competence to effect requisite performances across a wide variety of achievement situations". A substantial body of work indicates that GSE is related to task effort and performance, persistence, resilience, effective problem-solving and self-control (Bandura, 1986; Gist & Mitchell, 1992). We argue that individuals who have higher GSE will be more likely to report that there is a need for change and that change is appropriate than those low on GSE. Individuals high on GSE are likely to feel that they can cope with change, which will encourage them to identify opportunities for change. We also argue that GSE will be positively associated with change self-efficacy. Eden (1988) argued that GSE positively influences state specific self-efficacy across tasks and situations. Specifically, the tendency to feel efficacious across tasks and situations "spills over" into specific situations. Individuals who are high on GSE are likely to be responsive to signals from those around them that they support change, increasing their belief that there is principal support for change. We also suggest that individuals who are high on GSE will also be more likely to identify potentially positive outcomes from change efforts as their sense of competence will contribute to positive expectations about the outcomes of change. Finally, we argue that individuals high on GSE will report experiencing more positive emotions about change as they are likely to enjoy the challenge and opportunities to display and extend their skills in a changing workplace (see Figure 4.1). Thus, we propose that:

Hypothesis 1: GSE will be positively associated with discrepancy (1a), appropriateness of change (1b), change self-efficacy (1c), principal support for change (1d), valence of change (1e), and positive affect about change (1f).

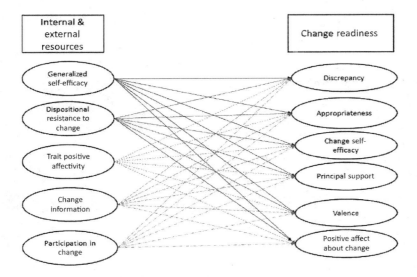

FIGURE 4.1 Model of theoretical relationships examined

Dispositional resistance to change

Oreg (2003) identified four dimensions of DRC. The first dimension, routine seeking, captures the extent to which an individual seeks out stable and routine environments. The second dimension, emotional reaction to change, focuses on the extent to which an individual feels uncomfortable and stressed in a changing workplace. The third dimension, short-term focus, assesses the extent to which individuals are concerned with the short-term inconvenience from change over the long-term potential gains that may arise from change. Finally, cognitive rigidity addresses an unwillingness to consider alternative ideas and perspectives. A number of empirical studies have recently examined DRC (e.g., Hon, Bloom, & Crant, 2014; Oreg & Berson, 2011; Rafferty & Jimmieson, in press; Xu, Payne, Horner, & Alexander, 2016), and suggest that this construct is an important antecedent of change attitudes and behaviors at work.

We propose that DRC will be negatively associated with all of the change beliefs and positive affect about change. In particular, employees who are high in DRC will be less positive about the need for change and will be less likely to consider change to be appropriate. In addition, individuals who are high in DRC will be less likely to develop a positive perception of their capability to perform at a high level in a changing workplace compared to those who are low on this trait. In addition, we propose that individuals who report high DRC will be less inclined to consider that their managers and colleagues are supportive of change, will expect less positive outcomes from change and will experience fewer positive emotions about change. Thus, we propose that;

> *Hypothesis 2: DRC will be negatively associated with discrepancy (2a), appropriateness (2b), change self-efficacy (2c), principal support for change (2d), valence (2e), and positive affect about change (2f).*

Trait positive affectivity

TPA refers to trait-based predispositions to experience high levels of energy, excitement and enthusiasm (Watson & Pennebaker, 1989). Research suggests that high TPA individuals lead a full, happy and interesting life, and maintain a generally high activity level (Watson, Clark, & Tellegen, 1988). Relatively few empirical studies have examined the role of TPA during change as researchers have tended focused on trait negativity affectivity (Begley & Czajka, 1993; Fugate, Kinicki, & Scheck, 2002). The available research suggests, however, that TPA is likely to be positively associated with positive employee responses to change (Iverson, 1996; Judge, Thoresen, Pucik, & Welbourne, 1999).

We propose that TPA will be positively associated with all of the change beliefs and positive emotions about change. In this respect, we argue that individuals who characteristically experience positive emotions are more likely than those low on TPA to report that there is a need for change and that change is appropriate. In addition, we argue that individuals who are high on TPA are likely to have a positive opinion of their change capabilities and due to their high levels of energy and excitement will encourage others to provide resources and information to support them during change. We also argue that people who are high in TPA will be more likely to report positive outcomes of change and will experience greater state positive affect about change. We propose that:

Hypothesis 3: TPA will be positively associated with discrepancy (3a), appropriateness of change (3b), change self-efficacy (3c), principal support for change (3d), valence of change (3e), and positive affect about change (3f).

Change information

One of the most common change process factors discussed in the literature is effective communication with employees (Bordia, Hobman, Jones, Gallois, & Callan, 2004; Schweiger & DeNisi, 1991). Effective change-related communication provides employees with high-quality information about how, when and why changes will occur (Wanberg & Banas, 2000). Empirical research has consistently demonstrated that the provision of high-quality change information reduces psychological uncertainty (Bordia, Hobman, et al., 2004; Bordia, Hunt, Paulsen, Tourish, & DiFonzo, 2004; Bordia, Jones, Gallois, Callan, & DiFonzo, 2006; Schweiger & DeNisi, 1991), as well as increasing acceptance, openness and commitment to change (Lawson & Angle, 1998; Martin, 1999; Miller et al., 1994; Wanberg & Banas, 2000).

We argue that when employees perceive that they are provided with quality information about change, then they will develop a better understanding of the need for change, will also understand the reasons behind change and will therefore be likely to consider change to be appropriate. In addition, when employees report receiving quality information about change they also will better understand what change requires to them, contributing to an enhanced sense of change self-efficacy. We also argue that when employees report that they receive quality information about change this enhances understanding and provides a sense of vicarious control of a situation, resulting in an enhanced likelihood of perceiving positive outcomes from change. As a result, we expect that change information will be positively associated with principal support and valence. Finally, we also propose that information will be associated with the experience of positive emotions in relation to change. Thus, we propose that:

Hypothesis 4: Change information will be positively associated with discrepancy (4a), appropriateness of change (4b), change self-efficacy (4c), principal support for change (4d), valence of change (4e), and positive affect about change (4f).

Change participation

Early research demonstrated that participation (in the form of management communicating the need for change and conducting group planning meetings) resulted in reduced resistance to job transfer (Coch & French, 1948). Traditionally, participation in change has been considered to involve the provision of opportunities to participate in a group discussion that leads to a decision about change (Woodman, 1989). Employee participation during change, especially in tactical planning (Piderit, 2000), has been discussed as empowering employees and providing them with a sense of agency and control (Armenakis et al., 1993; Gagné, Koestner, & Zuckerman, 2000). Empirical evidence has supported the importance of employee participation and opportunities for voice and self-discovery as a predictor of employee acceptance of change (Korunka, Weiss, Huemer, & Karetta, 1995; Lines, 2004; Wanberg & Banas, 2000).

We propose that participation in change will increase employees' understanding of the impetus and reasons for change, which will contribute to the belief that change is needed and appropriate. In addition, research indicates that participation in change builds agency and control which should contribute to greater change self-efficacy. We also propose that participation in change will provide access to other change-related resources such as managerial support and advice, contributing to a sense of principal support. We also argue that participation in change will enable employees to identify potential positive outcomes that can emerge from change implementation, which will enhance the perceived valence of change as well as create positive emotional responses to change. Thus, we propose that:

> *Hypothesis 5: Change participation will be positively associated with discrepancy (5a), appropriateness of change (5b), change self-efficacy (5c), principal support for change (5d), valence of change (5e), and positive affect about change (5f).*

Method

Participants and procedure

We collected data from a large provider of community and residential aged care services in Australia. This organization provides a broad range of services including services to older people, people with dementia, and people with disabilities and their carers who require support to remain living at home. Of the 488 employees invited to take part in the survey, 369 (75.6% response rate) completed a survey. Of these 369 surveys, 68 (18.4%) were completed electronically and 301 (81.6%) paper copies were completed. We asked respondents an open-ended question concerning what organizational changes they were experiencing. Three hundred and twenty-four employees provided a change description. We removed the 45 respondents from the analyses who did not provide a description of an organizational change that they were currently experiencing or who did not provide a valid change description (e.g., "change is always happening"). As such, analyses were conducted on the remaining 324 participants. One hundred and thirty-four of these respondents identified restructuring as most salient to them. Seventy-three respondents reported experiencing technological changes, followed by service changes (n = 50), and "other" changes (n = 57; e.g., "changes in government funding"). In addition, ten respondents focused on the way work is done (e.g., remote work) as the most salient change to them.

Of the 324 participants who provided a valid change description, 44 (13.6%) were male and 280 (86.4%) were female. The average age of these respondents was 49.4 years (SD = 10.10) and the average tenure in the organization was 5.26 years (SD = 4.18). Forty (12.3%) of these respondents were employed on a full-time basis while 233 (71.9%) were employed on a part-time basis, 48 (14.8%) respondents were employed casually, and 3 employees did not respond to this question. Seventy two percent (n = 236) of the respondents were employed as a community worker, 35 (10.8%) were employed as coordinators and 16 (4.9%) were employed as a community worker support officer.

Measures

The internal change resource measures were assessed using 1 (strongly disagree) to 5 (strongly agree) Likert scales. The external change resource measures and the change readiness dimensions were assessed with Likert scales ranging from 1 (strongly disagree) to 7 (strongly disagree).

Internal resources

Generalized self-efficacy. We used Chen et al.'s (2001) eight-item measure. An example item is "I will be able to achieve most of the goals that I have set for myself" (α = .90).

Dispositional resistance to change. DRC was assessed with 17 items (Oreg, 2003). Two items were reverse-scored. An example item assessing routine seeking is "I'd rather be bored than surprised" (α = .70).

Trait positive affectivity. TPA was assessed using the five highest loading positive affect items from the Positive and Negative Affect Scale (Watson et al., 1988). An example item is "In the last three months I have been enthusiastic" (α = .88).

External resources

Change information. Four items assessed this construct (Wanberg & Banas, 2000). An example item is "The information I have received about the implementation of change has been useful" (α = .92).

Change participation. Four items assessed this construct (Wanberg & Banas, 2000). An example item is "If I wanted to, I could have input into the decisions being made about the future of change programs" (α = .84).

Change readiness dimensions

We assessed all of the components of change readiness using items developed by Rafferty and Minbashian (submitted for publication).. Discrepancy was assessed

54 Alannah E. Rafferty and Nerina L. Jimmieson

using three items (α = .84). An example item is "This organizational change needs to be implemented to improve our operations". Appropriateness was assessed using three items (α = .92). An example item is "When I think about this change I realize it is appropriate for our organization". Change self-efficacy (α = .91) was assessed by four items. An example item is "I think I will be able to do all that is required by this change". Principal support for change (α = .82) was assessed using a four-item scale. An example item is "I believe top managers in this organization will continue to support this change effort into the future". Valence was assessed with a three-item scale (α = .88). An example item is "This change has important positive consequences for my future". Positive affect about change was assessed using a seven-item scale (α = .97). An example item is "I am excited by this change".

Control measures

We assessed a number of demographic characteristics including gender, age and organizational tenure as controls. In addition, we included employees' subjective perceptions of the extent of transformational change and the frequency of change as control measures. We expected that subjective perceptions of the extent of transformational change and the frequency of change would be associated with employees' perceptions of the internal and external resources as well as the change readiness dimensions (Rafferty & Griffin, 2006; Rafferty & Jimmieson, in press).

Rafferty and Griffin's (2006) three-item measure of transformational change was used (alpha = .78). This scale assesses employees' subjective perception that changes have been made to core aspects of the organization including strategy, structure and values. An example item is "Thinking about the degree of change occurring in your workplace, to what extent have you experienced large scale changes significantly changing your unit's values". The scale ranged from 1 "not at all" to 7 "a great deal".

Frequency of change was assessed using a four-item scale (Rafferty & Griffin, 2006). This scale assesses the extent to which employees subjectively report that change occurs very frequently within their organization. An example item is "Changes frequently occur in this unit". The scale ranged from 1 "strongly disagree" to 7 "strongly agree". This scale had a Cronbach alpha of .90.

Results

Table 4.1 displays the means, standard deviations and zero-order correlations among the study variables. Organizational tenure and the frequency of change and transformational change were significantly associated with a number of substantive scales and thus were included as control variables. In contrast, gender was not significantly associated with any of the substantive variables while age was only weakly associated with principal support.

TABLE 4.1 Descriptive statistics and zero-order correlations among the study variables

	Mean (SD)	1	2	3	4	5	6	7	8	9	10	11	12	13	14	15	16
1. Gender	1.86 (0.34)	–															
2. Age	49.36 (10.10)	−.14*	–														
3. Organizational tenure	5.26 (4.18)	−.06	.23***	–													
4. Transformational change	3.83 (1.36)	−.01	−.01	.06	(.79)												
5. Frequency of change	4.79 (1.28)	.06	.02	.24***	.32***	(.89)											
6. Generalized self-efficacy	4.06 (0.53)	.01	−.07	.01	−.02	.02	(.90)										
7. Dispositional resistance to change	2.73 (0.49)	−.04	−.00	.11*	.04	−.02	−.29***	(.70)									
8. Trait positive affectivity	3.47 (0.72)	.04	−.00	−.11	−.10	−.16**	.19***	−.27***	(.87)								
9. Change Information	4.44 (1.38)	−.07	.09	−.08	−.09	−.33***	.10	.01	.34***	(.92)							
10. Change Participation	3.89 (1.35)	−.10	−.01	−.14*	−.04	−.27***	.05	−.02	.21***	.67***	(.84)						
11. Discrepancy	4.74 (1.16)	.01	.02	−.02	.10	.16**	−.04	−.08	.07	.09	.09	(.84)					
12. Appropriateness	4.61 (1.33)	−.03	.01	−.10	−.01	−.19**	.06	−.14*	.25***	.38***	.40***	.47***	(.92)				
13. Change self-efficacy	5.29 (1.02)	.01	−.00	−.07	−.01	−.13*	.31***	−.24***	.34***	.37***	.30***	.20***	.45***	(.91)			
14. Principal support	4.99 (1.06)	−.04	.12*	−.06	.02	−.10	.11*	−.14*	.29***	.41***	.34***	.27***	.58***	.50***	(.82)		
15. Valence	4.50 (1.34)	−.04	.03	−.16**	−.06	−.25***	.04	−.15**	.27***	.40***	.45***	.34***	.73***	.43***	.59***	(.88)	
16. Positive affect about change	4.26 (1.36)	−.04	.01	−.18**	−.01	−.26***	.11	−.21***	.40***	.49***	.46***	.30***	.71***	.47***	.58***	.82***	(.97)

Notes: N ranges from 306–324. * $p < .05$, ** $p < .01$, *** $p < .001$.

Overview of analyses

Organizational tenure was assessed as a single indicator variable. Due to the large number of constructs included, the resources were assessed with reliability-corrected single indicator constructs (i.e., scale scores). In order to account for the imperfect reliability of scale scores, each of these latent variables was assessed by its corresponding scale score and the residual variance of the scale score fixed to (1-Cronbach alpha reliability)*scale variance (Hayduk, 1987). In all models, the internal and external resources were free to correlate with each other. In addition, the change beliefs and positive emotions about change also were free to correlate with each other in all models estimated. Relationships were estimated between organizational tenure, frequency of change and transformational change and all focal constructs in all models.

Analyses were conducted using LISREL 8.3. We conducted a two-step procedure when estimating relationships among the study variables (Anderson & Gerbing, 1988). First, we estimated a series of nested measurement models. We then estimated the saturated structural model to test the hypotheses. The fit of the models was assessed using both absolute and incremental fit indexes. Cut-off values of .06 for RMSEA (Hu & Bentler, 1999), .08 for the SRMR (Browne & Cudeck, 1993) and greater than .90 for the other fit indices are indicative of a good fitting model (Hu & Bentler, 1999).

Measurement models   To assess the factor structure of all measures simultaneously, we estimated a series of confirmatory factor analysis (CFA) models.[1] Each model included organizational tenure, transformational change, the frequency of change, the five scales assessing the resources and the items assessing the six change beliefs and positive emotions about change. The correlation matrix, consisting of product-moment correlations, was used as the input to LISREL 8.3. All model tests were based on this matrix and maximum likelihood estimation was used. The hypothesized 14-factor measurement model was the best fit to the data, $\chi^2(590) = 1235.3$, $p < .001$; RMSEA = .06, SRMR = .06, CFI = .97, NNFI = .96. All of the model parameters loaded significantly onto their hypothesized latent factor at $p < .001$, and the latent factors explained substantial amounts of item/scale variance (R^2 ranged from .35 to 1.00).

Structural model   We estimated the saturated structural model. This model was a good fit to the data, $\chi^2(553) = 1210.15$, $p < .001$; RMSEA = .06, SRMR = .06, CFI = .97, NNFI = .97. The results from the saturated structural model are used to test hypotheses. The structural relationships in the saturated model are displayed in Table 4.2.

Hypothesis testing   Hypotheses 1a) to 1f) specified relationships between GSE and the change beliefs and positive emotions about change. These hypotheses was partially supported. While GSE was significantly positively associated with principal

TABLE 4.2 Standardized parameter estimates in the saturated structural model

	Organizational tenure	Transformational change	Frequency of change	GSE	DRC	TPA	Change Information	Change Participation	Total Variance Explained
1. Change information	.01	.01	$-.35^{***}$						12
2. Change participation	$-.10$	.08	$-.29^{***}$						09
3. Discrepancy	$-.10$	.03	$.31^{***}$	$-.11$	$-.06$	.09	.10	.09	12
4. Appropriateness	$-.08$	.09	$-.06$	.03	$-.11^{*}$	$.15^{**}$	$.15^{*}$	$.24^{***}$	22
5. Change self-efficacy	$-.04$	.10	.05	.10	$-.22^{***}$	$.12^{*}$	$.15^{*}$	.12	17
6. Principal support for change	$-.05$	.11	.10	$.12^{*}$	$-.14^{**}$	$.15^{**}$	$.26^{***}$	$.15^{*}$	24
7. Valence	$-.12^{*}$	.07	$-.03$	$-.04$	$-.13^{**}$	$.17^{***}$	.09	$.33^{***}$	26
8. Positive affect about change	$-.05$	$.14^{*}$	$-.10$	.03	$-.21^{***}$	$.19^{***}$	$.22^{***}$	$.15^{**}$	29

Notes: N = 306–324. $^{*}p < .05$, $^{**}p < .01$, $^{***}p < .001$.

58 Alannah E. Rafferty and Nerina L. Jimmieson

support for change, $\beta = .12$, $p < .05$, it was not significantly associated with any of the other change beliefs or positive emotions about change.

Hypotheses 2a) to 2f) specified relationships between DRC and the change beliefs and positive emotions about change. Results indicated that DRC was significantly negatively associated with appropriateness of change, $\beta = -.11$, $p < .05$, change self-efficacy, $\beta = -.22$, $p < .001$, principal support for change, $\beta = -.14$, $p < .01$, valence, $\beta = -.13$, $p < .01$, and positive affect about change, $\beta = -.21$, $p < .001$. In contrast, DRC was not significantly associated with the discrepancy belief, $\beta = -.06$, *n.s.*

Hypotheses 3a) to 3f) specified relationships between TPA and the change beliefs and positive emotions about change. Results provided partial support for these hypotheses as TPA was significantly positively associated with appropriateness of change, $\beta = .15$, $p < .01$, change self-efficacy, $\beta = .12$, $p < .05$, principal support for change, $\beta = .15$, $p < .01$, valence of change $\beta = .17$, $p < .01$, and positive affect about change, $\beta = .19$, $p < .001$.

Hypotheses 4a) to 4f) specified the relationships between change information and the change beliefs and positive emotions about change. These hypotheses were partially supported. In particular, change information was significantly positively associated with appropriateness, $\beta = .15$, $p < .05$, change self-efficacy, $\beta = .15$, $p < .05$, principal support for change, $\beta = .26$, $p < .001$, and positive affect about change, $\beta = .22$, $p < .001$. In contrast, neither discrepancy $\beta = .10$, *n.s.*, nor valence, $\beta = .09$, *n.s.*, were significantly associated with change information.

Finally, Hypotheses 5a) to 5f) specified the relationships between change participation and change beliefs and positive emotions about change. Findings indicated that there was partial support for these hypotheses as change participation was significantly positively associated with appropriateness, $\beta = .24$, $p < .001$, principal support for change, $\beta = .15$, $p < .05$, valence, $\beta = .33$, $p < .001$, and positive affect about change, $\beta = .15$, $p < .01$. In contrast, change participation was not significantly associated with discrepancy about change, $\beta = .09$, *n.s.*, or change self-efficacy, $\beta = .12$, *n.s.*

Results indicated that organizational tenure was significantly negatively associated with valence, $\beta = -.12$, $p < .05$. Transformational change was significantly positively associated with positive affect about change, $\beta = .14$, $p < .05$, while the frequency of change was significantly negatively associated with change information, $\beta = -.35$, $p < .001$, change participation, $\beta = -.29$, $p < .001$, but positively associated with discrepancy, $\beta = .31$, $p < .001$. Overall, the structural model accounted for 12% of the variance in change information, 9% of the variance in change participation, 12% of the variance in discrepancy, 22% of the variance in appropriateness, 17% of the variance in change self-efficacy, 24% of the variance in principal support for change, 26% of the variance in valence and 29% of the variance in positive affect about change.

Discussion

The results of this study suggest that both internal and external resources are important in predicting change beliefs and positive emotions about change. Of particular note was that the control measures (organizational tenure and subjective perceptions of change impact and change frequency) and the internal and external resources were especially important in predicting valence and positive affect about change. In particular, we accounted for just under 30% of the variance in both valence and positive affect about change. These results are especially striking as researchers have not previously identified positive affect about change as a component of change readiness. As such, our knowledge of how to build positive emotions about change is lagging behind our knowledge of the other components of change readiness.

Our findings also indicated that, of the internal resources identified, both DRC and TPA were associated with a number of the change beliefs and positive emotions about change. In addition, both of the two external resources examined – change information and change participation – were associated with multiple change beliefs and positive emotions about change. Overall, this initial evidence provides support for the importance of both internal and external resources in predicting the components of change readiness.

Results revealed that GSE was positively associated with the valence of change. Surprisingly, GSE was not uniquely associated with change self-efficacy. In contrast, DRC was uniquely related to five of the six dimensions of change readiness, such that higher DRC was related to lower appropriateness, change self-efficacy, principal support for change, valence and positive affect about change. This finding is practically important because it suggests that some employees may enter an organization predisposed to be less ready for change compared to others who are low on this trait. If this is the case then, organizations may need to consider providing additional support to employees who report moderate to high levels of DRC. This support may involve coaching or mentoring employees in relation to taking a positive perspective on change.

TPA also was uniquely positively associated with appropriateness, principal support for change, valence and state positive affect about change. This dispositional trait appears to enable individuals to either identify or attract additional resources. For example, we have argued that individuals who are characteristically enthusiastic and optimistic may encourage others to provide more support during change as they are attractive and appealing to others. Thus, high TPA individuals may find themselves in the advantageous position of not only having a more positive emotional experience due to their dispositional makeup but they may also create a cycle whether others provide additional support to them because they are appealing and likable, which may be especially valued during periods of turmoil and chaos that often characterizes large-scale organizational changes.

Results indicated that both of the external resources were associated with change readiness. In particular, change information and change participation were associated with appropriateness, principal support for change and positive affect about change. Change information was uniquely associated with change self-efficacy while participation was positively associated with valence. These results support the importance of implementing positive change processes. Interestingly, the relationships between the external resources and the change readiness dimensions were slightly stronger than the relationships with the internal resources. This may suggest that even if one does not have a dispositional profile of internal resources to promote change readiness, if organizations introduce the right change processes then they may still be able to build change readiness.

We included employees' subjective perceptions of change impact and change frequency as control measures in analyses. Results indicated that, surprisingly, change impact, as assessed via employees' perceptions of the extent to which core aspects of the organization including strategy, structure and values had been changed, was uniquely *positively* associated with positive affect about change. One possible interpretation of this result is that employees' belief that change is transformational opens up opportunities and challenges that in turn result in the experience of positive emotions in response to change. However, we would encourage future research to explore this relationship using a different research design (i.e., a longitudinal design).

We also controlled for the effects of the frequency of change. We found that this aspect of the internal change context was negatively associated with change information and change participation and was positively associated with discrepancy about change. In a continuously changing environment, employees may experience depletion of their internal resources such that they have difficulty maintaining attention on change efforts as they feel pulled and pushed in all directions. Thus, the utility of positive change processes may be compromised as employees struggle to deal with the demands confronting them. Interestingly, results also revealed that, a higher frequency of change was associated with lower discrepancy about change. As such, in a frequently changing environment, it appears that employees may be getting the message that change is necessary but they may not necessarily be able to gather sufficient resources to respond positively to change in such an environment.

Organizational tenure also was included as a control variable and results revealed that this construct was negatively associated with valence. That is, as tenure in the organization increased employees were less likely to report positive outcomes as a result of change. This result is potentially concerning for organizations because it is often long-tenured employees who are most influential in an organization due to their expertise and insider knowledge of the company. If long-tenured employees have negative perceptions of the outcomes of change then this may get transmitted to other employees and then have an ongoing negative impact on collective change readiness. As such, organizations may find it useful to actively seek out the opinions regarding change of individuals with long tenure in the organization and if needed address any concerns so as to encourage the development of positive beliefs and emotions about change in this group of employees.

Theoretical and practical implications

A number of important theoretical contributions emerge from this study. First, to our knowledge, researchers have not simultaneously examined the change readiness dimensions to establish the unique predictors of the different dimensions. The results of this study provide initial evidence to suggest that internal and external resources were differentially related to the change readiness dimensions. Practically, such findings are important because it provides evidence that managing employees' change readiness requires a complex set of efforts designed to build employees' internal and external resources. Interestingly, evidence indicated that both internal and external resources were associated with the dimensions of change readiness. Of the three internal resources examined, DRC and TPA were most influential as reflected in their significant relationships with most of the dimensions of change readiness. In addition, both of the external resources − the provision of quality information about change and participation in change efforts − were associated with multiple dimensions of change readiness.

A second important contribution is that, to date, research has not yet empirically examined positive affect as a dimension of change readiness. As discussed previously, transformational change was positively associated with positive affect about change. In addition, TPA, change information and change participation were significantly positively associated with employees' reports that they experienced positive emotions about change. In contrast, DRC was negatively associated with positive emotions about change. Overall, we accounted for a considerable amount of the variance in employees' positive emotions about change. Based on these initial findings, it appears that if organizations seek to enhance individuals' positive emotional responses to change then they should simultaneously consider both the organizational context and resources, including both those internal and external to employees.

Strengths and limitations

As with all studies, this research has a number of strengths and limitations. In terms of strengths, we simultaneously examined all of the change readiness dimensions and identified resources that uniquely predict these different dimensions. We also included positive affect about change as a change readiness dimension, which has not previously been examined.

However, we also acknowledge several methodological limitations, including the reliance on self-report employee data and the cross-sectional nature of the research design. As such, we are not able to establish causality of the relationships that we examined. While we hypothesized that the internal and external resources predict the change readiness dimensions it also might be that individuals who have positive beliefs and positive affect about change report having more internal and external resources as a result. If we are to establish the direction of causality, we would need to conduct a longitudinal study with data on all constructs collected at all time points with at least three time points (Menard, 2002).

Future research

We identify three avenues for future research. First, while we examined the relationship between GSE and the change readiness dimensions, Judge, Locke, Durham, and Kluger (1998) identified a higher-order dispositional construct called core self-evaluations, defined as the "fundamental, subconscious conclusions that individuals reach about themselves, other people and the world" (p. 18). Judge et al. identified four personality traits that reflect core self-evaluations including self-esteem, GSE, emotional stability and locus of control. In the current study, GSE was only associated with principal support for change. However, perhaps a focus on the higher-order dispositional construct of core self-evaluation would reveal stronger relationships with the dimensions of change readiness.

Second, future research could explore if third-party (e.g., supervisors, colleagues) ratings of employees' change readiness are a viable alternative to self-report ratings. It seems reasonable to suggest that third-party raters would be able to make appropriate judgments as to employees' beliefs and emotions about change. Finally, we suggest that future research expands the focus to also incorporate outcomes into the model. For example, it would be particularly interesting to examine the extent to which the internal and external resources have indirect effects on outcomes such as change supportive behaviors and performance through the change readiness dimensions. To date, research in the change area has devoted little attention to the study of outcomes of change (Weiner, 2009). As such, we see value in exploring the role of both internal and external resources in driving outcomes during organizational change.

Notes

The collection of the data reported in this chapter was supported by an Australian Research Discovery Project DP130101680 awarded to the authors.

1 The nested measurement model comparisons are available from the first author.

References

Anderson, J. C., & Gerbing, D. W. (1988). Structural equation modeling in practice: A review and recommended two-step approach. *Psychological Bulletin, 103*(3), 411–423.

Armenakis, A. A., & Harris, S. G. (2002). Crafting a change message to create transformational readiness. *Journal of Organizational Change Management, 15*(2), 169–183.

Armenakis, A. A., Harris, S. G., & Feild, H. S. (1999). Making change permanent: A model for institutionalizing change interventions. In W. Pasmore & R. Woodman (Eds.), *Research in organizational change and development* (Vol. 12, pp. 97–128). Stamford, CT: JAI Press.

Armenakis, A. A., Harris, S. G., & Mossholder, K. W. (1993). Creating readiness for organizational change. *Human Relations, 46*(6), 681–703.

Ashford, S. J. (1988). Individual strategies for coping with stress during organizational transitions. *Journal of Applied Behavioral Science, 24*, 19–36.

Bandura, A. (1986). *Social foundations of thought and action: A social cognitive theory*. Englewood Cliffs, NJ: Prentice Hall.

Begley, T. M., & Czajka, J. M. (1993). Panel analysis of the moderating effects of commitment on job satisfaction, intent to quit, and health following organizational change. *Journal of Applied Psychology, 78*(4), 552–556.

Bordia, P., Hobman, E., Jones, E., Gallois, C., & Callan, V. J. (2004). Uncertainty during organizational change: Types, consequences, and management strategies. *Journal of Business and Psychology*, *18*(4), 507–532.

Bordia, P., Hunt, E., Paulsen, N., Tourish, D., & DiFonzo, N. (2004). Uncertainty during organizational change: Is it all about control? *European Journal of Work and Organizational Psychology*, *13*(3), 345–365.

Bordia, P., Jones, E., Gallois, C., Callan, V. J., & DiFonzo, N. (2006). Management are aliens! Rumors and stress during organizational change *Group and Organization Management*, *31*(5), 601–621.

Bouckenooghe, D. (2010). Positioning change recipients' attitudes toward change in the organizational change literature. *Journal of Applied Behavioral Science*, *46*(4), 500–531.

Browne, M. W., & Cudeck, R. (1993). Alternative ways of assessing model fit. In K. A. B. J. S. Long (Ed.), *Testing structural equation models* (pp. 136–162). Beverly Hills, CA: SAGE Publications.

Chen, G., Gully, S. M., & Eden, D. (2001). Validation of a new general self-efficacy scale. *Organizational Research Methods*, *4*(1), 62–83.

Coch, L., & French, J. R. P. (1948). Overcoming resistance to change. *Human Relations*, *1*, 512–532.

Crites, S. L., Fabringar, L. R., & Petty, R. E. (1994). Measuring the affective and cognitive properties of attitudes: Conceptual and methodological issues. *Personality and Social Psychology Bulletin*, *20*(6), 619–634.

Eden, D. (1988). Pygmalion, goal setting, and expectancy: Compatible ways to boost productivity. *Academy of Management Review*, *13*(4), 639–652.

Fugate, M., Kinicki, A. J., & Scheck, C. L. (2002). Coping with an organizational merger over four states. *Personnel Psychology*, *55*(905–928).

Gagné, M., Koestner, R., & Zuckerman, M. (2000). Facilitating acceptance of organizational change: The importance of self-determination. *Journal of Applied Social Psychology*, *30*, 1843–1852.

Gist, M., & Mitchell, T. R. (1992). Self-efficacy: A theoretical analysis of its determinants and malleability. *Academy of Management Review*, *17*(2), 183–211.

Hayduk, L. A. (1987). *Structural equation modeling with LISREL: Essentials and advances.* Baltimore, MD: Johns Hopkins University Press.

Hobfoll, S. E. (1989). Conservation of resources: A new attempt at conceptualizing stress. *American Psychologist*, *44*, 513–524.

Hobfoll, S. E. (2001). The influence of culture, community, and the nested self in the stress process: Advancing conservation of resources theory. *Applied Psychology: An International Review*, *50*, 337–370.

Hon, A. H.Y., Bloom, M., & Crant, M. (2014). Overcoming resistance to change and enhancing creative performance. *Journal of Management*, 919–941.

Hu, L., & Bentler, P. M. (1999). Cutoff criteria for fit indexes in covariance structure analysis: Conventional criteria versus new alternatives. *Structural Equation Modeling*, *6*(1), 1–55.

Iverson, R. D. (1996). Employee acceptance of organizational change: The role of organizational commitment. *The International Journal of Human Resource Management*, *7*(1), 122–149.

Judge, T. A., Locke, E. A., Durham, C. C., & Kluger, A. N. (1998). Dispositional effects on job and life satisfaction: The role of core evaluations. *Journal of Applied Psychology*, *83*(1), 17–34.

Judge, T. A., Thoresen, C. l. J., Pucik, V., & Welbourne, T. M. (1999). Managerial coping with organizational change: A dispositional perspective. *Journal of Applied Psychology*, *84*(1), 107–122.

Korunka, C., Weiss, A., Huemer, K.-H., & Karetta, B. (1995). The effect of new technologies on job satisfaction and psychosomatic complaints. *Applied Psychology: An International Review*, *44*(2), 123–142. doi:10.1111/j.1464-0597.1995.tb01070.x

Lawson, M. B., & Angle, H. L. (1998). Upon reflection: Commitment, satisfaction, and regret after a corporate relocation. *Group and Organization Management, 23*(3), 289–317.

Lines, R. (2004). Influence of participation in strategic change: Resistance, organizational commitment and change goal achievement. *Journal of Change Management, 4*(3), 193–215.

Martin, R. (1999). Adjusting to job relocation: Relocation preparation can produce relocation stress. *Journal of Occupational and Organizational Psychology, 72,* 231–235.

Menard, S. (2002). *Longitudinal research* (2nd ed.). Thousand Oaks, CA: SAGE Publications.

Miller, V. D., Johnson, J. R., & Grau, J. G. (1994). Antecedents to willingness to participate in a planned organizational change. *Journal of Applied Communication Research, 22,* 59–80.

Oreg, S. (2003). Resistance to change: Developing an individual differences measure. *Journal of Applied Psychology, 88*(4), 680–693.

Oreg, S., & Berson, Y. (2011). Leadership and employees' reactions to change: The role of leaders' personal attributes and transformational leadership style. *Personnel Psychology, 64,* 627–654.

Piderit, S. K. (2000). Rethinking resistance and recognizing ambivalence: A multidimensional view of attitudes toward an organizational change. *Academy of Management Review, 25*(4), 783–794.

Rafferty, A. E., & Griffin, M. A. (2006). Perceptions of organizational change: A stress and coping perspective. *The Journal of Applied Psychology, 91*(5), 1154–1162.

Rafferty, A. E., & Jimmieson, N. L. (in press). Subjective perceptions of organizational change and employee resistance to change: Direct and mediated relationships with employee well-being. *British Journal of Management.*

Rafferty, A. E., Jimmieson, N. L., & Armenakis, A. A. (2013). Change readiness: A multilevel review. *Journal of Management, 39*(1), 110–135.

Rafferty, A. E., & Minbashian, A. (submitted for publication). The cognitive and affective antecedents of change readiness: Direct and indirect relationships with change supportive behaviors.

Schweiger, D., & DeNisi, A. (1991). Communication with employees following a merger: A longitudinal field experiment. *Academy of Management Journal, 34,* 110–135.

Shaw, J. B., Fields, M. W., Thacker, J. W., & Fisher, C. D. (1993). The availability of personal and external coping resources: Their impact on job stress and employee attitudes during organizational restructuring. *Work and Stress, 7*(3), 229–246.

Wanberg, C. R., & Banas, J. T. (2000). Predictors and outcomes of openness to changes in a reorganizing workplace. *Journal of Applied Psychology, 85*(1), 132–142.

Watson, D., Clark, L. A., & Tellegen, A. (1988). Development and validation of brief measures of positive and negative affect: The PANAS scales. *Journal of Personality and Social Psychology, 54*(6), 1063–1070.

Watson, D., & Pennebaker, J. W. (1989). Health complaints, stress, and distress: Exploring the central role of negative affectivity. *Psychological Review, 96*(2), 234.

Weiner, B. J. (2009). A theory of organizational readiness for change. *Implementation Science, 4,* 67–75.

Woodman, R. W. (1989). Organizational change and development: New areas for inquiry and action. *Journal of Management, 15*(2), 205–228.

Xu, X., Payne, S. C., Horner, M. T., & Alexander, A. L. (2016). Individual difference predictors of perceived organizational change fairness. *Journal of Managerial Psychology, 31*(2), 420–433.

PART II

Emotions and cognitions and change outcomes

5

FEELINGS ABOUT CHANGE

The role of emotions and emotion regulation for employee adaptation to organizational change

Karen van Dam

Introduction

Adapting to dynamic and rapid changing environments has been a challenge for organizations and employees alike. Although organizational change is often crucial for the competitiveness of the organization, employees may perceive change as disrupting routines and a threat to achievements, expertise and relationships that have been acquired over time (Bartunek, Rousseau, Rudolph, & DePalma, 2006). Organizational change can thus evoke strong emotional responses in employees, which may turn into negative attitudes toward the change. Already in the 1940s, Coch and French (1948) pointed at frustration and aggression as emotional change responses that might cause resistance to change and other undesirable behaviors. Negative emotions can also cause lowered well-being, decreased commitment and job dissatisfaction (Kiefer, 2005).

While we often view emotions as irresistible forces that have a sweeping impact on behavior, most people do not like to be carried away by their emotions or "to be hijacked" (Goleman, 1995) by the emotional impact of the situation (Koole, 2009). Because pleasant emotions are generally preferred over unpleasant emotions (Mauss, Bunge, & Gross, 2007), employees in change situations may try to change or prevent negative affective responses and engage in emotion regulation. Effective emotion regulation might increase employees' openness to the change and protect their well-being (Van Dam, 2016). Emotions and emotion regulation during change have received research attention only recently.

The goal of this chapter is to delineate the role of emotions and emotion regulation as a part of employees' change responses. First, we will ask why change can act as an affective event: what are the reasons for employees to respond emotionally to change. Next, we focus on the concept and function of emotions, and how emotions relate to organizational change. Following, Gross' (1998, 2015) process model

68 Karen van Dam

of emotion regulation is discussed as an overarching, theoretical framework, that might explain which strategies employees use during organizational change. The chapter concludes with several suggestions for future research.

Organizational change as an affective event

It is generally acknowledged that organizational change can serve as a trigger of emotional responses (e.g., Elfenbein, 2007; Huy, 1999; Kiefer, 2005; Oreg, Bartunek, Lee, & Do, 2018; Piderit, 2000; Smollan & Sayers, 2009). Large-scale transformations, such as mergers, layoffs and reorganizations, as well as smaller-scale change, such as the introduction of new work methods or self-managing work teams, can evoke strong, often negative emotions in employees.

In the literature, various reasons have been proposed that might explain these affective responses. One reason relates to the (actual or anticipated) interruption of behavior and status quo that is often implied in organizational change. Change implementation can interrupt the daily workflow and result in increased work demands and stress (Bathge & Rigotti, 2013). Organizational change might also interrupt the practices, expertise, positions and relationships that have developed over time (Kiefer, 2005). Interruptions have generally been associated with emotional arousal (Carver & Scheier, 1990).

Employees' affective responses may also originate from sincere concerns about the outcomes of the change (Huy, 1999; Kiefer, 2005; Piderit, 2000). Employees might worry that the intended change will affect procedures, products, services or the future direction of the organization in such a way that it will negatively affect productivity, sales, customers or workers. In particular employees' expectation that their job is at stake can elicit strong affective responses (Wang, Patten, Currie, Sareen, & Schmitz, 2012). As such, the change may undermine employees' expectations that the organization will protect and promote their interests (Oreg et al., 2018), implying psychological contract breach (Zhao, Wayne, Glibkowski, & Bravo, 2007). Employees might also respond emotionally if the change prohibits them to act in line with their ethical principles (Piderit, 2000), or if the change involves a fundamental change in the organization's core identity of which employees are proud (Huy, 1999).

Affective responses can additionally result from perceptions of the change process. As many organizational changes are management-initiated and the process and outcome of the change are often unclear at the onset of the change, employees may experience loss of control and increased uncertainty (Allen, Jimmieson, Bordia, & Irmer, 2007). Employees' worries about the change can also result from perceptions of injustice regarding the change (Kiefer, 2005; Oreg & Van Dam, 2009). Perceptions of diminished control, uncertainty and injustice have been related to higher levels of stress and anxiety, and a decrease in job satisfaction, commitment and intentions to remain with the organization (e.g., Allen et al., 2007).

Whereas there are many different reasons for employees to respond to organizational change with emotions such as worry, anxiety and anger, it should be noted that not all instances of change will evoke negative feelings (Kiefer, 2005; Oreg et al., 2018). Sometimes, the need for change is so clear, and the expected outcomes for the organization or the individual are so positive, that a proposed change elicits positive feelings (Huy, 1999). In any case, it can be concluded that organizational change often serves as an affective event that can elicit different emotions in employees.

Emotions

What are emotions? Emotions are complex constellations of responses for dealing with adaptive problems (Baumeister, Vohs, DeWall, & Zhang, 2007; Mesquita & Frijda, 2011) that are characterized by four aspects (Frijda, 1988). First, emotions are short-lived responses to events that have meaning for the individual because they relate to a goal, need or expectation. Second, central to the emotional response is the subjective experience of an emotion that results from an awareness and appraisal of this situation's meaning. Third, the response usually includes physiological, bodily changes, such as increased heart rate or hormonal changes (e.g., adrenaline secretion). These bodily responses are meant to support the fourth component of emotions, that is action readiness; included in emotions are innate behavioral patterns that, on a basic evolutionary level, relate to approach (aggression) and avoidance (defense) tendencies. Together, the emotion process is characterized by a situation-attention-appraisal-response sequence (Frijda, 1988; Gross, 2015).

Although emotions are sometimes considered the cause of people acting foolish or destructive, and the expression of emotions may not be much appreciated in certain settings (Grandey, 2000), emotions do have important evolutionary qualities (Baumeister et al., 2007). As rapid information systems, emotions signal that something is happening that is relevant to us. At the same time, they prepare the body for action; the initial mobilization processes activate internal resources to direct attention and behavior for solving the problem at hand (Taylor, 1991). Whether people actually engage in action may depend on factors such as context, perceived consequences and previous experiences (Frijda, 1988). Emotions are also important for future self-regulation. By signaling how far one has moved toward a cherished goal, emotions can instigate processes of goal adjustment and learning (Baumeister et al., 2007; Carver & Scheier, 1990). In addition to these intrapersonal functions, emotions can also have interpersonal, social functions. For instance, the expression of particular emotions can signal the nature of interpersonal relationships, facilitate specific behaviors in the other person and provide incentives for desired social behavior (Hwang & Matsumoto, 2013). Taken together, emotions ensure that a matching takes place between the internal and external world (Frijda, 1988).

Emotions in organizational change

How do emotions relate to organizational change? Conform the situation-attention-appraisal-response sequence (Frijda, 1988), the first announcement of

70 Karen van Dam

change will initiate a process of appraisals (Lazarus, 1991; Liu & Perrewé, 2005) where the employee evaluates the anticipated change as compatible, or not, with important goals and needs (i.e., primary appraisal), and assesses what can be done (if so) in this situation and how this will affect both the situation and the employee (i.e., secondary appraisal). Note that the primary appraisal of the change can already elicit an emotional response, as a warning that something important is at stake (Frijda, 1988; Liu & Perrewé, 2005). In case of goal congruence, this first emotional response might be positive (e.g., excitement or enthusiasm). However, as the onset of change is generally characterized by ambiguity and uncertainty, most employees will perceive or expect goal incongruence and thus experience negative emotions, such as anger, anxiety and frustration (e.g., Bathge & Rigotti, 2013; Kiefer, 2005). Similarly, the secondary appraisal process can lead to, or extend, negative affective responses as these appraisals focus on the controllability and modifiability of the situation (Frijda, Kuipers, & Ter Schure, 1989), which might be rather limited in management-initiated organizational change.

As emotions are inherently motivational (Lazarus, 1991) and include action tendencies (Frijda, 1988), they will affect employees' attitudinal and behavioral response to the change (Oreg et al., 2018). Change research has shown that negative emotions can serve as antecedents of employees' change attitudes and withdrawal behavior (Fugate, Kinicki, & Prussia, 2008; Kiefer, 2005; Smollan & Sayers, 2009) and are indicative of employees' resistance to the change (Piderit, 2000; Oreg, 2006).

Given the complex and dynamic nature of most organizational changes, employees may experience a range of different emotions (Elfenbein, 2007; Klarner, By, & Diefenbach, 2011; Vince, 2006). For example, Vince (2006) noticed that the emotions of senior managers of a firm undergoing an acquisition ranged from anger at themselves and others, to shame, powerlessness, depression and fear, dependent on the aspect of the event they appraised. Moreover, emotions might alter over time, as the change proceeds and employees adapt to the change (Fugate et al., 2008; Klarner et al., 2011). Rafferty and Restubog (2010) noticed that employees' anxiety decreased as the number of formal change information sessions increased.

It will be clear that organizational change can elicit a number of different, often negative emotions. Yet, research suggests that people generally prefer positive feelings (Mauss et al., 2007). Reports of everyday emotion regulation show that people are inclined to down-regulate negative emotions (reducing their intensity or duration) and up-regulate positive emotions (Parkinson & Totterdell, 1999). It is therefore likely that employees in organizational change will try to enhance a positive state and engage in emotion regulation.

Emotion regulation

What is emotion regulation? Emotion regulation refers to individuals' deliberate and automatic attempts to influence which emotions they have, when they have them and how these emotions are experienced and expressed (Gross, 1998; Mauss et al., 2007). Emotion regulation can focus on each stage (i.e., situation-attention-appraisal-response) of the emotion process (Frijda, 1988; Gross, 1998). Taking these stages as a starting point, Gross (1998, 2015) proposed a process model of emotion regulation that delineates five distinct types (or families) of emotion regulation strategies.

Two strategies relate to the emotion provoking situation. (1) *Situation selection* refers to approaching or avoiding certain people, events and places in order to regulate emotions (Gross, 1998). (2) *Situation modification* relates to active efforts to directly change an affective or stressful situation in order to alter its emotional impact (Gross, 1998), and has been referred to as problem-focused coping in the stress and coping literature. Another two strategies address the attentional and appraisal phase of the emotion process. (3) *Attentional deployment* encompasses different ways of focusing on the situation, i.e., distraction, concentration and rumination. People can regulate their emotions by *distracting* themselves from the situation, either cognitively or behaviorally, for instance by thinking of pleasurable moments or engaging in alternative activities (Augustine & Hemenover, 2009; Gross, 1998). In contrast, people can *concentrate* on the problem or situation in an effort to understand the antecedents and consequences of this situation. Concentration may turn into *rumination* when people get stuck in continuous worrisome thoughts and circular thinking about the situation that is difficult to stop (Querstret & Cropley, 2012; Van Seggelen & Van Dam, 2016). (4) *Reappraisal* is an emotion regulation strategy that involves generating positive interpretations of the situation in order to alter its emotional impact (Aldao, Nolen-Hoeksema, & Schweitzer, 2010; Gross, 1998). The fifth type of emotion regulation, (5) *response modulation*, relates to individuals' efforts to change the emotional response at the physiological, experiential or behavioral level. Meta-analytic evidence (Aldao et al., 2010; Augustine & Hemenover, 2009; Webb, Miles, & Sheeran, 2012) indicates that some emotion regulation strategies (i.e., situation modification, distraction and reappraisal) generally result in more positive outcomes, such as affect repair and increased well-being, than other strategies (i.e., rumination and emotional suppression).

Emotion regulation in organizational change

How will employees regulate their change-related emotions? Unfortunately, little research has addressed this question. Still, there are some related studies that shed light on this issue (see also Elfenbein, 2007).

Situation selection as a strategy for emotion regulation is rather limited in case of large-scale organizational changes. As such changes are generally inevitable, employees have only few options. Employees can decide to withdraw from the organization; Fugate and colleagues (2008) found that negative change appraisals resulted in increased absenteeism, quit intentions and actual turnover behavior (see also Rafferty & Restubog, 2010). Employees can also decide to stay in the organization but avoid situations that are likely to elicit negative feelings, such as colleagues that are complaining about the change (Oreg, 2006) or even company meetings about the change, and seek out situations where they feel better.

72 Karen van Dam

Situation modification refers to employee attempts to do something about the change, for instance, through voice and participation in change implementation. Although change participation may not be primarily aimed at regulating ones' emotions, it can have beneficial effects on emotions because it can lead to a sense of ownership and control over the change process (Van Dam, Oreg, & Schyns, 2008) and to a work situation that is more attractive. Studies have found positive effects of change participation on employees' openness to change (Coch & French, 1948; Van Dam et al., 2008; Wanberg & Banas, 2000). Coping research however indicates that efforts to modify the situation will be effective mainly in situations that are malleable (Terry & Hynes, 1998). It is therefore possible that change situations where the input of participating employees is not used to modify the change might elicit negative emotions, such as frustration and cynicism.

Although employees' *attentional deployment* in change situations has not received much research attention, several studies have focused on distraction, concentration and rumination in other work settings (i.e., Querstret & Cropley, 2012; Sonnentag & Fritz, 2015; Van Seggelen & Van Dam, 2016). The findings of these studies generally support the conclusions of clinical and emotion research (e.g., Augustine & Hemenover, 2009) that distraction is an effective strategy for affect repair, whereas rumination can have detrimental effects on individuals' well-being and recovery processes. Querstret and Cropley (2012) for instance found that rumination increased work-related fatigue, partly by undermining employees' sleep quality. Similarly, research on recovery from work indicates that efforts to distract oneself from work (i.e., psychological detachment) contributes to employees' energetic state, work engagement and health (Sonnentag & Fritz, 2015). In a change situation, Van Dam (2016) found that rumination was positively associated with negative emotions and resistance to the change.

Employees who engage in *positive reappraisal* are actively trying to emphasize the positive aspects of the change and put the negative aspects into perspective. As such, positive reappraisal should be considered an act that affects employees' appraisal of the change as a challenge or a threat (cf. Lazarus, 1991). Change appraisals can have important consequences for employees' thoughts, feelings and behaviors toward the change (Fugate et al., 2008). Van Dam (2016) found that employees' efforts to positively reappraise the change situation related positively to challenge appraisals and positive emotions, and negatively to threat appraisals and negative emotions, which in turn predicted employees' openness to the change. Fugate et al. (2008) observed how threat appraisals were related to coping and negative emotions, which predicted voluntary turnover during the following year.

Employees' *response regulation* during change can take the form of either experience/arousal (down) regulation or emotional expression regulation. Employees in change situations may try to downplay their emotional arousal or feelings through, for instance, relaxation, mindfulness or other strategies. They might also engage in one the other emotion regulation strategies, such as distraction or reappraisal, to down-regulate their affective responses. Indeed, Van Dam (2016) noticed that employees who resisted the change more, and thus experienced more negative emotions, had put more effort in trying to distract their attention away from the change. It is important to note that change might serve as a chronic stressor, and that the physiological arousal resulting from the change may deplete individuals' resources and energy and, in the long run, may cause emotional exhaustion, poor performance and health problems (Sonnentag & Fritz, 2015). Moreover, sustained activation and negative affect might influence how change situations are appraised (Elfenbein, 2007; Tugate, Fredrickson, & Feldman-Barret, 2004); owing to increased arousal and negative emotions, employees are more likely to appraise a change as a hindrance stressor than as a challenge stressor (George & Jones, 2001). Given these consequences, arousal regulation deserves more attention in change research. Response regulation also applies to the display of emotions. While employees may have a need to express their emotions in change situations, organizations often consider emotional stages during change as unproductive that should be kept short (Kiefer, 2005). Emotional expression can have a number of different outcomes, such as emotional contagion. Because change happens within a social context, emotional contagion can serve as an important trigger of shared emotional responses to change (Bartunek et al., 2006). As negative emotional displays are not much appreciated, most organizations apply certain display rules that specify which emotions are appropriate and how they should be expressed to others (Grandey, 2000). Rules that emphasize suppression of negative emotions have been associated with lowered well-being (Brotheridge & Grandey, 2002), whereas rules that emphasize expression of positive emotions have been related to increased work engagement (Ybema & Van Dam, 2014). Studying a change situation, Smollan and Sayers (2009) noticed that especially in male-dominated environments change-related emotional displays were not much appreciated.

Future research

Although the role of emotions in organizations has received increasing attention in recent years and emotion regulation has been studied extensively in the fields of emotion and clinical psychology, the role of emotions and emotion regulation during organizational change has received limited research attention. As a consequence, there are many questions to be answered. To provide directions for future research, Ashkanasy's (Ashkanasy & Dorris, 2017) five-level model of emotions in organizations is used as a general framework for research suggestions.

Level 1 of this model refers to within-person processes and as such addresses many of the issues raised in this chapter. Future change research could investigate how the emotion-and-regulation process evolves over time, the order in which emotion regulation strategies are used, and whether this order would affect employee outcomes such as their well-being or attitudes towards the change. While much organizational research on emotions distinguishes between positive and negative emotions only, researchers are invited to focus on discrete emotions, such as anxiety or anger, as they may have different causes and outcomes (Elfenbein, 2007;

74 Karen van Dam

Kiefer, 2005; Oreg et al., 2018), and investigate the relationships of these discrete emotions with emotion regulation strategies.

Regarding level 2, the between-persons level, attention could be paid to individual differences, such as self-efficacy or trait affect, in affective responses and choice of regulation strategy. Research could also focus on the impact of employees' previous change experiences and their expectations on their affective responses.

Levels 3, 4 and 5 focus on the interpersonal, team/leadership and organizational level respectively. These levels might be especially important during change situations, as change is largely a social and contextual phenomenon. Future research could investigate how social and contextual variables affect employees' emotions and regulation during change (see also Klarner et al., 2011). For instance, emotional display rules and organizational emotional climate may determine how employees express their emotions during change (Ashkanasy & Dorris, 2017; Ybema & Van Dam, 2014). Moreover, in line with emotion contagion processes that lead to shared emotions, studies could investigate whether contagion also happens concerning emotion regulation, and, if so, how change agents or the change process may impact these contagion processes.

Besides suggestions on *what* to study, it is also important to consider *how* to study emotion and emotion regulation during change. Different methodologies might serve this purpose, each with their strengths and limitations. First, one could try to study these phenomena in real-life change settings. Given the dynamic nature of emotions and regulation, it is important to use longitudinal designs. Having (at least) three waves and using latent change scores is recommended to establish intrapersonal changes in emotions and regulation over time, and investigate both cross-lagged and reversed effects (McArdle, 2009; Ployhart & Vandenberg, 2010). Online and paper/pencil measures can be used to collect a dataset of sufficient size in organizations undergoing change. Possible limitations of this approach include 1 participation (organizations and change recipients may not be willing to provide data on multiple occasions); 2 timing (what would be the best time for data collection during the change, and how should the measurements be spaced); 3 awareness (participants might not always be fully aware of their emotional processes).

The second approach, diary or ESM methods, may overcome some of these limitations. In this approach, change recipients report their affective experiences on a day-to-day base (or more often) which helps to detect fluctuations and control for base level values. Owing to the increased number of observations per participant, this approach requires less participants, which accommodates limitation 1 but may raise another limitation, 4 generalization (is this smaller sample representative such that the findings can be generalized). Moreover, limitation 2, timing, is an issue; as organization change might take months or even years, in which period should we collect our data? In order to avoid limitation 3, awareness, wearables can be used that register participants' physical conditions, such as heart beat and blood pressure.

Finally, instead of field studies, experimental designs can be used where relevant aspects of the change are manipulated, and responses can be measured in different ways, for instance through registering participants' response time, and physiological responses. Vignette studies can be used to investigate how person characteristics, such as habitual emotion regulation and trait affect, impact participants' responses to specific change situations. While an experimental approach is useful for studying specific cause – effect relationships, the research setting differs considerably from the complexity involved in organizational change, and therefore, limitation 4, generalization, might be an issue.

Given the strengths and limitations of these approaches, a plea could be made to use different methodologies to overcome method-specific limitations and assess whether outcomes are method-dependent.

Conclusion

This chapter has delineated some of the ways in which emotions and emotion regulation can play a part in organizational change processes. Although this review is not comprehensive, it may serve as a trigger for organizations and researchers to pay more attention to the emotional aspect of organizational change. While emotions are often seen as irrational and the cause of problems during change implementation (Kiefer, 2005), they can be the expression of something valuable, indicating employees' perceptions, concerns, sense making and adaptation to the change (Bartunek et al., 2006; Carver & Scheier, 1990; Smollan & Sayers, 2009). As emotion generation and emotion regulation are inextricably connected (Mesquita & Frijda, 2011), organizations and researchers need to pay more attention to how employees regulate their emotions. Emotion regulation, like emotions, can imply strong motivational forces that can impact employee behavior and well-being at work. Employees will adjust to the change more easily when they apply adaptive regulation strategies such as positive reappraisal and distraction (Aldao et al., 2010; Augustine & Hemenover, 2009; Van Dam, 2016; Webb et al., 2012). Research with different methodologies is needed to investigate the specific mechanisms involved in employees' emotion regulation and adjustment to change. The practical implications of such research will help organizations in developing a shared meaning system and improve the emotional quality of organizational change.

References

Aldao, A., Nolen-Hoeksema, S., & Schweitzer, S. (2010). Emotion-regulation strategies across psychopathology: A meta-analytic review. *Clinical Psychological Review, 30,* 217–237.

Allen, J., Jimmieson, N. L., Bordia, P., & Irmer, B. E. (2007). Uncertainty during organizational change: Managing perceptions through communication. *Journal of Change Management, 7,* 187–210.

Ashkanasy, N. M., & Dorris, A. D. (2017). Emotions in the workplace. *Annual Review of Organizational Psychology and Organizational Behavior, 4,* 67–90.

Augustine, A. A., & Hemenover, S. H. (2009). On the relative effectiveness of affect regulation strategies: A meta-analysis. *Cognition and Emotion, 23,* 1181–1220.

Bartunek, J. M., Rousseau, D. M., Rudolph, J. W., & DePalma, J. A. (2006). On the receiving end: Sensemaking, emotion, and assessment of an organizational change initiated by others. *Journal of Applied Behavioral Science, 42,* 182–206.

76 Karen van Dam

Bathge, A., & Rigotti, T. (2013). Interruptions to workflow: Their relationship with irritation and satisfaction with performance, and the mediating roles of time pressure and mental demands. *Work & Stress, 27*, 43–63.

Baumeister, R. F., Vohs, K. D., DeWall, C. N., & Zhang, L. (2007). How emotion shapes behavior: Feedback, anticipation, and reflection, rather than direct causation. *Personality & Social Psychology Review, 22*, 167–203.

Brotheridge, C. M., & Grandey, A. A. (2002). Emotional labor and burnout: Comparing two perspectives of "people work". *Journal of Vocational Behavior, 60*, 17–39.

Carver, C. S., & Scheier, M. F. (1990). Origins and functions of positive and negative affect. *Psychological Review, 97*, 19–35.

Coch, L., & French Jr., J. R. (1948). Overcoming resistance to change. *Human Relations, 1*, 512–532.

Elfenbein, H. A. (2007). Emotions in organizations. *Academy of Management Annals, 1*, 315–386.

Frijda, N. H. (1988). The laws of emotion. *American Psychologist, 43*, 349–358.

Frijda, N. H., Kuipers, P., & Ter Schure, E. (1989). Relations among emotion, appraisal, and emotional action readiness. *Journal of Personality and Social Psychology, 57*, 212–228.

Fugate, M., Kinicki, A., & Prussia, G. E. (2008). Employee coping with organizational change: An examination of alternative theoretical perspectives. *Personnel Psychology, 61*, 1–36.

George, J. M., & Jones, G. R. (2001). Towards a process model of individual change in organizations. *Human Relations, 54*, 419–444.

Goleman, D. (1995). *Emotional intelligence: Why it can matter more than IQ*. London: Bloomsbury.

Grandey, A. A. (2000). Emotion regulation in the workplace: A new way to conceptualize emotional labor. *Journal of Occupational Health Psychology, 5*, 50–110.

Gross, J. J. (1998). The emerging field of emotion regulation: An integrative review. *Review of General Psychology, 2*, 271–299.

Gross, J. J. (2015). Emotion regulation: Conceptual and empirical foundations. In J. J. Gross (Ed.), *Handbook of emotion regulation* (2nd ed., pp. 3–20). New York: Guilford.

Huy, Q. N. (1999). Emotional capability, emotional intelligence, and radical change. *Academy of Management Review, 24*, 325–345.

Hwang, H., & Matsumoto, D. (2013). *Functions of emotions*. In R. Biswas-Diener & E. Diener (Eds.), *Noba textbook series: Psychology*. Champaign, IL: DEF Publishers. Retrieved from http://nobaproject.com/browse-content.

Kiefer, T. (2005). Feeling bad: Antecedents and consequences of negative emotions in ongoing change. *Journal of Organizational Behavior, 26*, 875–897.

Klarner, P., By, R. T., & Diefenbach, T. (2011). Employee emotions during organizational change: Towards a new research agenda. *Scandinavian Journal of Management, 27*, 332–340.

Koole, S. (2009). The psychology of emotion regulation: An integrative review. *Cognition and Emotion, 23*, 4–41.

Lazarus, R. S. (1991). Progress on a cognitive-motivational-relational theory of emotion. *American Psychologist, 46*, 819–834.

Liu, Y., & Perrewé, P. L. (2005). Another look at the role of emotion in the organizational change: A process model. *Human Resource Management Review, 15*, 263–280.

Mauss, I. B., Bunge, S. A., & Gross, J. J. (2007). Automatic emotion regulation. *Social and Personality Psychology Compass, 1*, 146–167.

McArdle, J. (2009). Latent variable modelling of differences and changes with longitudinal data. *Annual Review of Psychology, 60*, 577–605.

Mesquita, B., & Frijda, N. H. (2011). Commentary: An emotion perspective on emotion regulation. *Cognition and Emotion, 25*, 782–784.

Oreg, S. (2006). Personality, context and resistance to organizational change. *European Journal of Work and Organizational Psychology, 15*, 73–101.

Oreg, S., Bartunek, J., Lee, G., & Do, B. (2018). An affect-based model of recipients' responses to organizational change events. *Academy of Management Review, 43*, 65–86.

Oreg, S., & Van Dam, K. (2009). Organizational justice in the context of organizational change. *Netherlands Journal of Psychology, 65*, 127–135.

Parkinson, B., & Totterdell, P. (1999). Classifying affect regulation strategies. *Cognition and Emotion, 13*, 277–303.

Piderit, S. K. (2000). Rethinking resistance and recognizing ambivalence: A multidimensional view of attitudes toward an organizational change. *Academy of Management Review, 25*, 783–794.

Ployhart, R., & Vandenberg, R. (2010). Longitudinal research: The theory, design, and analysis of change. *Journal of Management, 36*, 94–120.

Querstret, D., & Cropley, M. (2012). Exploring the relationship between work-related rumination, sleep quality, and work-related fatigue. *Journal of Occupational Health Psychology, 17*, 341–353.

Rafferty, A. E., & Restubog, S. L. D. (2010). The impact of change process and context on change reactions and turnover during a merger. *Journal of Management, 36*, 1309–1338.

Smollan, R. K., & Sayers, J. G. (2009). Organizational culture, change and emotions: A qualitative study. *Journal of Change Management, 9*, 435–457.

Sonnentag, S., & Fritz, C. (2015). Recovery from job stress: The stressor-detachment model as an integrative framework. *Journal of Organizational Behavior, 36*, 72–103.

Taylor, S. E. (1991). Asymmetrical effects of positive and negative events: The mobilization-minimization hypothesis. *Psychological Bulletin, 110*, 67–85.

Terry, D. J., & Hynes, G. J. (1998). Adjustment to low-control situation: Reexaming the role of coping responses. *Journal of Personality and Social Psychology, 74*, 1078–1092.

Tugate, M. M., Fredrickson, B. L., & Feldman-Barret, L. (2004). Psychological resilience and positive emotional granularity: Examining the benefits of positive emotions on coping and health. *Journal of Personality, 72*, 1161–1190.

Van Dam, K. (2016, June). The role of emotion regulation for employee adaptation to organizational change: The case of reappraisal and attentional deployment. *EAWOP Small Group Meeting*, Athens, Greece.

Van Dam, K., Oreg, S., & Schyns, B. (2008). Daily work contexts and resistance to organizational change: The role of leader-member exchange, development climate, and change process characteristics. *Applied Psychology, an International Review, 57*, 313–334.

Van Seggelen, I., & Van Dam, K. (2016). Self-reflection as a mediator between self-efficacy and well-being. *Journal of Managerial Psychology, 31*, 18–33.

Vince, R. (2006). Being taken over: Managers' emotions and rationalizations during a company takeover. *Journal of Management Studies, 43*, 343–365.

Wanberg, C. R., & Banas, J. T. (2000). Predictors and outcomes of openness to changes in a reorganizing workplace. *Journal of Applied Psychology, 85*, 132–142.

Wang, J., Patten, S., Currie, S., Sareen, J., & Schmitz, N. (2012). Business mergers and acquisitions and the risk of mental disorders: A population-based study. *Occupational and Environmental Medicine, 69*, 569–573.

Webb, T. L., Miles, E., & Sheeran, P. (2012). Dealing with feeling: A meta-analysis of the effectiveness of strategies derived from the process model of emotion regulation. *Psychological Bulletin, 138*, 775–808.

Ybema, J. F., & Van Dam, K. (2014). The importance of negative and positive emotional display rules for emotional exhaustion and work engagement: A multi-group comparison. *Journal of Positive Psychology, 9*, 366–376.

Zhao, H., Wayne, S. J., Glibkowski, B. C., & Bravo, J. (2007). The impact of psychological contract breach on work-related outcomes: A meta-analysis. *Personnel Psychology, 60*, 647–680.

6

HOW WORKERS' APPRAISALS OF CHANGE INFLUENCE EMPLOYEE OUTCOMES

Karina Nielsen

Background

Organizations are constantly undergoing changes to ensure competitive advantage and address the challenges of operating in an ever-changing environment. It has been suggested that many organizational changes fail to achieve their objectives and that one possible explanation for this failure is that during organizational change, change agents often fail to consider the "human factor" (de Jong et al., 2016; Quinlan & Bohle, 2009). Bamberger et al. (2012) suggested that the process of organizational change, i.e. the way change is implemented, may influence the impact of such change on employee well-being. In the present chapter, I review the literature on organizational change and well-being from the perspective of employees. In doing so, I review the current state of the art of how cognitive appraisals of organizational change influence employees' well-being. The current literature has primarily focused on the appraisals of employees' position in the organization post change, i.e. has the change resulted in a better situation for the individual? Extending existing literature, I also present new results on how appraisals of the change process itself may influence employee outcomes.

There is a large body of research showing that organizational change mainly has a negative impact on employee well-being (de Jong et al., 2016), partly due to reduced autonomy and increased job demands as employees have to adjust to the new situation. In their review, de Jong et al. (2016) found that the change process had an impact on the outcomes for employees. For example, fears of losing your job increased but trust decreased. De Jong et al. (2016) identified several factors in the change process that had an impact on how employees reacted to the change process. Overall, they found that the impact of the change process is influenced by the extent to which employees are satisfied with the general management of changes in the workplace, i.e. if employees feel satisfied with the way change is organized this minimizes the negative impact of change. Other factors that may influence perceptions of change are communications about change and the provision of information, and perceptions of fair procedures concerning the change. Together, this body of research suggests that employees' appraisals of organizational change has an impact on employee well-being. In the present chapter, I use a broad definition of well-being. Danna and Griffin (1999) stated that well-being encompasses both health specific aspects such as psychological and physical symptoms, but also general job-specific outcomes such as job satisfaction, work enjoyment and work engagement.

Appraisals of organizational change

The way individuals appraise and give meaning to their experiences at work is a trigger to their well-being (Lazarus & Folkman, 1984). The cognitive appraisal theory of stress (CATS) provides an explanation of the links between perceptions of work and well-being (Lazarus & Folkman, 1984). Cognitive appraisal can be understood as the process by which individuals categorize an event as either posing a threat to their well-being, presenting a positive challenge that may improve their well-being and facilitate personal growth, or appearing neutral, i.e., having no potential effect on their well-being (Lazarus & Folkman, 1984). According to CATS, poor well-being is the result of an individual's appraisal that the demands of the situation exceed the individual's skills and resources to deal effectively with the situation (Lazarus & Folkman, 1984). According to CATS, there are two important elements to cognitive appraisal: (1) individuals appraise whether a situation may be of potential harm, may present a positive challenge or be neutral to their well-being, and (2) individuals appraise whether they have the ability to cope successfully with the situation. Numerous studies have found support for the importance of cognitive appraisal in employee well-being (Dewe, 1989; Dewe & Trenberth, 2012, Persson et al., 2012).

Lazarus and Folkman (1984) emphasized that a situation's novelty is central to the appraisal of whether a situation may be perceived to exceed the individual's resources. On the one hand, organizational change may be a potentially stressful situation. Employees may be unsure of the effects of the change: whether or not they are at risk of losing their job, whether they will be able to successfully perform new tasks associated with change or whether they will have to work with other colleagues and engage in new social relations and lose close colleagues (see e.g. Wiezer et al., 2011). On the other hand, organizational change may be perceived as a positive challenge because it brings about opportunities to influence how the future of the organization and the job should be designed (Pahkin, Mattila-Holappa, Nielsen, Widerszal-Bazyl, & Wiezer, 2014a). Organizational change and the open boundaries may be seen as an opportunity to craft a more interesting and challenging job. Cognitive appraisal theory thus suggests it is important to explore whether organizational changes are appraised to be good or bad, i.e. as an opportunity to enhance

80 Karina Nielsen

one's well-being or as a threat to one's well-being, and how these appraisals affect employees' well-being.

Previous research on employee appraisals and organizational change

A body of research has emerged in the organizational change literature examining the effects of employees' appraisals of whether they have benefited or not from a change, i.e. whether employees experience that they have either an improved or a worsened position within the organization after an organization change. In a study among white and blue collar workers in a multinational industrial company, Väänänen Ahola, Koskinen, Pahkin and Kouvonen (2004) studied the impact of a merger. They found that employees who appraised they had a deteriorated standing in the company after the merger reported higher levels of exhaustion and lower levels of work ability, i.e. they reported being less able to do their job, mentally, physically and compared to their peers. Taking these results one step further, Pahkin, Väänänen, Koskinen, Bergbom and Kouvonen (2011) found that employees who appraised they had a deteriorated standing in the company post-merger had a larger risk of psychiatric events, i.e. an increased risk of being hospitalized for any period of time during the follow-up period of five years, committing suicide or being prescribed psychotropic drugs. Experienced decline in one's own standing at work during an organizational merger has been found to elevate the risk of post-merger psychiatric morbidity five years later (Väänänen, Ahola, Koskinen, Pahkin & Kouvonen, 2011). Psychiatric morbidity was measured as hospitalization for psychiatric disorders, prescription of psychotropic drugs or registered suicide attempts (Väänänen et al., 2011).

It is not all bad news though. For employees with a sense of coherence, i.e. who have the ability to make sense of life, who believe they have the resources available to deal with life events and who evaluate external stimuli in a clear and structured way (Antonovsky, 1986), the negative impact on their standing had less of a negative impact on their mental health. A possible explanation for this finding may be that if people in general are able to make sense of the world and perceive they have a meaningful life then they are less affected by a deteriorated position at work (Pahkin, Väänänen, Koskinen, Bergbom, & Kouvonen, 2011).

Furthermore, rather than only focusing on negative aspects of employee well-being such as physical and mental symptoms of ill-health, Pahkin et al. (2014b) explored whether appraisals of one's standing in the organization were related not only to negative states of well-being, i.e. work ability, mental ill-health and exhaustion, but also whether positive well-being states could be the outcome of employees' positive appraisals of their standing within the organization post-change. Specifically, the authors looked at work enjoyment. In their study, which took place in the Finnish forestry industry, Pahkin et al. (2014b) found that employees who appraised their standing as deteriorated post-organizational change reported higher levels of stress and also enjoyed their work less compared to their colleagues who appraised the change experience positively. Pahkin et al. (2014b) then went on to explore the factors that may influence this negative appraisal. They found that a lack of opportunity to influence the change process resulted in a negative appraisal of their standing afterwards as did having a management that did not manage the change process well.

A limitation of the Pahkin et al. (2014b) study is that they only measured whether employees felt informed about the change, felt they had been involved and had their views heard but did not measure whether employees' appraisals of the change process were positive or negative, i.e. was involvement sufficient? As a result, they failed to capture the cognitive appraisals of the change process, but merely measured the perceived presence of management support and involvement, not whether the support and the level of involvement was perceived as problematic or positive by respondents. The underlying assumption of Pahkin et al.'s (2014b) measures of employees' involvement in the change process and the support of management is that there is an "objective" level over which an aspect of the work environment, in this case the change process, will have positive consequences for employee well-being (Cousins et al., 2004; Mackay, Cousins, Kelly, Lee, & McCaig, 2004). This view has been challenged on several accounts (Rick & Briner, 2000). First, it is near impossible to determine at which level the change process may change from being harmful to positive, or even neutral (Nielsen, Abildgaard, & Daniels, 2014; Rick & Briner, 2000). Second, there is an underlying assumption that two people involved in the same change process would experience the change in the same way (Daniels, 2011). Recent research has found that employees in similar jobs do not rate their work environment the same (Persson et al., 2012).

Based on Lazarus and Folkman's (1984) cognitive appraisal theory and the hindrance-challenge stressor approach (Cavanaugh, Boswell, Roehling, & Boudreau, 2000), it has been suggested that if the change process is perceived positively it may have a positive impact on employee well-being. The way individuals appraise and give meaning to their experiences at work is the trigger to their well-being (Lazarus & Folkman, 1984). If an aspect of the change process is perceived as potentially harmful and the individual fears he or she may not have the necessary resources to cope, the aspect will be appraised as problematic; conversely, when an aspect of the work environment is appraised to be beneficial and the individual has the resources to take advantage of the change, the change process will be appraised as good. Thus employees' appraisal of organizational change may impact their well-being. Building on previously unpublished data, I extend the existing literature on cognitive appraisals and organizational change to understand how employees' cognitive appraisals of specific change processes (Pahkin et al., 2014b) impact on their well-being. I explore the effects of a positive appraisals of the overall change process and, more specifically, the active role of line managers in supporting the process. The factors were found to be important in the study of Pahkin et al. (2014b) but, as mentioned above, the study failed to explore the appraisals of the process.

Case study: the effects of Danish mail delivery carriers' appraisal of change processes

National postal services are in many ways the "sick man of government agencies" (LA Times, 2015). The Danish postal service is no exception. Privatization and digitalization pose tremendous challenges for postal services. First, privatization has resulted in increased competition primarily in the area of parcel delivery. In January 2011, privatization was introduced in Denmark as part of a EU initiative that was also implemented in Belgium, Bulgaria, Estonia, Finland, France, Germany, Ireland, Italy, The Netherlands, Slovenia, Sweden, Great Britain and Austria (Transportstyrelsen, 2013). Second, recent years has seen a rapid decline in mail. People are increasingly using electronic media such as emails, text messaging and social media to communicate. Public bodies are also transitioning their communications and send official letters via electronic portals and emails. In 2010, 600 Danish private and public organizations and 3 million people were registered e-Boks, the national digital mail service. In total, 160 million letters were distributed via e-Boks in 2010.

The consequences of the changes in mail patterns are severe. In the Danish postal service alone, the past ten years have seen a reduction in mail of 52% (PostDanmark, 2014) with a 10% reduction in sent letters and 10% reduction in sent parcels in 2010 alone (PostDanmark, 2010). In 2008, on average 223 letters per inhabitant were sent. In 2012, this number had reduced to 123 (Transportstyrelsen, 2013). At the EU level, 9.71 billion letters were posted in 2007 compared to 8.22 billion in 2011. The number of parcels being sent on the other hand increased. In 2008, half a billion parcels were sent while in 2011, this amount had increased to .65 billion. Overall, in the EU, profits reduced 3.3%.

These reductions have resulted in major organizational changes in the Danish postal service. First, there have been major layoffs. In 2009, 18,049 full-time employees were employed in the postal service, but this number was reduced to 16,206 one year later, in 2010 (PostDanmark, 2010). Second, these changes have resulted in changes at the day-to-day running of the business. Where postal workers previously would have their own postal route, these routes are now continually changing with larger geographical areas having to be covered by one mail delivery carrier. In many cases, mopeds and cars are increasingly taking over where previously the mail was delivered using bicycles. Another result of the changes in mail on the day-to-day running of the business is that geographical postal areas are being merged. New technology is being introduced such as tracking devices and electronic signatures. Finally, new services are being introduced to maximize production, for example using cars to deliver "meals-on-wheels" to the elderly or keeping an eye on vacation homes in remote areas.

To understand the challenges of the Danish postal service better I conducted a longitudinal survey with one year between baseline and follow-up in two geographical areas of the postal service. In total, 495 employees responded to the questionnaire (response rates around 90% in both rounds). Of these, 43% were women, they were on average 42 years old and had on average worked 16 years in the postal service at baseline. I asked mail delivery service carriers about the changes they had experienced over the past 12 months. In 2011, only 7% of mail delivery carriers reported there had been no changes in the past 12 months. A total of 54% mail delivery carriers reported they had been given new work tasks, 52% reported new technology had been introduced, 60% reported differences in working hours, 62% reported they had experienced changes in the way work was organized and 60% reported changes to the work procedures. To understand more about what these changes meant I took a closer look into the consequences of changes in work organization. Of the total sample 60%, or 153 mail delivery carriers reported such a change.

Appraisals of change and well-being outcomes

As our review of the literature shows recent research has demonstrated that employees' appraisal of change impacts on their well-being, I expanded this line of thinking in the postal service project. Rather than asking about changes in position or standing, I asked directly about the appraisals of the change process itself. Based on interviews, we asked whether a certain aspect of the change was seen as problematic or a good aspect of the job (see also Nielsen, Stage, Abildgaard, & Brauer, 2013, Nielsen, Abildgaard, & Daniels, 2014). We developed two measures of the appraisal of the change process. First, we asked about the change process itself. Second, we asked about how mail delivery carriers felt their managers dealt with the change process. The items included in each scale can be found in Table 6.1.

I asked mail delivery carriers to rate their perceptions of appraisals at baseline and their well-being at follow-up 12 months later. As can be seen in the above figures, the changes were already undergoing at baseline. I conducted regression analyses to explore how appraisals of the change process and of the management of changes were related to well-being outcomes one year later. Employees who rated the overall change process positively reported being more engaged in their work one year later ($\beta = .24, p < .01$; measured by UWES (Schaufeli, Bakker, and

TABLE 6.1 Items included in measures of appraisals

The change process	Management's handling of changes
Time allowed to adjust to new initiatives	Consistent management's communication about changes
Time allocated to learn new tasks	My leader's management of colleagues' negative reaction to changes
Degree of influence over changes made	My leader's information about new initiatives
Degree of involvement over changes made	My leader's willingness to take on board input from employees concerning changes
Amount of changes made	My leader's ability to communicate about changes
Cronbach's alpha = .85	Cronbach's alpha = .83

Salanova, 2006), Cronbach's alpha = .93) and they were also more satisfied with their job overall (measured by one item, β = .13, p <.05). Employees who had rated the change process positively also reported better mental health (β = .20, p < .05, measured using the McHorney and Ware (1995) scale (Cronbach's alpha = .82).

We also asked employees to rate their job insecurity. We measured both quantitative job insecurity (the extent to which they fear losing their job) and qualitative job insecurity (the extent to which they fear changes to their job, but not job loss). We used Hellgren, Sverke and Isaksson (1999) to measure both types of job insecurity, alphas = .75 and .78, respectively. Although I found no effects of a positive appraisal of the change process on qualitative job insecurity (β = .11, NS), I did find that a positive appraisal of the change process was related to lower levels of quantitative job insecurity 12 months later (β = −.24, p < .01).

It may at a first glance seem surprising that it is the fear of losing your job that is reduced, not the fear of changes in the work process, however, there may be a logical explanation for this. It is possible that a positive appraisal does not change your view that changes are going to happen, particularly in the context of the postal service, where the decline in mail is obvious, also to mail delivery carriers. Previous studies on organizational change have explored the importance of the organizational context on job insecurity. In a qualitative study, Wiezer et al. (2011) found that employees who were given the chance to influence the change process reported having more faith in the decisions made by management and trusted them more. Trust and justice has been found to be related to job insecurity (Loi, Lam, & Chan, 2012; Sverke, Hellgren, & Näswall, 2002).

It is thus possible that a positive appraisal of the change process may result in employees experiencing the procedures are fair and that they can trust the organization and therefore they do not fear losing their job to the same extent. For example, if employees feel they have had a say over the change processes then they are more likely to perceive these as fair and trust that good decisions have been made. I tested these assumptions in mediational analyses, i.e. whether trust and justice could be the explanation for why a positive appraisal of the change process was related to lowered fears of losing your job. Mediation is tested in three steps. First, it is tested whether the predictor is related to the outcome (i.e. is appraisals of the change process related to job insecurity, the results of these tests are reported above). Second, it is tested whether the predictor is related to the mediator (e.g. is a positive change process related to trust?). Third, the predictor and the mediator are included in the same model and if the relationship between the predictor (e.g. appraisals of the change process) and the outcome (e.g. job insecurity) becomes either less significant or non-significant after the mediator (e.g. trust) is entered into the model, then there is either partial or full mediation at play: the explanation for why there is a relationship between appraisals of the process and job insecurity can be (partly) explained by the fact that employees trust their leaders. The Sobel (1982) procedure was employed to statistically establish the effect of the mediator on the predictor–outcome relationship. Trust and justice was measured at the same time as the appraisals of the process, i.e. at baseline. Appraisals of the change

Workers' appraisals of change **85**

process were positively associated with trust ($\beta = .35$, p. $< .001$). I did indeed find that trust could be the explanation for why positive appraisals of the change process led employees to fear less that they would lose their jobs. Trust fully mediated the relationship. After including trust, positive appraisals of the change process became non-significant ($\beta = -.19$, NS) after entering trust into the model, while trust was significantly related to quantitative job insecurity ($\beta = -.34$, $p < .01$). Sobel's test confirmed mediation was significant ($z = 2.66$, $p = .01$). Appraisals of the change process were significantly related to justice ($\beta = .24$, $p < .01$). Justice was a partial mediator of the relationship between employees' positive appraisal of the fear of losing your job. The relationship between positive appraisals of the change process and quantitative job insecurity became less significant ($\beta = -.22$, $p < .05$) after entering justice into the model while the relationship between justice and quantitative job insecurity was significant ($\beta = -.33$, $p < .01$). Sobel's test confirmed mediation was significant ($z = 3.62$, $p = .001$).

We also asked mail delivery carriers about how well they felt their leaders managed the change process. I analyzed how a positive appraisal of leaders' management of the change process was related to employee outcomes. I found that employees who held a positive view of their leader's management of the change reported being more engaged in their work ($\beta = .17$, $p < .01$) and more satisfied with their job in general ($\beta = .14$, $p < .05$). As with an overall positive appraisal of the process, employees' positive appraisal of the way their line managers managed the process led to fewer fears of losing one's job 12 months later ($\beta = -.13$, $p < .05$), but not to insecurity concerning changes in the job ($\beta = .00$, NS). A positive appraisal of the way line managers managed the change process was not related to mental health either ($\beta = .09$, NS).

As with the positive appraisal of the overall change process, a possible explanation for why the appraisals of leaders managing the change well led to fewer fears of being made redundant could be trust in management and perceptions of justice. It is possible that if employees see that their leaders manage the change well this will result in them developing a general sense of trust in leaders and they feel that they are being treated fairly. In the qualitative study by Wiezer et al. (2011), employees reported the importance of leaders' handling of changes. Employees needed to "give restructuring a face", i.e. they needed leaders to be the face of organizational change on the ground and inform and acknowledge the difficulties of implementing change.

Mediational analyses supported these assumptions. Appraisals of the line manager's handling of the process was significantly related to trust ($\beta = .46$, $p < .001$). When entering trust in the model testing the relationship between employees' appraisals of line managers' handling of the change process and quantitative job insecurity, the relationship between these appraisals and fears of losing your job became non-significant ($\beta = -.10$, NS) and the relationship between trust and quantitative job insecurity was significant ($\beta = -.36$, $p < .01$). This result suggests full mediation. Sobel's test confirmed mediation was significant ($z = 3.97$, $p = .001$). Also justice mediated the relationship between employees' cognitive appraisals of

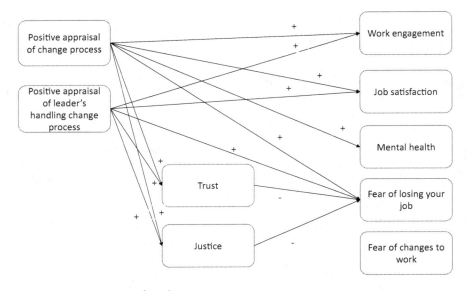

FIGURE 6.1 Summary of results

how well their leaders managed the change process. Appraisals of managers' handling of the process was positively related to justice ($\beta = .42$, $p < .001$). When entering justice into the model, the relationship between the appraisal of leaders and quantitative job insecurity became non-significant ($\beta = -.12$, NS) and the relationship between justice and quantitative job insecurity was significant ($\beta = -.33$, $p < .01$). Sobel's test confirmed mediation was significant ($z = 4.36$, $p = .001$). In Figure 6.1, a summary of the results is presented.

Discussion

Overall, I conclude that organizations need to consider the human factor. Employees are not just passive recipients of organizational change but actively appraise whether the change is good or bad for them and whether the change process itself is considered problematic or positive. These appraisals influence employees' well-being and therefore organizations need to ensure employees appraise the change and the changes processes in a positive light. These findings carry important recommendations for organizations. Change agents need to consider how they can communicate about change. Change agents need to formulate a vision for what can be achieved through change. This may help promote appraisals of an improved position in the organization. Such communication may be a necessary, but not sufficient, requirement. Change agents should identify ways in which employees can be involved in decisions regarding how work should be organized and designed after the change. Third, the change process and the active role of leaders handling change has a positive impact on quantitative job insecurity, which can partially be explained by an increased trust and perceptions of fairness. Trust and fairness are often reduced during times of organizational change (de Jong et al., 2016) and our results indicate that managing the process well may prevent such decline. Fourth, organizations should also consider whether managers, and in particular, line managers, are equipped to manage change effectively. They may need additional training. Finally, ongoing monitoring of the process and employees' appraisals of the change may highlight areas for improving the change process.

References

Antonovsky, A. (1986). Intergenerational networks and transmitting the sense of coherence. In N. Datan, A. Greene, & H. W. Reese (Eds.), *Life-span developmental psychology* (pp. 211–222). Hillsdale, NJ: Lawrence Erlbaum Associates.

Bamberger, S. G., Vinding, A. L., Larsen, A., Nielsen, P., Fonager, K., Nielsen, R. N., & Omland, Ø. (2012). Impact of organisational change on mental health: A systematic review. *Occupational and Environmental Medicine, 69*(8), 592–598.

Cavanaugh, M. A., Boswell, W. R., Roehling, M. V., & Boudreau, J. W. (2000). An empirical examination of self-reported work stress among US managers. *Journal of Applied Psychology, 85*(1), 65.

Cousins, R., Mackay, C. J., Simon, D. C., Kelly, P. J., Kelly, C., & McCaig, R. H. (2004). Management standards and work-related stress in the UK. *Work & Stress, 18*, 113–136.

Daniels, K. (2011). Stress and well-being are still issues and something still needs to be done: Or why agency and interpretation are important for policy and practice. In G. P. Hodgkinson & J. K. Ford (Eds.), *Review of Industrial and Organizational Psychology* (pp. 1–45). Chichester: Wiley.

Danna, K., & Griffin, R. W. (1999). Health and well-being in the workplace: A review and synthesis of the literature. *Journal of Management, 25*(3), 357–384.

de Jong, T., Wiezer, N., de Weerd, M., Nielsen, K., Mattila-Holappa, P., & Mockałło, Z. (2016). The impact of restructuring on employee well-being: A systematic review of longitudinal studies. *Work & Stress, 30*(1), 91–114.

Dewe, P. (1989). Examining the nature of work stress: Individual evaluations of stressful experiences and coping. *Human Relations, 42*(11), 993–1013.

Dewe, P., & Trenberth, L. (2012). Exploring the relationships between appraisals of stressful encounters and the associated emotions in a work setting. *Work & Stress, 26*(2), 161–174.

Hellgren, J., Sverke, M., & Isaksson, K. (1999). A two-dimensional approach to job insecurity: Consequences for employee attitudes and well-being. *European Journal of Work and Organizational Psychology, 8*(2), 179–195.

LA Times (2015). The obvious solution to the Postal Service's problems that no one notices. Retrieved December 14, 2016, from www.latimes.com/business/hiltzik/la-fi-mh-postal-service-s-problems-20151001-column.html

Lazarus, R. S., & Folkman, S. (1984). *Stress, appraisal, and coping.* New York: Springer Publishing Company.

Loi, R., Lam, L. W., & Chan, K. W. (2012). Coping with job insecurity: The role of procedural justice, ethical leadership and power distance orientation. *Journal of Business Ethics, 108*(3), 361–372.

Mackay, C., Cousins, R., Kelly, P., Lee, S., & McCaig, R. H. (2004). "Management Standards" and work-related stress in the UK: Policy background and science. *Work & Stress, 18*, 91–112.

88 Karina Nielsen

McHorney, C. A., & Ware Jr, J. E. (1995). Construction and validation of an alternate form general mental health scale for the Medical Outcomes Study Short-Form 36-Item Health Survey. *Medical Care, 1,* 15–28.

Nielsen, K., Abildgaard, J. S., & Daniels, K. (2014). Putting context into organizational intervention design: Using tailored questionnaires to measure initiatives for worker wellbeing. *Human Relations, 67*(2), 1537–1560.

Nielsen, K., Stage, M., Abildgaard, J. S., & Brauer, C. V. (2013). Participatory intervention from and organizational perspective: Employees as active agents in creating a healthy work environment. In G. Bauer & G. Jenny (Eds.), *Concepts of salutogenic organizations and change: The logics behind organizational health intervention research* (pp. 327–350). Dordrecht, The Netherlands: Springer Publications.

Pahkin, K., Mattila-Holappa, P., Nielsen, K., Widerszal-Bazyl, M., & Wiezer, N. (2014a). A *sound change: Ways to support employees' well-being during organizational restructuring.* Warsaw: Central Institute for Labour Protection – National Research Institute.

Pahkin, K., Nielsen, K., Väänänen, A., Mattila-Holappa, P., Leppänen, A., & Koskinen, A. (2014b). Importance of change appraisal for employee well-being during organizational restructuring: Findings from the Finnish paper industry's extensive transition. *Industrial Health, 52*(5), 445–455.

Pahkin, K., Väänänen, A., Koskinen, A., Bergbom, B., & Kouvonen, A. (2011). Organizational change and employees' mental health: The protective role of sense of coherence. *Journal of Occupational and Environmental Medicine, 53*(2), 118–123.

Persson, R., Hansen, Å. M., Kristiansen, J., Nordander, C., Balogh, I., Ohlsson, K. . . . Ørbæk, P. (2012). Can the job content questionnaire be used to assess structural and organizational properties of the work environment? *International Archives of Occupational and Environmental Health, 85,* 45–55.

PostDanmark. (2010). *Årsrapport 2010. PostDanmark – En del af PostNord* (Annual report. Post Danmark – a part of PostNord). Retrieved November 23, 2016, from www.postnord. com/globalassets/global/danmark/dokument/rapporter/ars-rapporter/postdanmark/ post-danmark-arsrapport-2010.pdf

PostDanmark. (2014). *Årsrapport 2014. PostDanmark – En del af PostNord* (Annual report. Post Danmark – a part of PostNord). Retrieved November 23, 2016, from www.postnord.dk/ da/Documents/Finansiel-info/arsrapport-2014.pdf

Quinlan, M., & Bohle, P. (2009). Overstretched and unreciprocated commitment: Reviewing research on the occupational health and safety effects of downsizing and job insecurity. *International Journal of Health Services, 39*(1), 1–44.

Rick, J., & Briner, R. (2000). Psychosocial risk assessment: Problems and prospects. *Occupational Medicine, 50,* 310–314.

Schaufeli, W. B., Bakker, A. B., & Salanova, M. (2006). The measurement of work engagement with a short questionnaire a cross-national study. *Educational and Psychological Measurement, 66*(4), 701–716.

Sobel, M. E. (1982). Asymptotic confidence intervals for indirect effects in structural equation models. *Sociological Methodology, 13,* 290–312.

Sverke, M., Hellgren, J., & Näswall, K. (2002). No security: A meta-analysis and review of job insecurity and its consequences. *Journal of Occupational Health Psychology, 7*(3), 242–264.

Trafikstyrelsen. (2013). *Redegørelse om postmarkedet 2013* (Review of postal market 2013). Retrieved December 16, 2016, from www.trafikstyrelsen.dk/DA/Erhvervstransport/ Posttilsyn/Statistik/~/media/866C3B7AEB764E86901C53E127504F48.ashx

Väänänen, A., Ahola, K., Koskinen, A., Pahkin, K., & Kouvonen, A. (2011). Organisational merger and psychiatric morbidity: A prospective study in a changing work organisation. *Journal of Epidemiology and Community Health, 65,* 682–687.

Väänänen, A., Pahkin, K., Kalimo, R., & Buunk, B. P. (2004). Maintenance of subjective health during a merger: The role of experienced change and pre-merger social support at work in white-and blue-collar workers. *Social Science & Medicine, 58*(10), 1903–1915.

Wiezer, N., Nielsen, K., Pahkin, K., Widerszal-Bazyl, M., de Jong, T., Mattila-Holappa, P., & Mockałło, Z. (2011). *Exploring the link between restructuring and employee well-being.* Warsaw: Central Institute for Labour Protection – National Research Institute.

7

DYNAMICS OF TRUST AND FAIRNESS DURING ORGANIZATIONAL CHANGE

Implications for job crafting and work engagement

Janne Kaltiainen, Jukka Lipponen and Paraskevas Petrou

Employees' perceptions of their leaders' characteristics and actions can make or break organizational changes (e.g., Fugate, 2012; Rafferty, Jimmieson, & Restubog, 2013). Especially trust in leaders and fairness perceptions have been shown to play a key role for employees' change reactions and subsequent adjustment (for reviews see Taylor, 2015; Van Dam, Oreg, & Schyns, 2008). While trust has been defined in numerous ways in organizational literature (see McEvily & Tortoriello, 2011), we use "trust" as an overarching concept that incorporates evaluations of leaders' characteristics (e.g., integrity, competence, benevolence) and readiness to be vulnerable to the actions of another party (Mayer, Davis, & Schoorman, 1995). By fairness, we refer to employees' perceptions of leaders' actions regarding the fairness of procedures, explanations, treatment and outcome allocations during the change event (Ambrose & Schminke, 2009; Colquitt, 2001).

Building on theoretical frameworks and recent empirical findings, in this chapter we present a research model about how trust and fairness perceptions of organizational leadership can influence employee work engagement (i.e., a work-related state of mind characterized by vigor, dedication and absorption; Schaufeli, Bakker, & Salanova, 2006) during organizational change. We suggest that trust and fairness have the potential to boost employee work engagement via appraisals of the change, and by enhancing proactive employee behaviors targeted at improving one's work environment (i.e., job crafting). We end by proposing a reciprocal feedback loop between change appraisals and work engagement. We present our research model in Figure 7.1.

While trust and fairness perceptions can be relatively stable, organizational change events can trigger changes in these evaluations as uncertain environments make trust and fairness evaluations particularly salient (Dirks & Ferrin, 2002; Lind, 2001). Considering that employees' trust in leaders and fairness perceptions play a vital role in the success of organizational changes, and as studies have shown trust in

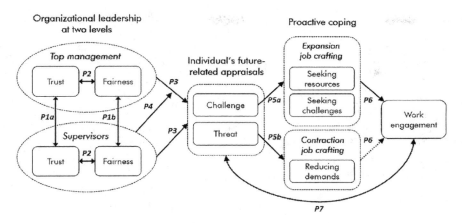

FIGURE 7.1 Proposed research model

Note: P = proposition.

management often decreases during significant organizational changes (e.g., Lines, Selart, Espedal, & Johansen, 2005; Morgan & Zeffane, 2003), it is important to understand how these perceptions develop.

Trickling trust and fairness between top management and supervisors

Organizations' leadership is typically structured at different hierarchical levels, of which we focus on the top management and immediate supervisors. Prior research has shown a trickle-down effect, wherein employees' perceptions of top management (e.g., justice perceptions) influence how employees' perceive their supervisors (e.g., Wo, Ambrose, & Schminke, 2015). Supporting the notion of opposite direction, a study by Fulmer and Ostroff (2017) found that trust can trickle also upwards: trust in direct leaders was positively related to trust in top leaders over time with a two-week time lag between measurement time points. In a similar vein, fairness scholars have shown that fairness perceptions of a particular entity, such as supervisory fairness, can influence overall fairness evaluations of an organization and its processes (Blader & Tyler, 2003; Holtz & Harold, 2009). In general, the results of trust and justice transfers are in line with the convergence model (Sluss & Ashforth, 2008), which suggests that generalization often occurs across nested entities that are structurally tied and resemble each other (e.g., supervisor, top management and organization).

> *Proposition 1a: Employees' evaluations of top management's and supervisor's trust have a positive reciprocal relationship.*
>
> *Proposition 1b: Employees' perceptions of top management's and supervisor's fairness have a positive reciprocal relationship.*

Dynamics between trust and fairness perceptions

In addition to the proposed transfers among different organizational entities, another important aspect for understanding the development of trust and fairness perceptions is the notion that they influence each other. Research literature has found that perceptions of fair procedures, treatment and outcome allocations are essential for building trust (for meta-analytical reviews see Colquitt et al., 2013; Dirks & Ferrin, 2002). These studies have mainly built on social exchange theory (Blau, 1964), which posits that being treated in a favorable way creates an obligation to respond in a positive manner. Thus, trust in leaders is expected to gradually build over time when employees perceive that their leaders have acted in a fair manner towards them.

Conversely, scholars have also argued that employees' trust in leaders may actually reflect an important antecedent of justice perceptions (e.g., Holtz, 2013; Lewicki, Wiethoff, & Tomlinson, 2005). The basic argument for this is two-fold (Holtz, 2013). First, humans' ability to infer others' intentions and characteristics quickly is an important evolved cognitive ability (Todorov, 2011). Thus, trustworthiness evaluations are formed rapidly and are, therefore, inherently present in the very early stages of a relationship. Second, as a result of cognitive processing shortcuts, our prior assessments of exchange partners affect how we perceive their actions. As people have a fundamental tendency to seek information consistent with their current beliefs or theories (i.e., confirmation bias; Wason, 1960), trust-related cognitions towards a leader are expected to color one's perceptions of leader's actions.

The notion that trust-related cognitions can influence subsequent fairness perceptions has received growing empirical support from experimental (Holtz, 2015) and longitudinal survey studies (Colquitt & Rodell, 2011; Holtz & Harold, 2009; Holtz & Hu, 2017). As the only study conducted during an organizational change, Kaltiainen, Lipponen, and Holtz (2017) found that justice perceptions and employee's trust in top management were reciprocally related over three phases of a merger with one-year measurement time lags.

Proposition 2: Employees' perceptions of leaders' (i.e., top management and supervisors) fairness and trust have a positive reciprocal relationship.

From trust and fairness to change appraisals

Trust in management and perceptions of individual supervisors' fair treatment can alleviate employees' feelings of uncertainty (e.g., Dirks & Ferrin, 2002; Lind, 2001) and have a positive effect on future-related change appraisals by mitigating threat and enhancing challenge appraisals (see Fugate, 2013; Mishra & Spreitzer, 1998). By change appraisals, we refer to one's negative (threat) and positive (challenge) expectations and cognitive evaluations regarding one's adjustment to change and change-related benefits or harms for oneself (Fugate, 2013; Lazarus & Folkman, 1984). Thus, appraisals represent the personal meaning and impact of change. Additionally, challenge and threat are not mutually exclusive as events can include potentially harmful and beneficial aspects (Lazarus & Folkman, 1984).[1] In top-down change processes, top management is typically responsible for the original decision, while supervisors implement the change at lower levels. Thus, if these responsible entities are perceived to be fair, competent, benevolent and reliable, there are fewer reasons to expect that the change implementation will fail or that one will be mistreated, thus mitigating employees' negative, and enhancing positive, change appraisals.

The coexistent effects of fairness information originating from top management and supervisor levels are important for two reasons. First, they have been shown to affect employees' change perceptions and reactions (e.g., Rodell & Colquitt, 2009; Tyler & De Cremer, 2005). Second, research has found interactive effects between different sources of fairness information (e.g., Luo, 2007). In addition, Koivisto, Lipponen and Platow (2013) found that organizational fairness decreased employees' feelings of change-related threat particularly when also the supervisor treated employees fairly.

> *Proposition 3: Employees' perceptions of leaders' (i.e., top management and supervisors) fairness and trust are positively related to challenge appraisals, and negatively related to threat appraisals.*
>
> *Proposition 4: Employees' perceptions of supervisors moderates the relationship between perceptions of top management and change appraisals. Specifically, the relationship from top management fairness and trust on change appraisals (i.e., negative relationship to threat; positive relationship to challenge) will be stronger when the supervisor is trusted and perceived to be fair.*

Taken together, in order to manage the impact that organizational change has on employees and their future-related appraisals, it is of paramount importance for leaders at different hierarchical levels to be trustworthy and lead employees fairly. This is especially so because appraisals are expected to act as an antecedent of employees' job crafting.

Crafting the change: the role of appraisals and implications for work engagement

Existing literature increasingly suggests that for organizational change to succeed, it is crucial that employees take initiative and become active change agents (Ghitulescu, 2013). Therefore, especially during organizational changes, proactive behaviors are important as they provide the necessary tools for handling novel situations, facilitate new work-roles to emerge and thus, enhance adjustment (Griffin, Neal, & Parker, 2007).

One such proactive behavior is job crafting, which refers to actions employees take in order to adjust and improve their job characteristics (Wrzesniewski & Dutton, 2001). In the context of organizational change (Petrou, Demerouti, Peeters, Schaufeli, & Hetland, 2012), job crafting has generally been proposed to take three forms: seeking resources (e.g., asking others for advice or feedback), seeking challenges (e.g., taking up additional and motivating tasks) or reducing demands (e.g., eliminating one's emotional or cognitive job demands). More recent literature suggests that two distinct types of motivation tend to drive job crafting behaviors (Bruning & Campion, 2017) in such a way that job crafting can either "expand" or "contract" one's job (Wang, Demerouti, & Le Blanc, 2017, p. 187). On one hand, behaviors that expand the job (e.g., seeking resources and challenges) help employees increase their job scope and, thus, learn and grow. On the other hand, behaviors that contract the job (e.g., reducing demands) help employees cope with stressors and protect themselves.

Drawing from coping and appraisal literature (Fugate, 2013; Lazarus & Folkman, 1984), we posit that challenge and threat appraisals have differential effects on facets of job crafting. To elaborate, challenge appraisal is associated with positive expectations towards the change and more productive coping efforts, such as promotive behaviors. Therefore, we propose that challenge is positively related to expansion job crafting (i.e., seeking resources and challenges). As threat appraisal is, on the other hand, associated with negative expectations for one's adjustment and personal change-related outcomes and disadvantageous coping behaviors, such as avoidance and self-protection, we posit that threat increases contraction job crafting (i.e., reducing job demands).[2] Naturally, organizational change often increases job demands for many employees (Tvedt, Saksvik, & Nytrø, 2009). When such an increase in demands is an integral part of the change, most employees will fail to reduce these job demands. In such cases, employees could, however, choose to reduce other job demands (e.g., the ones that exist prior to change), in order to cope with or simply survive the new job demands.

Job crafting research has supported our propositions. While organizational changes with excessive impact (and, therefore, potential threat) lead employees to limit their job scope (Kira, Balkin, & San, 2012), a positive motivational orientation of employees toward the changes leads employees to increase their job scope (Herscovitch & Meyer, 2002). Similarly, a longitudinal survey study with a time lag of one year by Petrou, Demerouti and Schaufeli (2015) found that while excessive change led employees to reduce their job demands, positive employee orientation toward the changes increased seeking challenges and resources.

Proposition 5a: Challenge appraisals are positively related to seeking resources and challenges.

Proposition 5b: Threat appraisals are positively related to reducing demands.

Given that employees craft their jobs in the face of organizational change, what are the implications for their work engagement? Among the existing studies that aim to answer this question, general consensus seems to exist around the fact that job crafting plays a dual role in that respect: On the one hand, seeking resources and seeking challenges have been found to relate to increased work engagement, possibly because they increase employees' job scope and motivation. On the other hand, reducing demands has non-substantial or even negative links with work engagement, because it is a form of employee withdrawal that reduces one's job scope (Petrou et al., 2012; Petrou, Demerouti, & Schaufeli, 2016; Petrou, Demerouti, & Xanthopoulou, 2017).

> *Proposition 6: Seeking resources and challenges is positively related to work engagement. This relationship is stronger than the relationship between reducing demands and work engagement.*

Feedback loop between appraisals and work engagement

In addition to proposing that the relationship from change appraisals to work engagement is mediated by job crafting, we also expect direct and reciprocal effects between appraisals and work engagement. First, according to transactional stress theory (Lazarus & Folkman, 1984), appraisals play a central role in shaping employee affective states and behavioral reactions. Thus, as work engagement refers to an affective-motivational state (Schaufeli et al., 2006), we posit a direct effect from appraisals to work engagement. Second, our proposition of the feedback loop, i.e., work engagement having beneficial effects on change appraisals, draws from the literature on positive effects of psychological resources (i.e., positive self-belief, affect or motivation; Fredrickson, 2001; Hobfoll, 2002). The more psychological resources one has, the more one is expected to perceive the change event as a positive challenge, and less as a negative threat (Fugate, 2013; Lazarus & Folkman, 1984). This is because an event is perceived as a threat when the situational demands exceed the resources one has, while the perception of sufficient resources results in appraising the change as a challenge. Accordingly, scholars have proposed that being immersed in one's work and experiencing it as fulfilling (i.e., being work engaged) increases positive expectations and adjustment to stressful situations (Hobfoll, 2011; Van den Heuvel, Demerouti, Schaufeli, & Bakker, 2010).

While there are no published studies to date that have examined the relationship between work engagement and individual's future-related appraisals of a change event, there is preliminary evidence in favor of our proposition. Specifically, prior studies have found that individual's positive psychological (pre)dispositions, such as hope and optimism, are positively related to work engagement (for reviews see Bailey, Madden, Alfes, & Fletcher, 2017; Halbesleben, 2010). Furthermore, the proposed feedback cycle received support in a recent longitudinal study as Kaltiainen, Lipponen, Vakola and Fugate (2017) found reciprocal relations over time between work engagement and change appraisals (i.e., threat and challenge) in the context of an organizational merger.

> *Proposition 7: Challenge appraisals have a positive and threat appraisals have a negative reciprocal relationship with work engagement.*

Implications for future research

While our research model (see Figure 7.1) draws from prior empirical research findings, several of its aspects warrant for further studies. Next, we highlight several possible avenues for future research.

Implication 1: As uncertain circumstances are expected to amplify changes in employees' trust and justice perceptions (e.g., Dirks & Ferrin, 2002; Lind, 2001), organizational changes present an intriguing context for examining trust and justice perception transfers between hierarchical levels of leadership. However, we are not aware of studies examining this proposition during organizational change events.

Implication 2: Significant organizational changes are often associated with early-stage employee-leader relationships (e.g., new employees joining the organization or changes in top management as a result of a merger or acquisition, or changes in supervisors due to team restructuring). Thus, change events provide a noteworthy opportunity to examine how early-stage trust evaluations develop over time and how they influence fairness perceptions (see also Holtz, 2013).

Implication 3: While studies have shown that trust in leaders and fairness perceptions are associated with employees' change appraisals (see Fugate, 2013), we are not aware of studies testing the possible differences that employees' perceptions of different levels of leadership have on change appraisals. This could provide important information for organizations looking for the most efficient ways to direct their leadership-related resources in order to enhance employees' adjustment and well-being during organizational changes.

Implication 4: We have not been able to identify studies examining our proposition of change appraisals mediating the relationships from employees' leader-related justice and trust perceptions to job crafting. Thus, we see that studies testing this proposition would further our understanding regarding conditions for employees' proactive coping and successful adjustment.

Implication 5: Although we have proposed that reducing demands may even harm engagement during organizational changes, this is based on limited evidence and future research could test alternative propositions. For example, one possibility is that this effect could be non-linear (e.g., an average amount of reducing demands is perhaps beneficial). Another possibility is that this effect is dependent on the situation (e.g., perhaps the beneficial effects occur only for specific types of organizational change) or on the employee (e.g., motivational style or personality).

Furthermore, we call for further longitudinal studies to shed light on the role of time (Pitariu & Ployhart, 2010) within organizational change literature. Such studies could provide further information on the duration of effects, and whether the strength of effects or change trajectories vary across different phases of organizational change processes (cf. Fortin, Cojuharenco, Patient, & German, 2016).

Similarly, we propose that future organizational change studies should not limit their scope to unidirectional models (i.e., from antecedents to outcomes via specific processes). Recent literature has argued that reciprocal models (i.e., feedback loops) are necessary in order to capture the dynamism of employees' trust and justice perceptions (Holtz, 2013), changes in fairness perceptions (Jones & Skarlicki, 2013) and the relationships among stressors, responses and adjustment as they develop during stressful events (e.g., Bliese, Edwards, & Sonnentag, 2017). Furthermore, longitudinal reciprocal models enable researchers to further our understanding about the direction of cause-and-effect relations by testing competing theoretical propositions. As stated by the creators of one cornerstone of the stress literature: "In contrast to the unidirectional, static, antecedent-consequent model, the transactional model views the person and the environment in a dynamic, mutually reciprocal, bidirectional relations. What is a consequence at Time 1 can become an antecedent at Time 2" (Lazarus & Folkman, 1984, p. 293).

Implications for practice

Organizations that undergo change should follow a holistic approach and recognize that both trust and fairness could be and should be built at different levels of the organization, namely, both at the supervisor and top management level. To enhance trust and fairness perceptions, it is important that leaders and managers are perceived to share common values with the employees, demonstrate consistency in their actions and decisions over time and across people, aim for the common good, be competent and effective, provide opportunities for employees to express their opinions, treat others with respect and be ready to trust others. Trust and fairness are important because they enhance each other and help employees appraise change as a challenge and less as a threat. Leaders can foster positive change appraisals also by providing support (e.g., showing care and commitment for employees' well-being and being available for help and assistance; see Fugate, 2013; Oreg, Vakola, & Armenakis, 2011). Challenge appraisals will empower employees to engage in expansive forms of job crafting that will help them learn and grow, even in the face of organizational changes.

Although job crafting is primarily an individual strategy, we do not posit that it is entirely the responsibility of employees to engage in it and to solve organizational deficiencies. While organizations cannot impose job crafting on employees, they can provide job crafting opportunities. This can be done either via job design (i.e., creating autonomous jobs and providing freedom to employees to craft their jobs if they wish) or via voluntary job crafting training that has been shown to benefit employees during organizational change (Van den Heuvel, Demerouti, & Peeters, 2015).

Notes

1 In our research model we focus on future-related appraisals, and thus, exclude harm appraisal as it refers to occurred harms or benefits (e.g., Fugate, 2013).
2 However, this relationship most likely is not linear, as hopelessness (i.e., high threat appraisal) can also diminish proactive coping efforts (Lazarus & Folkman, 1984).

98 Janne Kaltiainen et al.

References

Ambrose, M. L., & Schminke, M. (2009). The role of overall justice judgments in organizational justice research: A test of mediation. *Journal of Applied Psychology, 94*(2), 491–500. doi:10.1037/a0013203

Bailey, C., Madden, A., Alfes, K., & Fletcher, L. (2017). The meaning, antecedents and outcomes of employee engagement: A narrative synthesis. *International Journal of Management Reviews, 19*(1), 31–53. doi:10.1111/ijmr.12077

Blader, S. L., & Tyler, T. R. (2003). A four-component model of procedural justice: Defining the meaning of a "Fair" process. *Personality and Social Psychology Bulletin, 29*(6), 747–758. doi:10.1177/0146167203029006007

Blau, P. (1964). *Exchange and power in social life*. New York: Wiley.

Bliese, P. D., Edwards, J. R., & Sonnentag, S. (2017). Stress and well-being at work: A century of empirical trends reflecting theoretical and societal influences. *Journal of Applied Psychology, 102*(3), 389–402. doi:10.1037/apl0000109

Bruning, P. F., & Campion, M. A. (2017). A role-resource approach-avoidance model of job crafting: A multi-method integration and extension of job crafting theory. *Academy of Management Journal*. Advance online publication. doi:10.5465/amj.2015.0604

Colquitt, J. A. (2001). On the dimensionality of organizational justice: A construct validation of a measure. *Journal of Applied Psychology, 86*(3), 386–400. doi:10.1037/0021-9010.86.3.386

Colquitt, J. A., & Rodell, J. B. (2011). Justice, trust, and trustworthiness: A longitudinal analysis integrating three theoretical perspectives. *Academy of Management Journal, 54*(6), 1183–1206. doi:10.5465/amj.2007.0572

Colquitt, J. A., Scott, B. A., Rodell, J. B., Long, D. M., Zapata, C. P., Conlon, D. E., & Wesson, M. J. (2013). Justice at the millennium, a decade later: A meta-analytic test of social exchange and affect-based perspectives. *Journal of Applied Psychology, 98*(2), 199–236. doi:10.1037/a0031757

Dirks, K. T., & Ferrin, D. L. (2002). Trust in leadership: Meta-analytic findings and implications for research and practice. *Journal of Applied Psychology, 87*(4), 611–628. doi:10.1037/0021-9010.87.4.611

Fortin, M., Cojuharenco, I., Patient, D., & German, H. (2016). It is time for justice: How time changes what we know about justice judgments and justice effects. *Journal of Organizational Behavior, 37*(1), 30–56. doi:10.1002/job.1958

Fredrickson, B. L. (2001). The role of positive emotions in positive psychology: The broaden-and-build theory of positive emotions. *American Psychologist, 56*(3), 218–226. doi:10.1037/0003-066X.56.3.218

Fugate, M. (2012). The impact of leadership, management, and HRM on employee reactions to organizational change. In J. J. Martocchio, A. Joshi, & H. Liao (Eds.), *Research in personnel and human resources management* (Vol. 31, pp. 177–208). Bingley, UK: Emerald Group Publishing.

Fugate, M. (2013). Capturing the positive experience of change: Antecedents, processes, and consequences. In R. By, A. Michel, & S. Oreg (Eds.), *The psychology of organizational change* (pp. 15–39). Cambridge: Cambridge University Press.

Fulmer, C. A., & Ostroff, C. (2017). Trust in direct leaders and top leaders: A trickle-up model. *Journal of Applied Psychology, 102*(4), 648–657. doi:10.1037/apl0000189

Ghitulescu, B. E. (2013). Making change happen: The impact of work context on adaptive and proactive behaviors. *The Journal of Applied Behavioral Science, 49*(2), 206–245. doi:10.1177/0021886312469254

Griffin, M. A., Neal, A., & Parker, S. K. (2007). A new model of work role performance: Positive behavior in uncertain and interdependent contexts. *Academy of Management Journal, 50*(2), 327–347. doi:10.5465/amj.2007.24634438

Halbesleben, J. R. B. (2010). A meta-analysis of work engagement: Relationships with burn-out, demands, resources, and consequences. In A. B. Bakker & M. Leiter (Eds.), *Work engagement: A handbook of essential theory and research* (pp. 102–117). Hove: Psychology Press.

Herscovitch, L., & Meyer, J. P. (2002). Commitment to organizational change: Extension of a three-component model. *Journal of Applied Psychology, 87*(3), 474–487. doi:10.1037/0021-9010.87.3.474

Hobfoll, S. E. (2002). Social and psychological resources and adaptation. *Review of General Psychology, 6*(4), 307–324. doi:10.1037/1089-2680.6.4.307

Hobfoll, S. E. (2011). Conservation of resources theory: Its implication for stress, health, and resilience. In S. Folkman (Ed.), *The Oxford handbook of stress, health, and coping* (pp. 127–147). Oxford: Oxford University Press.

Holtz, B. C. (2013). Trust primacy: A model of the reciprocal relations between trust and perceived justice. *Journal of Management, 39*(7), 1891–1923. doi:10.1177/0149206312471392

Holtz, B. C. (2015). From first impression to fairness perception: Investigating the impact of initial trustworthiness beliefs. *Personnel Psychology, 68*(3), 499–546. doi:10.1111/peps.12092

Holtz, B. C., & Harold, C. M. (2009). Fair today, fair tomorrow? A longitudinal investigation of overall justice perceptions. *Journal of Applied Psychology, 94*(5), 1185–1199. doi:10.1037/A0015900

Holtz, B. C., & Hu, B. (2017). Passive leadership: Relationships with trust and justice perceptions. *Journal of Managerial Psychology, 32*(1), 119–130. doi:10.1108/JMP-02-2016-0029

Jones, D. A., & Skarlicki, D. P. (2013). How perceptions of fairness can change: A dynamic model of organizational justice. *Organizational Psychology Review, 3*(2), 138–160. doi:10.1177/2041386612461665

Kaltiainen, J., Lipponen, J., & Holtz, B. C. (2017). Dynamic interplay between merger process justice and cognitive trust in top management: A longitudinal study. *Journal of Applied Psychology, 102*(4), 636–647. doi:10.1037/apl0000180

Kaltiainen, J., Lipponen, J., Vakola, M., & Fugate, M. (2017, May). *Am I going to make it? Dynamic relations between changes in work engagement and change appraisals throughout organizational mergers.* Paper presented at the Congress of the European Association of Work and Organizational Psychology, Dublin, Ireland.

Kira, M., Balkin, D. B., & San, E. (2012). Authentic work and organizational change: Longitudinal evidence from a merger. *Journal of Change Management, 12*(1), 31–51. doi:10.108 0/14697017.2011.652374

Koivisto, S., Lipponen, J., & Platow, M. J. (2013). Organizational and supervisory justice effects on experienced threat during change: The moderating role of leader in-group representativeness. *Leadership Quarterly, 24*(4), 595–607.

Lazarus, R. S., & Folkman, S. (1984). *Stress, appraisal, and coping.* New York: Springer.

Lewicki, R. J., Wiethoff, C., & Tomlinson, E. (2005). What is the role of trust in organizational justice? In J. Greenberg & J. A. Colquitt (Eds.), *Handbook of organizational justice* (pp. 247–272). Mahwah, NJ: Lawrence Erlbaum Associates.

Lind, E. A. (2001). Fairness heuristics theory: Justice judgments as pivotal cognitions in organizational relations. In J. Greenberg & R. Cropanzano (Eds.), *Advances in organizational justice* (pp. 56–88). Stanford, CA: Stanford University Press.

Lines, R., Selart, M., Espedal, B., & Johansen, S. T. (2005). The production of trust during organizational change. *Journal of Change Management, 5*(2), 221–245. doi:10.1080/14697010500143555

Luo, Y. (2007). The independent and interactive roles of procedural, distributive, and interactional justice in strategic alliances. *Academy of Management Journal, 50*(3), 644–664. doi:10.5465/amj.2007.25526452

Mayer, R. C., Davis, J. H., & Schoorman, F. D. (1995). An integrative model of organizational trust. *Academy of Management Review, 20*(3), 709–734. doi:10.5465/amr.1995.9508080335

McEvily, B., & Tortoriello, M. (2011). Measuring trust in organisational research: Review and recommendations. *Journal of Trust Research, 1*(1), 23–63. doi:10.1080/21515581.2011.552424

Mishra, A. K., & Spreitzer, G. M. (1998). Explaining how survivors respond to downsizing: The roles of trust, empowerment, justice, and work redesign. *Academy of Management Review, 23*(3), 567–588. doi:10.5465/amr.1998.926627

Morgan, D., & Zeffane, R. (2003). Employee involvement, organizational change and trust in management. *The International Journal of Human Resource Management, 14*(1), 55–75. doi:10.1080/09585190210158510

Oreg, S., Vakola, M., & Armenakis, A. (2011). Change recipients' reactions to organizational change: A 60-year review of quantitative studies. *Journal of Applied Behavioral Science, 47*(4), 461–524. doi:10.1177/0021886310396550

Petrou, P., Demerouti, E., Peeters, M. C. W., Schaufeli, W. B., & Hetland, J. (2012). Crafting a job on a daily basis: Contextual correlates and the link to work engagement. *Journal of Organizational Behavior, 33*(8), 1120–1141. doi:10.1002/job.1783

Petrou, P., Demerouti, E., & Schaufeli, W. B. (2015). Job crafting in changing organizations: Antecedents and implications for exhaustion and performance. *Journal of Occupational Health Psychology, 20*(4), 470–480. doi:10.1037/a0039003

Petrou, P., Demerouti, E., & Schaufeli, W. B. (2016). Crafting the change: The role of employee job crafting behaviors for successful organizational change. *Journal of Management*. Advance online publication. doi:10.1177/0149206315624961

Petrou, P., Demerouti, E., & Xanthopoulou, D. (2017). Regular versus cutback-related change: The role of employee job crafting in organizational change contexts of different nature. *International Journal of Stress Management, 24*(1), 62–85. doi:10.1037/str0000033

Pitariu, A. H., & Ployhart, R. E. (2010). Explaining change: Theorizing and testing dynamic mediated longitudinal relationships. *Journal of Management, 36*(2), 405–429. doi:10.1177/0149206308331096

Rafferty, A. E., Jimmieson, N. L., & Restubog, S. L. D. (2013). When leadership meets organizational change: The influence of the top management team and supervisory leaders on change appraisals, change attitudes, and adjustment to change. In S. Oreg, A. Michel, & R. T. By (Eds.), *The psychology of organizational change* (pp. 143–194). New York: Cambridge University Press.

Rodell, J. B., & Colquitt, J. A. (2009). Looking ahead in times of uncertainty: The role of anticipatory justice in an organizational change context. *Journal of Applied Psychology, 94*(4), 989–1002. doi:10.1037/a0015351

Schaufeli, W. B., Bakker, A. B., & Salanova, M. (2006). The measurement of work engagement with a short questionnaire: A cross-national study. *Educational and Psychological Measurement, 66*(4), 701–716. doi:10.1177/0013164405282471

Sluss, D. M., & Ashforth, B. E. (2008). How relational and organizational identification converge: Processes and conditions. *Organization Science, 19*(6), 807–823. doi:10.1287/orsc.1070.0349

Taylor, S. (2015). The roles of justice in the midst of organizational change. In R. Cropanzano & M. L. Ambrose (Eds.), *The Oxford handbook of justice in the workplace* (pp. 577–604). Oxford: Oxford University Press.

Todorov, A. (2011). Evaluating faces on social dimensions. In A. Todorov, S. T. Fiske, & D. Prentice (Eds.), *Social neuroscience: Toward understanding the underpinnings of the social mind* (pp. 54–76). New York: Oxford University Press.

Tvedt, S. D., Saksvik, P. Ø., & Nytrø, K. (2009). Does change process healthiness reduce the negative effects of organizational change on the psychosocial work environment? *Work & Stress, 23*(1), 80–98. doi:10.1080/02678370902857113

Tyler, T. R., & De Cremer, D. (2005). Process-based leadership: Fair procedures and reactions to organizational change. *The Leadership Quarterly, 16*(4), 529–545. doi:10.1016/j.leaqua.2005.06.001

Van Dam, K., Oreg, S., & Schyns, B. (2008). Daily work contexts and resistance to organisational change: The role of leader–member exchange, development climate, and change process characteristics. *Applied Psychology, 57*(2), 313–334. doi:10.1111/j.1464-0597.2007.00311.x

Van den Heuvel, M., Demerouti, E., & Peeters, M. C. W. (2015). The job crafting intervention: Effects on job resources, self-efficacy, and affective well-being. *Journal of Occupational and Organizational Psychology, 88*(3), 511–532. doi:10.1111/joop.12128

Van den Heuvel, M., Demerouti, E., Schaufeli, W. B., & Bakker, A. B. (2010). Personal resources and work engagement in the face of change. In J. Houdmont & S. Leka (Eds.), *Contemporary occupational health psychology: Global perspectives on research and practice* (Vol. 1, pp. 124–150). Chichester: John Wiley & Sons.

Wang, H.-J., Demerouti, E., & Le Blanc, P. (2017). Transformational leadership, adaptability, and job crafting: The moderating role of organizational identification. *Journal of Vocational Behavior, 100*, 185–195. doi:10.1016/j.jvb.2017.03.009

Wason, P. C. (1960). On the failure to eliminate hypotheses in a conceptual task. *Quarterly Journal of Experimental Psychology, 12*(3), 129–140. doi:10.1080/17470216008416717

Wo, D. X. H., Ambrose, M. L., & Schminke, M. (2015). What drives trickle-down effects? A test of multiple mediation processes. *Academy of Management Journal, 58*(6), 1848–1868. doi:10.5465/amj.2013.0670

Wrzesniewski, A., & Dutton, J. E. (2001). Crafting a job: Revisioning employees as active crafters of their work. *Academy of Management Review, 26*(2), 179–201. doi:10.5465/amr.2001.4378011

8

ORGANIZATIONAL CHANGE

Implications for the psychological contract[1]

Maria Tomprou and Samantha D. Hansen

Organizational change is a critical event in employees' organizational life, often creating *disruptions* in their psychological contract (Morrison & Robinson, 1997; Schalk & Freese, 1997). The psychological contract is a cognitive schema, or mental model, that comprises employee perceptions of their and their organization's obligations to one another (Rousseau, 1995). For instance, an employee may believe that, in exchange for contributing hard work and loyalty, the organization is obligated to provide advancement opportunities and pay increases. This schema affects what employees attend to, how they interpret organizational experiences and how they behave (Rousseau, 2001a). Disruptions to the psychological contract, like those associated with organizational change, can compromise these processes, impacting employee perceptions, attitudes and behaviors toward the organization. Indeed, the study of organizational change has seen significant development in recent years, encouraging greater attention to the importance of relationship management rather than a narrow focus on the perceived legitimacy of the change, typical in past work (e.g., Huy, Corley, & Kraatz, 2014; Stensaker & Langley, 2010). In this chapter, we draw on recent theoretical advances in the study of psychological contracts (i.e., the dynamic phase model of psychological contract processes and the post-violation model; Rousseau, Hansen, & Tomprou, 2018; Tomprou, Rousseau, & Hansen, 2015) to explore perceptions of psychological contract disruption in the context of organizational change and the circumstances under which these disruptions lead to positive and negative outcomes for employees and the change effort. We discuss the roles of employees and organizations in promoting successful change efforts. Ultimately, such efforts will impact the viability of functional psychological contracts during and following change efforts.

The impact of organizational change on psychological contracts

Psychological contract obligations may become particularly challenging to manage during change interventions. Whether narrow (e.g., job redesign) or broad (e.g., culture change), change is likely to interfere with the organization's ability to fulfill its obligations to employees (e.g., Freese, Schalk, & Croon, 2011; Turnley & Feldman, 1998) and with the stability of the composition of the psychological contract (e.g., Chaudhry, Coyle-Shapiro, & Wayne, 2011). Indeed, employee perceptions of obligations may shrink or expand depending on the changes implemented. Even minor organizational changes will necessitate change to the psychological contract to reflect the new arrangement. Successful change of the psychological contract is critical to the lasting health of the employee-employer relationship (Rousseau et al., 2018).

Organizational changes can have positive or negative consequences for employees and their psychological contracts. For instance, Schalk and Roe (2007) reported that during change, many employees experience positive events (e.g., bonuses and promotions). Further, qualitative studies (Bellou, 2007; van de Heuvel, Schalk, Freese, & Timmerman, 2016) found that employees experience positive emotions and enlargement of their psychological contract (e.g., increased job opportunities and autonomy) during organizational change. However, in many change scenarios, the employer is no longer able to meet particular obligations (Dulac, Coyle-Shapiro, Henderson, & Wayne, 2008). Budget cuts may mean that flexible scheduling or bonuses can no longer be guaranteed. Further, oversights during the change process can result in failure to adequately manage employees' psychological contracts, causing inadvertent psychological contract breach, or a perceived discrepancy between organizational obligations and actual delivered inducements (Robinson & Morrison, 2000). Indeed, resistance to change may be an indicator of perceived breach (Ford, Ford, & D'Amelio, 2008). Perceptions of breach are associated with negative employee affect (e.g., feelings of violation), attitudes and behavior (Zhao, Wayne, Glibkowski, & Bravo, 2007), all of which damage effective organizational functioning and can interfere with the success of the change intervention (Lo & Aryee, 2003).

Several studies have reported a positive relationship between organizational change and psychological contract breach (e.g., Conway, Kiefer, Hartley, & Briner, 2014; Lo & Aryee, 2003). Others, such as Freese et al. (2011), found that change was associated with decreased perceived fulfillment of organizational policies and reward obligations and increased feelings of violation. And still others reported no significant relationship between organizational change and breach (e.g., Robinson & Morrison, 2000; Tomprou, Nikolaou, & Vakola, 2012). Such conflicting findings suggest that organizational changes may have either positive or negative consequences for employee goals and that there is some variability in terms of how easily the psychological contract "recovers" from organizational change efforts. In some cases, organizational change may be easily incorporated into the psychological contract; in other cases, the change may cause a disruption that requires significant time and effort for revision. In the following section, we describe recent theoretical work that is relevant to enhancing understanding of psychological contract processes during organizational change.

Psychological contract change during organizational change

Building on foundational psychological contract theory (Rousseau, 1989, 1995) and research, Rousseau, Hansen and Tomprou (2017) present a dynamic phase model of psychological contract processes that explains how employees' psychological contracts are created, maintained and changed over the course of the employment relationship. Employees cycle through Creation, Maintenance, Repair and Renegotiation as a function of changing circumstances and personal goals. During Creation employees develop their psychological contract schema as a function of pre-existing expectations and organizational information (e.g., employer promises, Rousseau, 2001a; De Vos, Buyens, & Schalk, 2003). When stable, employees then transition into the Maintenance phase, the status quo of the relationship, wherein they make contributions to, and receive inducements from, the organization in ways consistent with the psychological contract, all while subconsciously monitoring this exchange. Minor discrepancies between obligations and inducements/contributions that do not interfere with personal goal attainment or elicit strong affect can trigger small effortless changes to the psychological contract through the process of *assimilation* (e.g., employees are asked to use a new tagline on their sign-lines, reflecting the changing organizational culture). In contrast, major discrepancies (e.g., demotion/promotion) between perceived obligations and inducements *disrupt* the relationship and create strong affect, triggering a shift out of Maintenance and into either Repair (in the case of negative affect) or Renegotiation (in the case of positive affect). In either case, the employee works to create a new or revised psychological contract which will enable a transition back into Maintenance. Such disruptions are likely during organizational change efforts.

Changes to the psychological contract may reflect increases or decreases in perceived employee and employer obligations. In some change scenarios, employees may need to adopt new responsibilities, thus requiring expansion of their psychological contract obligations to the organization. In other cases, employees' obligations to the organization may decrease (e.g., dropping down to part-time). How employees react to such circumstances will depend on whether the change facilitates or hinders personal goals. For example, Huy et al. (2014) found that managers who initially supported a change initiative, later opposed it when it became clear that the organization failed to follow through on its promises. In other scenarios employees must revise their perceptions of organizational obligations downward to reflect the new reality. This change may be accompanied by the belief that employees owe less to the organization in return (e.g., resulting in reduced performance and citizenship behavior; Dulac, Coyle-Shapiro, Henderson, & Wayne, 2008; Robinson & Morrison, 2000) which may interfere with the success of the change intervention and create lasting effects on the relationship (Lo & Aryee, 2003). Thus, careful management of the psychological contract during change is paramount, as sustaining positive relationships can facilitate successful organizational change and smooth transition back into Maintenance (Huy et al., 2014; Rousseau et al., 2017; Stensaker & Langley, 2010). In the following sections, we explore various factors relevant to promoting and maintaining functional psychological contracts during times of change.

Promoting functional psychological contracts during organizational change

Consistent with reports of positive emotions among employees during organizational change (e.g., Schalk & Roe, 2007), at times change initiatives may benefit employees, causing a positive disruption to the psychological contract. For example, organizational change resulting in greater work-life balance or career opportunities would be viewed as desirable by employees who strive to reach such goals (Rousseau et al., 2017). Indeed, van de Heuvel et al. (2016) found that attitudes toward change were related positively to psychological contract fulfillment and to a broadening of obligations when change agents communicated "what's in it" for employees.

Following from the dynamic phase model of psychological contract processes (Rousseau et al., 2017) there are two main reasons why organizational change efforts might serve as a positive disruption to the employee-employer relationship. First, as noted, the organizational change initiative may satisfy personal goals and lead to obligation fulfillment through the delivery of valued inducements. For example, discussions with a new manager may result in training opportunities that the previous boss did not support, but that the employee desires. Second, change initiatives may provide an opportunity for employees to request customized work arrangements, especially for high performers and veterans (Rosen, Slater, Chang, & Johnson, 2013), to secure resources for personal goals (Hornung, Rousseau, & Glaser, 2008). As such, when possible, organizations can support their change efforts by being cognizant of important employee goals (e.g., allow employees to participate in designing changes that will impact them) and by supporting employees to attain those goals in the new work arrangement. Organizational change agents play a critical role in this process. Studies of change agents such as front-line managers have demonstrated that these individuals engage in active efforts to manage renegotiations and repairs with subordinates during planned change, and also negotiate politically with upper management to push these agreements forward (e.g., Stensaker & Langley, 2010).

Avoiding and addressing disruptions during organizational change

Disruptions to psychological contracts are common during organizational change (Lo & Aryee, 2003; Turnley & Feldman, 1998). Although some disruptions may be seen as positive, allowing for quick revision of the psychological contract and return to Maintenance, oftentimes changes cause negative disruptions. According to the dynamic phase model of psychological contract processes (Rousseau et al., 2018), negative disruptions are more likely to occur when change initiatives interfere severely with employee goals (e.g., the organization fails to meet an obligation that the employee believes has already been "paid for" through his or her contributions). As noted, when change creates a negative disruption, employees engage in a downward revision of their perceived obligations, resulting in reduced contributions (e.g., civic virtue withdrawal; Lo & Aryee, 2003). As such, it is imperative that organizations undertaking change engage in efforts designed to avoid negative disruptions and generate plans for how they will address and resolve negative disruptions when they are inevitable. Further, it is important to recognize that both parties can play a role in overcoming negative disruptions.

Employer efforts

What can organizations do during Maintenance to minimize the likelihood that employees will view organizational change as a negative disruption? Change agents can focus equally on managing employee relationships and change implementation. The former strategy is often overlooked; agents tend to be more preoccupied with how they will accomplish the change than with recipients' concerns about the consequences of the change (Gioia, Thomas, Clark, & Chittipeddi, 1994). As such, open two-way communication, wherein the employer considers employee goals, will help to reduce the potential for negative disruption. Further, agents who offer justifications that establish the appropriateness and rationale of change efforts are effective in creating readiness for change and increasing the likelihood and speed of acceptance (Armenakis, Harris, & Mossholder, 1993; Rousseau & Tijoriwala, 1999).

Despite employer efforts to avoid negative disruption, it is often unavoidable and employees transition into Renegotiation or Repair and attempt to modify their psychological contract. Theory and research offer potential guidance to promote psychological contract restoration in such cases. An important element is trust in the employer. Robinson (1996) found that trust mediated the relationship between breach and employee contributions. Similarly, disentangling different psychological contract types (i.e., relational and transactional), Montes and Irving (2008) found that trust mediated the effects of relational psychological contracts on feelings of violation. Although full restoration of organizational trust is unlikely, the trust repair literature offers guidance to help offset the negative outcomes of disruption (Tomlinson, Dineen, & Lewicki, 2004). During an organizational change, Rousseau and

Tijoriwala (1999) showed that social accounts such as explanations and justifications about the change resulted in increased perceived legitimacy of the change and contributed to reduced psychological contract breach. Further, trust can be restored if the transgressor offers a sincere and timely apology, admitting personal culpability (Tomlinson et al., 2004). However, in a study of post-violation experiences, little support was found that apology is seen as a form of employer reparation (Tomprou, Rousseau, & Griep, 2018). Instead, reparative acts such as offering alternatives and credible justifications contributed to violation resolution. Bottom, Gibson, Daniels and Murnighan (2002) also reported that offers of penance are more effective than verbal apologies alone. Ultimately, change agents need to pay greater attention to employees and promote bilateral conversations (e.g., use of surveys to improve implementation) rather than focusing solely on the success of the change. However, it is crucial that employees also play a role. Research has shown that employees reported greater resolution to a violation when *they* personally initiated resolution efforts (Tomprou et al., 2018).

Employee efforts

One important way employees can contribute to managing disruptions during organizational change is through their efforts to activate certain social networks (i.e., structures of social ties in the workplace). Social networks are an important source of information during organizational change (Battilana & Casciaro, 2013; Krackhardt & Hanson, 1993) and can be used to influence change adoption, especially among employees who are neutral about the change and when the change diverges minimally from regular practices (Battilana & Casciaro, 2013). As such, social networks are likely highly relevant during Maintenance. Social networks influence employees' psychological contract by their association with specific goals (Ho, 2005). Networks offer two primary functions, the exchange of information and the exercise of social influence (Krackhardt & Hanson, 1993) which can assist with personal goal achievement. People cognitively activate their social networks depending on their goals (e.g., job search, reduce the threat of job loss; Shea, Menon, Smith, & Emich, 2015) and the situation.

Organizational change is a situational trigger that may prompt people to activate different aspects of their networks. We argue that, in Maintenance, employees who easily adapt to the change and revise their psychological contract so it is congruent with the new reality are more likely to activate and mobilize stronger ties with change agents and contacts who favor the initiative. By doing so, employees may gain in-depth information about change initiatives and actively be involved and influence decisions. In contrast, employees who are more resistant to adopting the new terms because of misalignment with personal goals, and who experience change as a negative disruption, are more likely to activate and mobilize their ties with employees holding similar beliefs. While transitioning to Repair, such employees are more likely to refrain from attending to updates and upcoming events related to the change and as such, become more marginalized. Research found that Facebook users are more likely to "unfriend" individuals with political views different than theirs (John & Dvir-Gvirsman, 2015). We expect a similar pattern of behavior in relation to social networks and employees' tendencies to sustain or revise their psychological contract. Further, positive affect, like that associated with positive disruptions, activates larger and more sparsely connected social network structures (likely highly salient during Renegotiation or when making restoration efforts during Repair), whereas negative affect, like that associated with negative disruptions, activates smaller, redundant social network structures (Shea et al., 2015) which are likely highly salient after psychological contract breach. Based on these findings, we argue that employees who are more negatively affected by organizational change may activate smaller and denser social networks and develop stronger ties with opponents of the change. In contrast, those who share positive feelings about the change may mobilize a larger subset of their organizational network, and develop strong ties with change agents and employees in favor of the change. Employees who seek broad network structures may be more likely to locate opportunities to manage losses and new benefits, adding positively to their psychological contract revision.

Joint efforts

Whether during Renegotiation or Repair, employees can be active agents for self-benefit (Petrou, Demerouti, & Schaufeli, 2015) and work with their employer toward revising their employment relationship. Relevant to this "proactivity" is the "zone of negotiability" which dictates the resources available for negotiation by individuals and their organization (Rousseau, 2001b; Rousseau & Schalk, 2000; Rosen et al., 2013) and how change recipients tend to activate certain social networks to gain access to information contingent on their goals (e.g., supporting or resisting the change) (Shea, Menon, Smith, & Emich, 2015). Although heavily influenced by social norms (Rousseau & Schalk, 2000), we argue that the zone of negotiability is also relevant at the level of the employee-employer exchange, playing a critical role in the success of psychological contract revision efforts.

The size of the zone of negotiability determines the resources available for negotiation (Rousseau, 2001b; Rosen et al., 2013). We argue that two critical factors affect the zone of negotiability during organizational change: employee voice and organizational flexibility. Employee voice describes the discretionary provision of information intended to improve organizational functioning and is a problem-focused coping mechanism that employees use to bring a perceived violation to the attention of their boss (Turnley & Feldman, 1998; Tomprou et al., 2015). Despite positive intentions, sometimes voicing can challenge the status quo of the organization and its power holders (Detert & Burris, 2007, p. 869), thus compromising the success of the negotiation. Organizational flexibility refers to change agents' openness to modify their plans to match employees' concerns, and focuses on the nature of the change initiative rather than employer willingness. For example,

The psychological contract **109**

TABLE 8.1 Zone of negotiability in employment relationships during organizational change

	High Organizational Flexibility	Low Organizational Flexibility
High Employee Voice	Wide zone of negotiability – Expand psychological contract – Smooth and fast adoption of change	Moderate zone of negotiability – Compliant psychological contract – Challenging and slow adoption of change
Low Employee Voice	Idle zone of negotiability – Narrow psychological contract – No resistance to adopt change	Narrow zone of negotiability – Damage to psychological contract – Unlikely adoption of change

radical changes may offer limited flexibility and therefore limit the negotiability zone, whereas changes that are more accommodative in nature may enable greater flexibility and therefore enhance the negotiability zone (Rousseau, 1996).

Crossing the two key factors that influence the zone of negotiability results in four possible scenarios with implications for psychological contract change (see Table 8.1). First, when both organizational flexibility and employee voice are high, the zone of negotiability will be wide because employees will view the change as an opportunity to revise terms of their contract and gain access to goal-consistent resources. As a result, employees may adopt the change more readily. Second, when employee voice is high but organizational flexibility is low, the zone of negotiability may be moderate. In such cases, employees who voice concerns may be more proactive in seeking alternatives such as engaging in social network activation to reduce or avoid any potential damage to the relationship whilst seeking more information about "what's in it" for them from other stakeholders. Although some change agents may perceive such voice as "resistance to change", thus threatening the initiative (e.g., Ford et al., 2008), others may acknowledge the value of voice and respond positively to it. Regardless of the parties' true motives, change will progress slowly as employees seek to comply with the changes while maintaining the relationship. Third, when organizational flexibility is high but employee voice is low, the zone of negotiability may remain untapped, as resources available for negotiation fail to be utilized. In such cases, employees are likely to hold a transactional psychological contract (i.e., quid pro quo), choosing not to contribute to the change effort. Although they may eventually adopt the change, the opportunity for the organization to benefit from employee participation is missed. Finally, when both organizational flexibility and employee voice are low, the zone of negotiability will be narrow; employees may feel unsafe to speak up because of the potential consequences (Edmondson, 1999). Although they may adapt to the change, it is unlikely that their psychological contract will be restored due to organizational rigidity and their inaction (Tomprou et al., 2015). Ideally, organizations should strive for a wide zone of negotiability; if employees view it as narrow, they will withdraw either by revising their psychological contract downward or by exiting the organization.

Conclusion

Organizational change can trigger positive and/or negative disruptions in the employment relationship that require changes to employees' psychological contracts. Indeed, organizational change means modification of the psychological contract (increases or decreases in perceived obligations), whether through the process of assimilation during Maintenance, or as a result of major disruptions that rock the psychological contract foundation in Repair or through cooperative discussion during Renegotiation (Rousseau et al., 2018). Given the limited body of knowledge on psychological contracts during organizational change, we drew on recent theoretical advancement in the study of psychological contracts to help understand how organizations and employees can each work to promote positive, and address negative, reactions to change. We underscored the importance of employee proactivity and the relevance of social networks in various phases of the employment relationship. Further, we highlighted the role that employers play during Maintenance to promote positive acceptance of organizational change as well as employers' role in mitigating negative reactions to organizational change following disruption. Finally, we adopted the concept of "zone of negotiability" to show how employees and employers can work jointly to affect change acceptance, and as a result, successfully negotiate a functional psychological contract.

We hope that these ideas stimulate further research on psychological contract processes during organizational change. Although the post-violation model (Tomprou et al., 2015) suggests that several factors may be relevant to overcoming severe negative disruptions (e.g., coping style, employee resources and organizational responsiveness), little empirical work has explored important topics such as key mechanisms affecting the success of repair efforts following negative disruptions. Such knowledge would be particularly helpful when undertaking radical change efforts where there is a strong likelihood that existing agreements will be damaged. Ultimately, the existing body of work suggests that effective management of psychological contracts is critical to the success of change efforts as it can reduce negative attitudes toward the change and increase the perceived legitimacy of the change (van den Heuvel, Schalk, & van Assen, 2015; Rousseau & Tijoriwala, 1999).

Note

1 We would like to thank the anonymous reviewer for her insightful comments.

References

Armenakis, A. A., Harris, S. G., & Mossholder, K. W. (1993). Creating readiness for organizational change. *Human Relations*, *46*(6), 681–703.

The psychological contract **111**

Battilana, J., & Casciaro, T. (2013). Overcoming resistance to organizational change: Strong ties and affective cooptation. *Management Science, 59*(4), 819–836.

Bellou, V. (2007). Psychological contract assessment after a major organizational change: The case of mergers and acquisitions. *Employee Relations, 29*, 68–88.

Bottom, W. P., Gibson, K., Daniels, S. E., & Murnighan, J. K. (2002). When talk is not cheap: Substantive penance and expressions of intent in rebuilding cooperation. *Organization Science, 13*(5), 497–513.

Carver, C. S., & Scheier, M. F. (2004). Self-regulation of action and affect. In R. F. Baumeister & K. D. Vohs (Eds.), *Handbook of self-regulation: Research, theory, and applications* (pp. 13–39). New York: Guildford Press.

Chaudhry, A., Coyle-Shapiro, J. A. M., & Wayne, S. J. (2011). A longitudinal study of the impact of organizational change on transactional, relational, and balanced psychological contracts. *Journal of Leadership & Organizational Studies, 18*(2), 247–259.

Conway, N., Kiefer, T., Hartley, J., & Briner, R. B. (2014). Doing more with less? Employee reactions to psychological contract breach via target similarity or spillover during public sector organizational change. *British Journal of Management, 25*(4), 737–754.

Detert, J. R., & Burris, E. R. (2007). Leadership behavior and employee voice: Is the door really open? *Academy of Management Journal, 50*(4), 869–-884.

De Vos, A., Buyens, D., & Schalk, R. (2003). Psychological contract development during organizational socialization: Adaptation to reality and the role of reciprocity. *Journal of Organizational Behavior, 24*(5), 537–559.

Dulac, T., Coyle-Shapiro, J. A., Henderson, D. J., & Wayne, S. J. (2008). Not all responses to breach are the same: The interconnection of social exchange and psychological contract processes in organizations. *Academy of Management Journal, 51*(6), 1079–1098.

Edmondson, A. (1999). Psychological safety and learning behavior in work teams. *Administrative science quarterly, 44*(2), 350–383.

Ford, J. D., Ford, L. W., & D'Amelio, A. (2008). Resistance to change: The rest of the story. *Academy of Management Review, 33*(2), 362–377.

Freese, C., Schalk, R., & Croon, M. (2011). The impact of organizational changes on psychological contracts: A longitudinal study. *Personnel Review, 40*(4), 404–422.

Gioia, D. A., Thomas, J. B., Clark, S. M., & Chittipeddi, K. (1994). Symbolism and strategic change in academia: The dynamics of sensemaking and influence. *Organization Science, 5*(3), 363–383.

Ho, V. T. (2005). Social influence on evaluations of psychological contract fulfillment. *Academy of Management Review, 30*(1), 113–128.

Hornung, S., Rousseau, D. M., & Glaser, J. (2008). Creating flexible work arrangements through idiosyncratic deals. *Journal of Applied Psychology, 93*, 655–664.

Huy, Q. N., Corley, K. G., & Kraatz, M. S. (2014). From support to mutiny: Shifting legitimacy judgments and emotional reactions impacting the implementation of radical change. *Academy of Management Journal, 57*(6), 1650–1680.

John, N. A., & Dvir-Gvirsman, S. (2015). "I Don't Like You Any More": Facebook unfriending by Israelis during the Israel–Gaza conflict of 2014. *Journal of Communication, 65*(6), 953–974.

Krackhardt, D., & Hanson, J. R. (1993). Informal networks: The company behind the chart. *Harvard Business Review, 4*, 104–111.

Lo, S., & Aryee, S. (2003). Psychological contract breach in a Chinese context: An integrative approach. *Journal of Management Studies, 40*, 1005–1020.

Montes, S. D., & Irving, P. G. (2008). Disentangling the effects of promised and delivered inducements: Relational and transactional contract elements and the mediating role of trust. *Journal of Applied Psychology, 93*(6), 1367–1381.

Morrison, E. W., & Robinson, S. L. (1997). When employees feel betrayed: A model of how psychological contract violation develops. *Academy of Management Review, 22*(1), 226–256.

Petrou, P., Demerouti, E., & Schaufeli, W. B. (2015). Crafting the change the role of employee job crafting behaviors for successful organizational change. *Journal of Management, 20*(4), 470–480. 0149206315624961.

Robinson, S. L. (1996). Trust and breach of the psychological contract. *Administrative Science Quarterly, 41*(4), 574–599.

Robinson, S. L., & Morrison, E. W. (2000). The development of psychological contract breach and violation: A longitudinal study. *Journal of Organizational Behavior,* 525–546.

Rosen, C. C., Slater, D. J., Chang, C. H., & Johnson, R. E. (2013). Let's make a deal: Development and validation of the ex post i-deals scale. *Journal of Management, 39*(3), 709–742.

Rousseau, D.M. (1989). Psychological and implied contracts in organizations. *Employee Responsibilities and Rights Journal, 2,* 121–138.

Rousseau, D. M. (1995). *Psychological contracts in organizations: Understanding written and unwritten agreements.* Thousand Oaks, CA: SAGE Publications.

Rousseau, D. M. (1996). Changing the deal while keeping the people. *The Academy of Management Executive, 10*(1), 50–59.

Rousseau, D. M. (2001a). Schema, promise and mutuality: The building blocks of the psychological contract. *Journal of Occupational and Organizational Psychology, 74*(4), 511–541.

Rousseau, D. M. (2001b). The idiosyncratic deal: Flexibility versus fairness? *Organizational Dynamics, 29*(4), 260–273.

Rousseau, D. M., Hansen, S. D., & Tomprou, M. (2018, under review). *A dynamic phase model of psychological contract processes.*

Rousseau, D. M., & Schalk, R. (2000). *Psychological contracts in employment: Cross cultural perspectives.* Thousand Oaks, CA: SAGE Publications.

Rousseau, D. M., & Tijoriwala, S. A. (1999). What's a good reason to change? Motivated reasoning and social accounts in promoting organizational change. *Journal of Applied Psychology, 84*(4), 514–528.

Schalk, R., & Freese, C. (1997). New facets of commitment in response to organizational change: Research trends and the Dutch experience. In C. L. Cooper & D. M. Rousseau (Eds.), *Trends in organizational behavior* (Vol. 4, pp. 107–123). Chichester: John Wiley & Sons.

Schalk, R., & Roe, R. E. (2007). Towards a dynamic model of the psychological contract. *Journal for the Theory of Social Behaviour, 37*(2), 167–182.

Shea, C. T., Menon, T., Smith, E. B., & Emich, K. (2015). The affective antecedents of cognitive social network activation. *Social Networks, 43,* 91–99.

Stensaker, I. G., & Langley, A. (2010). Change management choices and trajectories in a multidivisional firm. *British Journal of Management, 21*(1), 7–27.

Tomlinson, E. C., Dineen, B. R., & Lewicki, R. J. (2004). The road to reconciliation: Antecedents of victim willingness to reconcile following a broken promise. *Journal of Management, 30*(2), 165–187.

Tomprou, M., Nikolaou, I., & Vakola, M. (2012). Experiencing organizational change in Greece: The framework of psychological contract. *The International Journal of Human Resource Management, 23,* 385–405.

Tomprou, M., Rousseau, D. M., & Griep, Y. (2018, under review). Resolution in the aftermath of psychological contract violation.

Tomprou, M., Rousseau, D. M., & Hansen, S. D. (2015). The psychological contracts of violation victims: A post-violation model. *Journal of Organizational Behavior, 36*(4), 561–581.

Turnley, W. H., & Feldman, D. C. (1998). Psychological contract violations during corporate restructuring. *Human Resource Management, 37*(1), 71–83.

van den Heuvel, S., Schalk, R., Freese, C., & Timmerman, V. (2016). What's in it for me? A managerial perspective on the influence of the psychological contract on attitude towards change. *Journal of Organizational Change Management, 29*, 263–292.

van den Heuvel, S., Schalk, R., & van Assen, M. A. (2015). Does a well-informed employee have a more positive attitude toward change? The mediating role of psychological contract fulfillment, trust, and perceived need for change. *The Journal of Applied Behavioral Science, 51*(3), 401–422. 0021886315569507.

Zhao, H. A. O., Wayne, S. J., Glibkowski, B. C., & Bravo, J. (2007). The impact of psychological contract breach on work-related outcomes: A meta-analysis. *Personnel Psychology, 60*(3), 647–680.

9

MEASURING CHANGE RECIPIENTS' REACTIONS

The development and psychometric evaluation of the CRRE scale

Ioannis Tsaousis and Maria Vakola

In a rapid and fast-changing social and economic environment, organizations seek ways of adapting quickly to constant and ongoing changes. Continuous change is said to be a fact of life for organizations and their members and many authors suggest that success in change implementation is increasingly reliant on positive reactions on the part of change recipients (Jacobs, van Witteloostuijn, & Christe-Zeyse, 2013; Oreg, Vakola, & Armenakis, 2011; Oreg, 2003; Paterson & Cary, 2002; Piderit, 2000; Wanberg & Banas, 2000). Negative reactions from change recipients can be responsible for dysfunctional outcomes such as low job satisfaction, intention to quit, low organizational commitment and low trust in the organization (Paterson & Cary, 2002). In addition, it is well documented that positive attitudes and reactions contribute to change success – to the extent that some authors indicate this to be one of the most critical factors in change implementation (Oreg et al., 2011).

The existing literature has frequently overlooked the possibility that change recipients may distinguish between attitude or dispositions to organizational change in general (that varies from dispositional resistance to commitment to change in general) and attitudes to a specific organizational change. For example, a change recipient may hold a positive attitude toward change in general, but may develop a negative reaction toward a specific change project (such as restructuring) that takes place in his/her workplace because of poor implementation or lack of involvement. The present research aims to close this gap by developing a new instrument, called CRRE Change Recipients' Reactions Scale, that assesses reactions to a specific organizational change following the tridimensional nature of attitudes – namely, cognitive, affective and behavioral. So far, even though the existing change management literature has practically overlooked the distinction between attitudes to organizational change in general and attitudes to specific organizational change, psychologists have demonstrated that conceptually, attitude can explain the general tendency to engage in relevant behaviors, and a reaction is a relatively strong predictor of a single behavior involving *a particular attitude* object (Eagly & Chaiken, 1993).

This is a well-known dilemma called "bandwidth-fidelity" (Cronbach & Gleser, 1965). "Bandwidth" refers to the ability to view psychological constructs using a wide-angle lens and consequently understand the "big picture"; however, using this approach also implies a loss of detail. "Fidelity", on the other hand, refers to the ability to define aspects of the issue at hand more precisely, providing a more detailed view by "zooming in". However, this results in less resonance with broader themes or criteria. Practitioners as well as researchers are faced with this dilemma when deciding whether to use narrow versus broad scales in the description of human behavior, which creates confusion.

This confusion has led some change management scholars to put specificity on the agenda for change management. Recently, Du Gay and Vikkelso (2012) have argued that if change continues to be assessed as an abstract and generic entity without specification, there will be some unfortunate consequences for the precise assessment and practical management of particular organizational change. In an attitudinal context, there is strong evidence suggesting that to predict a more specific behavior criterion, a more specific measure of attitude should be used (Eagly & Chaiken, 1993; Jaccard, King, & Pomazal, 1977). Among the few change researchers to have adopted this distinction are Lau and Woodman (1995), who suggest that a person may have an attitude toward change in general while at the same time reacting differently toward a change currently being faced, depending on the specific issues and contexts involved. For example, some recipients can be generally supportive of their organization's willingness to improve things, yet vary in their support and commitment to working overtime to implement a specific change project.

Within this context, there are several issues related to the measurement of change reactions that need to be addressed. First, not only conceptually but also methodologically, some researchers fairly often use instruments developed to measure attitudes toward change in general (e.g., Dunham, Grube, Gardner, Cummings, & Pierce, 1989) to assess employees' reactions toward a specific change, which adds confusion to the change management research (Oreg et al., 2011). Second, some self-report instruments, while considered as measures of attitudes toward change (either general or specific), have not yet gone through systematic and rigorous psychometric evaluation (i.e., there is less sound evidence regarding their content, concurrent and construct validity evidence), and are still either unpublished and/ or being used as pilot versions. These measures include the Inventory of Attitudes Toward Change (IATC; Dunham et al., 1989), the Specific Attitude Toward Change (SATC; Lau, 1990) and the Change Attitude Scale (CAS; Oreg, 2006).

In our examination of the scales used to measure recipients' reactions, we found several additional measures that focus on single reaction toward organizational change. For example, Axtell et al. (2002) used an openness to change scale which follows a cognitive approach of measuring change or Armstrong-Stassen's (1998) emotional reactions scale which aims at capturing negative emotions regarding change (for a full list please see Oreg et al., 2011).

Responding to a call for specificity in change management research we believe that the new scale will contribute to both research and practice. With this scale, we offer both researchers and practitioners the opportunity to capture how change recipients think, feel and intend to behave toward the specific change at hand. Apart from regaining the specificity, the present research relies on the tridimensional nature of attitudes – namely, cognitive, affective and behavioral (Breckler, 1984). This framework is the most prominent framework for the study of attitudes in organizational change and it offers accuracy in understanding change recipients' reactions facilitating our effort to formulate a plan to deal with them effectively. A review of past empirical research reveals three different emphases in the conceptualization of attitudes to change based on the predominant tripartite view (Oreg et al., 2011; Piderit, 2000; Elizur & Guttman, 1976): a *cognitive reaction* (e.g., sense making, decision satisfaction, change commitment, perceived fairness); an *affective reaction* (e.g., stress associated with change, pleasantness, change-related satisfaction, affective organizational change commitment, etc.); and a *behavioral reaction* (e.g. active support and involvement, withdrawal behaviors, resistance, etc.).

We present the four phases of the development of the CRRE scale: (1) Development of the items and the extraction of the factor solution; (2) verification of the obtained factor solution; (3) examination of the reliability of the scale; and (4) justification of the concurrent, convergent, divergent and incremental validity of the scale. We administered the CRRE scale in various change contexts to address the specificity issue and to examine the stability of its psychometric properties across different change programs.

Method

Participants

Six different samples were used during the various developmental stages of the CRRE scale. The first sample consisted of 205 employees from various organizations (46.34% males) and was used to examine the factor structure of the initial version of the CRRE via exploratory factor analysis (EFA). The mean age of the participants was 38.21 years ($SD = 9.51$). The second sample consisted of 331 (64.34% were males; *Mean age* = 35.26, $SD = 7.55$) employees working in a Telecom and IT company and was used to replicate the factor structure obtained from the EFA as well as to estimate the internal consistency of the scale. The third sample was used for estimating the test-retest reliability of the scale. It was consisted of 126 MBA students (98 females; *Mean age* = 27.17, $SD = 8.06$) who completed the CRRE scale twice, with an interval of four weeks between administrations. The fourth sample consisted of 237 employees (54.43% of whom were males) working in a large private telecommunication company; the mean age of this sample was 35.06 ($SD = 9.20$). The fifth sample consisted of 161 employees (56.5% females; *Mean age* = 39.32, $SD = 10.11$) working in a large public bank which was involved in a large restructuring program. Finally, the sixth sample consisted of 79 employees

(77.2% were females) working in a large retail company; the mean age was 37.32 ($SD = 9.14$). The last three samples were used to examine the concurrent, convergent, divergent and incremental validity of the CRRE scale.

Item development

In this phase, we focused on determining the basic dimensions of the concept model and writing appropriate items to measure them. The conceptual model adopted was the *Tripartite Attitude Model* or *ABC model*, according to which the attitude concept is composed of three components: *cognition, affect* and *behavior* (Breckler, 1984; Eagly & Chaiken, 1993). Two organizational psychologists, both experts in organizational change, independently developed 45 items each (15 per dimension) based on the adopted theoretical model. Next, the two authors using certain criteria and guidelines (e.g., syntactical or grammatical errors, vague and unclear sentences, double negative items, conceptually irrelevant items, etc.) came up with 71 items (25 cognitive, 24 emotional and 22 behavioral) that formed the initial version of the CRRE scale.

Procedure

All participants were asked to complete either the initial (first sample) or the final (all other samples) version of the CRRE scale. The third sample completed the CRRE scale twice, with an interval of four weeks between administrations. The fourth sample was additionally asked to complete the Dispositional Measure of Employability scale. The fifth sample was additionally asked to complete the Readiness to Change Questionnaire. Finally, the sixth sample was additionally asked to complete the Resistance to Change scale, the Commitment to Change scale, the Job Satisfaction Scale, the Intention to Quit scale, the Work Engagement scale, the Work Exhaustion scale and the Work Personality Inventory. In all cases, the HR departments took the responsibility for administering and collecting the questionnaire booklets. An internal memo was sent to all employees setting out the scope of the study and informing them of confidentiality issues. However, if a participant wanted to be debriefed, he/she could report his/her name in order to receive by post his/her personal results.

Results

Initially, response distributions were examined to determine whether the items consisting the initial version of the scale were appropriate (e.g., neither too high nor too low scores so as to avoid ceiling or floor effects, low variability, etc.) and to establish that their distributions followed a normal curve. After this procedure, 12 items were eliminated, reducing the total number of items in the initial version of the scale to 59. Next, we developed a core cluster of items, a *prototype*, for each of the hypothetical constructs we intended to measure (Tsaousis, 1999). This *prototype* was composed of highly inter-correlated items which represent the core characteristics (i.e., the operational definition) of each hypothetical construct. Next, all items were correlated with all other *prototypes*, and those with the highest correlations on one *prototype* but low correlations on all the other *prototypes* were selected (Hinkin, 1999; Worthington, 2006). At the end of this phase, 30 items (ten for each dimension) were retained.

Factor structure of the CRRE scale

In the next step, the data were subjected to principal-axis factor analysis with oblique rotation (due to the inter-correlation among the factors) to define the factor structure of the final version of the scale. Items were retained only if they had a loading of 0.40 or higher on a factor and did not have high secondary loading (< .40) on another factor (Field, 2000). Three eigenvalues > 1 were found (10.47, 1.67 and 1.61), together explaining 65.50% of the total variance. Several researchers recommend parallel analysis (PA) as the best factor retention method (e.g., Patil, Singh, Mishra, & Todd Donavan, 2008). PA is a Monte Carlo simulation technique which compares the observed eigenvalues extracted from the correlation matrix to be analyzed with those obtained from random data sets. Factors or components are retained as long as the ith eigenvalue from the actual data is greater than the ith eigenvalue from the random data. The results from the PA indicated that only the first three eigenvalues exceeded the respected averaged eigenvalues that resulted from repeated random data reconstructions (Watkins, 2000). After rotating the solution, we eliminated the items that either did not meet the above inclusion criteria or had poor conceptual (e.g., similar meaning) and psychometric (e.g., lower factor loadings) qualities. The final version of the CRRE scale consisted of 21 items. Each sub-scale consisted of seven items – according to Hinkin (1999), this is enough to adequately tap the domain of interest. Table 9.1 presents the corresponding results.

Next, we examined whether the obtained three-factor solution could be replicated in new sample of employees. For that, Confirmatory Factor Analysis (CFA) was used. Model parameters were estimated using maximum likelihood parameter estimates with standard errors and a mean-adjusted chi-square test statistic (MLM or Satorra-Bentler χ^2) that is robust to non-normality. To assess how well the CFA model represented the data, the following criteria were used as cutoffs for good fit: $\chi^2/df < 3.0$ (< with 2.5 being ideal); CFI and TLI > .90 (with > .95 being ideal); RMSEA (with 90% confidence intervals), and SRMR < 0.08 (with < .05 being ideal) (Brown, 2015). To determine the best fitting model for the sample, two competing models of interest were estimated. The first model was the unidimensional model of attitudes toward a specific organizational change, in which all 21 items were loaded onto a general latent variable. The next model was the three-factor model, which included the three assumed latent constructs (factors) – the cognitive, the emotional and the behavioral – each of which consisting of seven items as their observed indicators.

Measuring change recipients' reactions **119**

TABLE 9.1 Factor structure of the CRRE Scales

Items	Emotional	Behavioral	Cognitive
This change is unpleasant for me.[a]	**.93**	.02	−.02
I feel uncomfortable with the change that they are trying to implement.[a]	**.85**	.01	.00
This change is giving me a headache.[a]	**.85**	−.05	.03
This change makes me emotionally tired.[a]	**.85**	−.03	.00
I do not like this change.[a]	**.83**	.10	.06
Due to this change, I am not satisfied with my job anymore.[a]	**.63**	.10	.12
I am happy with this change.	**.61**	.23	.09
I share whatever knowledge or information I have to help this change be successful.	**−.19**	.77	.05
I am willing to help this change be successful.	**.19**	.73	.00
I will work longer hours to implement this change successfully.	**.08**	.72	.00
I am trying to convince others about the benefits of this change.	**.13**	.70	.14
I am fighting for the success of this change.	**.01**	.69	−.08
I am trying to encourage my colleagues to adopt this change.	**.14**	.67	.17
I will strongly support the implementation of this change.	**.28**	.58	.09
I believe that this change will benefit this organization.	**−.07**	.01	.91
I believe that this change will be very effective for this organization.	**.02**	−.08	.86
I believe that this change will meet its aims.	**−.12**	.05	.82
I believe that this change is appropriate for this organization.	**.14**	−.08	.76
This change will have a positive impact on this organization.	**−.01**	.17	.71
This change will not help the development of this organization.[a]	**.12**	.09	.55
I am skeptical about the outcomes of this change.[a]	**.22**	−.01	.54
%Variance	**49.87**	7.99	7.65

Notes: [a] reversed items. Permission to use the CRRE scale free of charge and for a limited period is provided only for research purposes. Administration instructions should be requested from the first author to adapt to the specific content of the change under consideration.

The results showed that the three-factor model provided the best fit. Particularly, the obtained fit indices suggested acceptable fit to the observed data: χ^2 (186, N = 331) = 354.73, $\chi^2/$ df = 1.91, $p < .001$; CFI = .953, TLI = .947, RMSEA = .052 (90% CI = .044 − .061), and SRMR = .051. Furthermore, all the factor indicators and path loadings were substantial, statistically significant and in the expected direction. The corresponding fit indices for the one-factor model were: χ^2 (189,

$N = 331) = 1006.46, \chi^2/ df = 5.33, p < .001; CFI = .773, TLI = .748, RMSEA = .114$ (90% CI = .107 − .121), and SRMR = .085), indicating a not adequate fit. Furthermore, the chi-square difference between the two contrasted models showed that the three-factor model provided a significantly better fit than did the one-factor model $(\Delta\chi^2 = 651.73, \Delta df = 3, p < .001)$.

Reliability of the CRRE scale

First, we examined the internal consistency and the homogeneity of the CRRE sub-scales using the omega (ω) or composite reliability index (Raykov, 2004), and the mean inter-item correlations (MIC). Omega index of reliability is more robust and more precise than alpha coefficient, especially when the aim is to estimate the internal consistency reliability of composite scores within a latent variable framework (Raykov, 2004). To provide additional support to the reliability of the measure, the MIC, an index of the homogeneity of a scale, was also computed. The omega estimates were .89 (MIC = .54) for the cognitive aspect, .93 (MIC = .65) for the emotional aspect, and .90 (MIC = .55) for the behavioral aspect. The omega for the total scale was .97 (MIC = .58). Next, we assessed the stability of the scale over time. Test-retest reliability is the most obvious form of investigating changes over time (Nunnally & Bernstein, 1994). Test-retest estimates were .85 for the cognitive aspect, .85 for the emotional aspect and .88 for the behavioral aspect. The test-retest coefficient for the total scale was .88.

Validity of the CRRE scale

To examine the concurrent, convergent, divergent and incremental validity of the CRRE scale we correlated CRRE sub-scales with scales that are theoretically relevant to organizational change (i.e., personality traits, readiness to change, intensions to quit, job satisfaction, etc.). The results from this analysis are presented in Table 9.2.

The direction and magnitude of all reported coefficients provide strong evidence regarding the concurrent, convergent and divergent validity of the CRRE sub-scales. Particularly, it was found that all CRRE sub-scales were correlated positively with all sub-scales from the Readiness to Change Questionnaire (RCQ) and Commitment to Change Scale (CCS). These results could be considered as evidence of the concurrent validity of the CRRE, due to the conceptual equivalence of the two measures with what the CRRE scale measures. All CRRE sub-scales were also found to be positively related to Dispositional Measure of Employability (DME), Overall Job Satisfaction Score and Work Engagement Scale. On the other hand, they were negatively correlated to Resistance to Change Scale (RCS), Intention to Quit Scale and Work Exhaustion Scale. The lower part of the table presents correlations among the CRRE sub-scales and personality traits as measured by the Work Personality Inventory (WPI; Tsaousis, 2015). As can be seen, Extraversion and Openness to Experience were positively correlated with all CRRE sub-scales.

TABLE 9.2 Correlation coefficients of the CRRE sub-scales with various criterion scales

Criterion Scales	CRRE Cognitive	CRRE Emotional	CRRE Behavioral	CRRE Overall
CRRE Scale				
CRRE Cognitive		.67**	.56**	.84**
CRRE Emotional			.67**	.92**
CRRE Behavioral				.85**
Dispositional Measure of Employability (DME)				
Openness to Change at Work	.45**	.39**	.60**	.52**
Work & Career Proactivity	.26**	.19**	.38**	.30**
Career Motivation	.21**	.03	.27**	.19**
Work & Career Resilience	.39**	.25**	.51**	.41**
Work Optimism	.39**	.36**	.45**	.45**
Work Identity	.29**	.13*	.41**	.29**
Readiness to Change Questionnaire (RCQ)				
Appropriateness	.84**	.75**	.71**	.90**
Leadership Support	.61**	.34**	.43**	.53**
Change Efficacy	.48**	.36**	.59**	.55**
Personal Valence	.31**	.54**	.20*	.43**
Change Commitment Scale (CCS)				
Overall Commitment to Change Score	.73**	.65**	.86**	.82**
Resistance to Change Scale (RTC)				
Overall Resistance to Change Score	−.36**	−.38**	−.23*	−.35**
The Michigan Org. Assessment Questionnaire				
Overall Job Satisfaction Score	.48**	.51**	.39**	.50**
Intentions to Quit Scale				
Overall Intentions to Quit Score	−.23*	−.45**	−.26**	−.35**
Work Engagement Scale				
Overall Work Engagement Score	.43**	.53**	.44**	.52**
Work Exhaustion Scale				
Overall Work Exhaustion Score	−.18	−.35**	−.18	−.26*
Work Personality Inventory (WPI)				
Extraversion	.32**	.33**	.29**	.34**
Neuroticism	−.53**	−.52**	−.39**	−.52**
Openness to Experience	.34**	.51**	.39**	.46**
Agreeableness	.22	.25*	.08	.20
Conscientiousness	.04	.30**	.09	.16

Notes: * $p < 0.05$, ** $p < 0.01$.

On the other hand, Emotional Stability was negatively correlated with all aspects of the CRRE scale.

CRRE sub-scales demonstrated also evidence for divergent validity, by exhibiting low or even no correlations with theoretically unrelated traits. For example, the CRRE cognitive dimension was weakly correlated with Agreeableness and Conscientiousness personality dimensions and Work Exhaustion. The same pattern of results reported for the CRRE behavioral dimension and the above-mentioned dimensions. Finally, the CRRE emotional dimension showed very low correlations with Career Motivation, Work & Career Motivation and Work identity.

Finally, to test the incremental validity of the CRRE scale, a hierarchical multiple regression was used. The order of entry of predictors into the hierarchical regression analysis was determined *a priori*, as suggested by Cohen and Cohen (1983). Each of the demographic characteristics (e.g., gender and age) and personal characteristics (e.g., dispositional resistance to change and dispositional employability) was entered first to predict both job satisfaction and intention to quit; then, the CRRE sub-scales were added to the equations to ascertain any increase in explained variance. This analysis indicated that the addition of the CRRE sub-scales in step 2 increased the explained variance of job satisfaction (when CRRE sub-scales were entered, $\Delta R^2 = .10, p < .01$) and intention to quit (when CRRE sub-scales were entered, $\Delta R^2 = .07, p < .01$).

Discussion

The goal of this research was to develop a new measure of reactions toward a specific organizational change. On the basis of an initial principal-axis factor analysis, 21 items were identified to represent the three theoretical core dimensions of the conceptual adopted model (i.e., *Tripartite Attitude Model*). The first factor involves feelings, moods, emotions and evaluations (i.e., positive, negative or neutral) about a specific organizational change. The second factor is related to the actual actions an employee intends to take in relation to the specific organizational change he/she is facing. Finally, the third factor refers to an individual's beliefs, perceptual responses and thoughts regarding a specific change policy which he/she has to deal with in his/her working environment. This three-factor solution was replicated in a new sample of employees via CFA, providing strong support for the content validity of the new instrument. Furthermore, due to high inter-correlations among the three scales of the measure, a one-factor model was tested to see if there was a substantial overlap among the scales. The results showed that this model could not successfully fit the data, providing further support for the tridimensional nature of the scale.

All CRRE sub-scales demonstrated also high internal consistency, with omega values ranging from .89 to .97. Moreover, the MIC index provided further support for the homogeneity of the three scales, with corresponding values ranging from .54 to .65. Finally, test-retest data over a four-week period suggested that the CRRE sub-scales have temporal stability, with values ranging from .85 to .88. Finally, three independent studies revealed substantial correlations between the

Measuring change recipients' reactions 123

CRRE sub-scales and theoretically related constructs, providing evidence for the concurrent, convergent and divergent validity of the scale. In particular, all CRRE sub-scales were correlated with several constructs hypothesized to make up its nomological network, including personality traits, dispositional employability, job satisfaction, intention to quit, work engagement and work exhaustion (Fugate & Kinicki, 2008; Fugate, Kinicki, & Ashforth, 2004; Vakola, Tsaousis, & Nikolaou, 2004; Wanberg & Banas, 2000). The CRRE sub-scales' correlations with these personal and contextual variables, although moderate in magnitude, are within the usual range for variables from the organizational context.

In addition to convergent validity, the current research also provides some evidence for the divergent and incremental validity of CRRE sub-scales. Divergent validity was demonstrated by low correlations with constructs that are theoretically unrelated to the concept of change. From this perspective, the cognitive and the behavioral dimensions of CRRE showed very weak correlations with Agreeableness, Conscientiousness and work exhaustion, while the emotional dimension of CRRE exhibited weak correlations with several sub-scales of employability (i.e., Work & Career Proactivity, Work Motivation and Work Identity). Finally, the CRRE sub-scales add incremental validity to the prediction of both job satisfaction and intention to quit, in that they act as key criteria which provide unique information that improves the prediction over and above the theoretically relevant factors of dispositional employability and readiness to change.

One of the main advantages of the CRRE scale over existing psychometric instruments for organizational change is that the CRRE measures reactions toward a *specific* organizational change. Matching attitude specificity with measurement specificity accomplishes two things. First, it increases the accuracy of the measurement within the specified domain, and second, it increases the predictability of the instrument because of this increased accuracy (Eagly & Chaiken, 1993; Robinson, Stimpson, Huefner, & Hunt, 1991). Indeed, when organizational change is to be measured, one should take into consideration the specific characteristics of the change program itself (impact, process, planning, etc.) and the impact this specific change might have on change recipients' reactions to change. For example, you may have an employee who is dispositionally resistant toward anything new but has become very positive toward a restructuring program because he/she strongly believes that this is what the organization needs to move forward. This is why it is very important for both researchers and practitioners to be able to measure not only attitudes in general or dispositional tendencies toward change, but also the reactions to a specific change situation that an employee has to cope with.

Furthermore, although there are alternative instruments measuring specific reactions towards organizational change (e.g. Readiness to Change Questionnaire – RCQ, Commitment to Change Scale – CCS, Resistance to Change – RTC, etc.) none of these measures follows the tripartite model for assessing the individual's specific reactions towards change. This conceptualization offers a more comprehensive understanding of why people decide to react in a particular way on a specific change process, since it views the different components of the model (i.e., cognitive, affective and behavioral) as three distinct classes of information upon which evaluative judgments are based (Chaiken & Stangor, 1987).

This study has also some limitations. One potential limitation might be the fact that the present investigations were limited to the use of self-report instruments of organizational change and related constructs. More research is needed to examine the relationship between the CRRE sub-scales and observation- and performance-based instruments of constructs related to specific organizational change programs. Validity evidence using multi-trait, multi-method techniques and/or longitudinal designs could overcome the problem of common-method variance due to the cross-sectional design used in this study, and strengthen the empirical evidence regarding the construct and predictive validity of the CRRE scale. Furthermore, cross-validation in different cultural settings is needed. Although no empirical evidence exists to date, cultural differences may be present regarding both the level and the internal structure of the construct.

Overall, the results from this study led us to conclude that the CRRE scale is a valuable instrument with strong psychometric properties. This instrument is effective because it facilitates both researchers and practitioners' attempts to accurately capture change recipients' reactions to a current change. Conceptually, this measure is a response to a call to regain specificity in change management research. We believe that change cannot be assessed as an abstract and generic entity without specification, because this may have some unfortunate consequences for accurate assessment both in research and in practice.

APPENDIX

Change Recipients' Reactions (CRRE) Scale

Listed below are several statements regarding your beliefs and attitudes about the change that take place at your organization. Please read the following sentences and indicate the degree to which you agree or disagree by selecting the appropriate number on the following scale.

①	②	③	④	⑤
Strongly Disagree	**Disagree**	**Neutral**	**Agree**	**Strongly Agree**

1 I feel uncomfortable with the change that they are trying to implement.	①	②	③	④	⑤
2 I believe that this change will benefit this organization.	①	②	③	④	⑤
3 This change is unpleasant for me.	①	②	③	④	⑤
4 This change will not help the development of this organization.	①	②	③	④	⑤
5 I believe that this change is appropriate for this organization.	①	②	③	④	⑤
6 I share whatever knowledge or information I have to help this change be successful.	①	②	③	④	⑤
7 I am willing to help this change be successful.	①	②	③	④	⑤
8 I believe that this change will be very effective.	①	②	③	④	⑤
9 I am skeptical about the outcomes of this change.	①	②	③	④	⑤
10 Due to this change, I am not satisfied with my job anymore.	①	②	③	④	⑤
11 I am trying to encourage my colleagues to adopt this change.	①	②	③	④	⑤

(Continued)

12 This change is giving me a headache	①	②	③	④	⑤
13 I strongly support the implementation of this change.	①	②	③	④	⑤
14 I am happy with this change.	①	②	③	④	⑤
15 I believe that this change will meet its aims.	①	②	③	④	⑤
16 I am trying to convince others about the benefits of this change.	①	②	③	④	⑤
17 This change makes me emotionally tired.	①	②	③	④	⑤
18 I will work longer hours to implement this change successfully.	①	②	③	④	⑤
19 This change will have a positive impact on this organization.	①	②	③	④	⑤
20 I am fighting for the success of this change.	①	②	③	④	⑤
21 I do not like this change.	①	②	③	④	⑤

Note: You can replace the words "this change" with the name of the change under consideration (i.e., this restructuring, this merger etc.).

References

Armstrong-Stassen, M. (1998). The effect of gender and organizational level on how survivors appraise and cope with organizational downsizing. *Journal of Applied Behavioral Science, 34*, 125–142.

Axtell, C., Wall, T., Stride, C., Pepper, K., Clegg, C., Gardner, P., & Bolden, R. (2002). Familiarity breeds content: The impact of exposure to change on employee openness and well-being. *Journal of Occupational and Organizational Psychology, 75*, 217–231.

Breckler, S. J. (1984). Empirical validation of affect, behavior, and cognition as distinct components of attitude. *Journal of Personality and Social Psychology, 47*, 1191–1205.

Brown, A. T. (2015). *Confirmatory factor analysis for applied research* (2nd ed.). New York: Guilford Press.

Chaiken, S., & Stangor, C. (1987). Attitudes and attitude change. *Annual Review of Psychology, 38*, 575–630.

Cohen, J., & Cohen, P. (1983). *Applied multiple regression/correlation analysis for the behavioral sciences* (2nd ed.). Hillsdale, NJ: Lawrence Erlbaum Associates.

Cronbach, L. J., & Gleser, G. C. (1965). *Psychological tests and personnel decisions* (2nd ed.). Urbana, IL: University of Illinois Press.

Du Gay, P., & Vikkelsø, S. (2012). Exploitation, exploration and exaltation: Notes on a metaphysical (re) turn to 'one best way of organizing'. *Research in the Sociology of Organizations, 37*, 249–279.

Dunham, R. B., Grube, J. A., Gardner, D. G., Cummings, L. L., & & Pierce, J. L. (1989). The development of an attitude toward change instrument. *Academy of Management Annual Meeting*, Washington, DC.

Eagly, A., & Chaiken, S. (1993). *The psychology of attitudes.* Orlando, FL: Harcourt Brace Jovanovich College Publishers.

Elizur, D., & Guttman, L. (1976). The structure of attitudes toward work and technological change within an organization. *Administrative Science Quarterly, 21*, 611–622.

Field, A. (2000). *Discovering statistics using SPSS for Windows.* Thousand Oaks, CA: SAGE Publications.

Fugate, M., & Kinicki, A. J. (2008). A dispositional approach to employability: Development of a measure and test of its implications for employee reactions to organizational change. *Journal of Occupational and Organizational Psychology, 81*, 503–527.

Fugate, M., Kinicki, A. J., & Ashforth, B. E. (2004). Employability: A psycho-social construct, its dimensions, and applications. *Journal of Vocational Behavior, 65,* 14–38.

Hinkin, R. T. (1999). A brief tutorial on the development of measures for use in survey questionnaires. *Organizational Research Methods, 1,* 104–121.

Jaccard, J., King, G., & Pomazal, R. (1977). Attitudes and behavior: An analysis of specificity of attitudinal predictors. *Human Relations, 30,* 817–824.

Jacobs, G., van Witteloostuijn, A., & Christe-Zeyse, J. (2013). A theoretical framework of organizational change. *Journal of Organizational Change Management, 26,* 772–792.

Lau, C. M. (1990). *A schematic approach to organizational change: The development of a change schema instrument.* Paper presented at the annual meeting of the Academy of Management.

Lau, C. M., & Woodman, R. W. (1995). Understanding organizational change: A schematic perspective. *Academy of Management Journal, 38,* 537–554.

Nunnally, J. C., & Bernstein, I. H. (1994). *Psychometric theory* (3rd ed.). New York: McGraw-Hill.

Oreg, S. (2003). Resistance to change: Developing an individual differences measure. *Journal of Applied Psychology, 88,* 680–693.

Oreg, S. (2006). Personality, context, and resistance to organizational change. *European Journal of Work and Organizational Psychology, 15,* 73–101.

Oreg, S., Vakola, M., & Armenakis, A. A. (2011). Change recipients' reactions to organizational change: A sixty-year review of quantitative studies. *Journal of Applied Behavioral Science, 47,* 461–524.

Paterson, J. M., & Cary, J. (2002). Organizational justice, change anxiety, and acceptance of downsizing: Preliminary tests of an AET-based model. *Motivation and Emotion, 26,* 83–103.

Patil, V., Singh, S., Mishra, S., & Todd Donavan, D. (2008). Efficient theory development and factor retention criteria: Abandon the 'eigenvalue greater than one' criterion. *Journal of Business Research, 61,* 162–170.

Piderit, S. K. (2000). Rethinking resistance and recognizing ambivelence: A multidimensional view of attitudes toward an organizational change. *Academy of Management Review, 25,* 783–794.

Raykov, T. (2004). Point and interval estimation of reliability for multiple-component measuring instruments via linear constraint covariance structure modeling. *Structural Equation Modeling: A Multidisciplinary Journal, 11*(3), 342–356.

Robinson, P. B., Stimpson, D. V., Huefner, J. C., & Hunt, H. K. (1991). An attitude approach to the prediction of entrepreneurship. *Entrepreneurship Theory and Practice, 15,* 13–31.

Tsaousis, I. (1999). The trait personality questionnaire: A Greek measure for the five factor model. *Personality and Individual Differences, 26*(2), 262–274.

Tsaousis, I. (2015, May). *The Work Personality Inventory (WPI): Development and psychometric properties.* Paper presented at the 15th Hellenic Conference of Psychological Research, University of Cyprus, Cyprus.

Vakola, M., Tsaousis, I., & Nikolaou, I. (2004). The role of emotional intelligence and personality variables on attitudes towards organizational change. *Journal of Managerial Psychology, 19,* 88–110.

Wanberg, C. R., & Banas, J. T. (2000). Predictors and outcomes of openness to changes in a reorganizing workplace. *Journal of Applied Psychology, 85,* 132–142.

Watkins, M. W. (2000). *Monte Carlo PCA for parallel analysis* [computer software]. State College, PA: Ed & Psych Associates.

Worthington, L. R. (2006). Scale development research: A content analysis and recommendations for best practices. *The Counseling Psychologist, 34,* 806–838.

PART III

Organizational-level and team-level facilitators of change

10

DESTRUCTIVE UNCERTAINTY

The toxic triangle, implicit theories and leadership identity during organizational change

Pedro Neves and Birgit Schyns

Introduction

The importance of leadership for effective and successful change management has long been recognized, particularly for the reduction of resistance of change (Coch & French, 1948; Kotter & Schlesinger, 1979, 2008), which has been identified as one of the main sources of failure (Szabla, 2007). In fact, behaviors such as involving members in decision-making processes or providing social and technical support have become increasingly central in the planning and enactment of change efforts. This is due to changes in the macroeconomic context itself, which made organizational change and adaptation more frequent, inevitable and unanticipated (Herscovitch & Meyer, 2002; Shin, Taylor, & Seo, 2012). This led researchers to argue – and rightly so – that the current main task for management is precisely the leadership of organizational change, as managers have to develop a new skillset that moves away from the traditional top-down approach and builds on bottom-up, shared, flexible and agile strategies that foster collaboration and cooperative problem-solving (Graetz, 2000).

This approach, that highlights the efforts undertaken by leaders (beyond their technical ability) preparing for and during change efforts, is common to the main models of change management. Armenakis and colleagues' (Armenakis & Harris, 2002; Armenakis, Harris, & Mossholder, 1993) model of readiness for change highlights the importance of how change leaders craft the change message, the influence strategies they use and their attributes, such as trustworthiness, credibility or expertise. Herscovitch and Meyer's (2002) model of commitment to organizational change also presupposes that the main antecedents of employees' commitment to any particular change effort revolve around effective leadership and trust in management (Meyer, Srinivas, Lal, & Topolnytsky, 2007). Authors more focused on providing practical guidance to managers (e.g., Kanter, Stein, & Jick, 1992; Kotter,

1995, 2007; Luecke, 2003) assume a similar perspective: if you want to effectively manage change, you should make sure leaders follow a certain number of steps which normally include creating a vision, establishing a sense of urgency and communicating effectively.

Despite having employees as the main target of all interventions, this "change agent-centric" (Ford, Ford, & D'Amelio, 2008) perspective focuses on the role of the leader and top-down processes. As By, Hughes and Ford (2016) recently recognized, two of change management's greatest myths are that (1) it is the individual leader that matters; and (2) leadership itself is enough to guarantee effective change. Although there is now a stronger appreciation that leadership is a combination of leaders, followers and situations (Hollander, 1978), the reigning models overemphasize the role of the leader in this process. This is not surprising, given the attractiveness of leadership as an explanation of organizational events. In his work on the Romance of Leadership, Meindl (1990) argued that "the faithful belief in leadership is itself beneficial in providing a sense of comfort and security, in reducing feelings of uncertainty, and in providing a sense of human agency and control" (p. 464).

Moreover, it presumes that what leaders report is an accurate interpretation of what actually takes place in reality while neglecting the possibility that multiple sense-making processes occur simultaneously. Consequently, if an individual resists change, it is either due to the poor strategy and/or influence tactics used by the leader (By et al., 2016) or due to that specific employee's inherent predisposition to resist any change effort (Oreg, 2003). However, a recent study conducted by Neves (2014) showed that the leader's behavior itself during change may be influenced by employees and the dynamics of the workplace. He found that reports of abusive supervision increased significantly for organizations that experienced downsizing but only among employees with a submissive profile (low core self-evaluations and co-worker support). These results suggest that change processes are influenced by leaders, followers and the context.

Thus, we build on this recent evidence to argue here that the failure of change efforts is a result of the lack of understanding of the dynamics of individual and collective resistance to change (Ford et al., 2008). While we agree that leaders matter for change management, the first aim of this chapter is to present an organizational change model that proposes a fuller understanding of individual and collective reactions to change, particularly the interplay between leaders, followers and context.

Moreover, while the overarching goal of change researchers is to help organizations effectively deal with change, one should also pay attention to the consequences of negative organizational practices, such as abusive supervision, ostracism and social exclusion, as well as deviant and counterproductive behaviors (Neider & Schriesheim, 2010). Given the pervasiveness of such behaviors, our second aim is to shift the focus to the toxic side of change management. Specifically, we argue that change efforts fail faster and more abruptly when there is a combination of factors: leaders enacting destructive behaviors, followers demonstrating a susceptible stance and the environment facilitating such behaviors. In that sense, our model is aligned with what Padilla, Hogan and Kaiser (2007) call "the toxic triangle".

Destructive uncertainty **133**

Finally, because we are discussing how these conditions negatively affect change management, our aim is to put forth some strategies that help organizations deal with these negative spirals of toxicity. We argue that the toxic triangle elements are not independent of each other and that granting-claiming processes and implicit theories (Shondrick & Lord, 2010) can serve as boundary conditions in the potentially toxic change process. If these expectations and role prototypes are developed and communicated highlighting principled rather than vicious elements, the toxic triangle might turn into a virtuous triangle.

In conclusion, our chapter contributes to the change management and leadership literatures by: (1) discussing how, in the context of organizational change, leaders affect and are affected by followers and context; (2) focusing on the understudied "dark side" of change management, and particularly the toxic triangle; and (3) integrating how implicit theories of what one should do are often as important as what one actually does.

Toxic triangle and change management

According to the toxic triangle framework, destructive leadership is the end result of a combination of factors pertaining to the leader, the follower and the surrounding context (Padilla et al., 2007) and, under certain organizational dynamics, can stem from the interactions between "seemingly good, well-intentioned professionals" (Fraher, 2016, p. 34).

We start with the most salient element of the triangle: the leader. Padilla et al. (2007) suggest that a number of characteristics of the leader contribute to destructive leadership. *Charisma* and charismatic leaders tend to be romanticized given their ability to articulate an inspirational vision and to foster the impression that their mission is of outstanding importance (Conger, Kanungo, & Menon, 2000). Charismatic leadership, which has often been suggested as a necessary leadership style for change (Conger et al., 2000), has the potential to be positive as well as destructive (House & Howell, 1992), as it might lead to a biased, exaggerated view of the leader's actions. In combination with Romance of Leadership, charisma might inadvertently contribute to the emergence of groupthink or create barriers to the discussion of ideas contradicting the leaders' view. Leaders' *need for power*, that is, their desire to have an impact on others (Litwin & Stringer, 1968), and *narcissism* (i.e., grandiosity, entitlement, dominance and superiority, Paulhus & Williams, 2002) contribute to destructive leadership, especially in times of change, as they will see change as an opportunity for self-promotion and to exert and extend their power. The two remaining themes, *negative life themes* and *ideology of hate* pertain to the leader's personal life story, rhetoric and worldview (Padilla et al., 2007). Such rhetoric is often linked to resistance to change (Oreg, 2006) and has the potential to cascade down to all employees in the organization. Moreover, recent research has shown that individuals with prior experiences of family undermining have a stronger tendency to engage in abusive supervisory behaviors as adults (Kiewitz et al., 2012).[1]

Followers also contribute to the destructive leadership process. Padilla et al. (2007) identify two separate profiles of followers that contribute to destructive leadership: conformers and colluders (see also Thoroughgood, Padilla, Hunter, & Tate, 2012). *Conformers* (lost souls, authoritarians and bystanders) are motivated to comply with destructive leaders due to fear about the consequences of not following. This might be pronounced during change processes as leaders might be seen as more influential during uncertainty. *Colluders* (acolytes and opportunists) actively participate and contribute to the destructive leadership process. In change processes, colluders might assume that their status and influence increases when they work with the leader.

Finally, conducive environments are characterized by four factors (Padilla et al., 2007): instability, perceived threat, cultural values and absence of checks and balances as well as institutionalization. *Instability* (which is a core characteristic of change) often increases the power of the leader (Waldman, Ramírez, House, & Puranam, 2001) and paves the way to justify harsher, more radical measures in order to restore the status quo – or create a new one. The *perception of imminent threat* also contributes to a favorable environment for destructive behaviors. When groups believe their future is in jeopardy, they are more likely to increase in-group strengthening behaviors (Wohl, Branscombe & Reysen, 2010). Again, this is particularly troublesome during change processes when the change itself can be regarded as a threat to identity, status, etc., and actions intended to defend such identity such as enacting unethical behaviors to protect the organization (unethical pro-organizational behavior; Umphress, Bingham, & Mitchell, 2010) may emerge.

The *cultural values* of the organization, for example the endorsement of (un) ethical values (Schaubroeck et al., 2012), and the broader social context determine which behaviors are expected, tolerated or endorsed. During change, values might be less clearly defined and, thus, there is more leeway for destructive behaviors. Finally, when there is *no system of checks and balances and institutionalization*, centralized systems where power lies in the hands of a few often emerge. Change can create power vacuums that bear the risk of a lack of check and balances. There is evidence showing the interaction between the three elements of the toxic triangle (e.g., Thoroughgood, Hunter, & Sawyer, 2011). This framework has been particularly useful to interpret complex cases such as the Penn State scandal (Powers, Judge, & Makela, 2016; Thoroughgood & Padilla, 2013).

In the context of change, it is important to look further at the dynamics involved in the interplay between the elements of the toxic triangle. We posit that each single element is not enough to drive a toxic change process. Indeed, the other elements can counteract the influence of one factor to prevent a toxic change process from occurring. For example, a narcissistic, power-seeking change leader will see his/ her ability to engage in destructive leadership behaviors diminished if confronted with followers who refuse to conform/ collude. Similarly, if this leader is part of an organization which embraces positive values, his/her behaviors will not be tolerated. The same principle of counteracting the emergence of a toxic change process applies to conducive change environments where a positive leader emerges or where followers engage in civil disobedience; or to a group of susceptible followers who report to a positive, effective leader or operate in a change context characterized by psychological safety, diversity and trust.

However, these three elements tend to feed off one another and create a vicious circle (Ashforth, 1994) which not only sustains the destructive process, but generates greater destructive potential. Interventions relating to each of the elements of the toxic triangle can neutralize the emergence of this vicious circle (Padilla et al., 2007). Organizations should (1) screen for the dark characteristics during leader selection and development; (2) empower and develop followers in order to reduce conformism; and (3) invest in the creation of a system of checks and balances. While each of these strategies is noteworthy, we argue that this approach is hardly sustainable in the long-term as it treats each component individually, rather than targeting the overall processes. We assume a Gestalt perspective of change management (Chidiac, 2013), and argue that an effective management of the change process requires a holistic understanding of what change means to the different stakeholders.

In this context, it is relevant to examine more closely what change means for the expectations towards leaders and followers and how those expectations can interact to facilitate or hinder a toxic change process. Specifically, we argue that implicit leadership theories (e.g., Eden & Leviatan, 1975) and implicit followership theories (e.g., Sy, 2010) can be specific to change processes and that those implicit theories influence the claiming and granting process of leadership (DeRue & Ashford, 2010; Shondrick & Lord, 2010) in the context of change.

Leaders and environments in change: ILTs

ILTs refer to prototypes, or cognitive structures or schemas specifying traits and behaviors expected from leaders, which are activated when encountering a "leader" (Lord & Maher, 1991). They are built on abstract representations of typical leaders as well as shaped by previous experiences with other individuals, as these experiences transfer from one leader to the another (Ritter & Lord, 2007).

ILTs serve as sense-making mechanisms (Shondrick & Lord, 2010), which guide the actions and expectations of both followers and leaders. According to the leadership categorization approach (Lord, Foti, & de Vader, 1984), ILT can differ in terms of their level of abstraction. The highest level of abstraction is leaders versus non-leaders. Lower levels comprise different types of leaders, such as political versus business leaders. We argue here that ILTs can also be specific to change, that is, that the ILT of leaders for change might differ from ILT of leaders in stable environments. For example, Offerman, Kennedy, and Wirtz's (1994) dedication and masculinity attributes might be seen as highly important during turbulent, uncertain periods, proposing a "we do whatever it takes" approach. Similarly, the perceived need for a highly charismatic leader might be enhanced during change, thus creating the idea that what is needed is someone extraordinary with exceptional powers and qualities (Levay, 2010) whose actions and influence processes should not be interfered with. On the other hand, some ILTs such as sensitivity might be seen as less relevant in that context (Offerman et al., 1994) as change often comes with difficult decisions and hard measures, making sensitivity seemingly less relevant. That is, leaders who fit the change leadership prototype better might be more likely to emerge in change processes but also might be exactly the ones potentially jeopardizing the process and contributing to a toxic change process.

Followers and environments in change: IFTs

Sy (2010) identified several follower prototypes and anti-prototypes in attempt to define implicit followership theories. Followership prototypes include industry, enthusiasm and being a good citizen, while the anti-prototypes emphasize conformity, insubordination and incompetence.

Similar to ILTs, IFTs might be change specific. For example, during particularly difficult moments, organizations might endorse followership roles that highlight a combination of industriousness and conformity (i.e., hardworking individuals that do not create problems by asking too many questions), which might induce an accepting stance in response to the demands of change. Moreover, and as Sy (2010) argued, the endorsement of either prototypical or antiprototypical roles might lead organizations to completely different assessments: organizations which sanction antiprototypical roles might engage in more punitive actions (e.g., be more severe if an individual has a hard time adjusting to the new practices), while those that sanction prototypical roles might focus more on the potential positives and be more lenient, which might unintentionally perpetuate certain behaviors. Since dissent is vital to reduce conformity risks and is often a form of productive resistance (Cunha, Neves, Clegg, & Rego, 2015), other stakeholders might fail to recognize the potential of followers who are less congruent with their own (and those endorsed by the organization) IFTs in a change context.

Leaders and followers in change: claiming-granting process

Drawing on a social perspective of identity, DeRue and Ashford (2010) proposed a model of identity construction. The process builds on the claiming (actions that assert one's identity as leader or follower) and granting (actions that bestows an identity as a leader or follower) of roles and their underlying identities, where "claims are reciprocated by grants and grants are reciprocated by claims" (DeRue & Ashford, 2010, p. 628). Claiming and granting is based on ILTs in the sense that leaders who think that they fit their own ILTs are more likely to claim a leader identity. Those who fit others' ILTs are more likely to be granted leadership. During change, as we argued before, ILTs and IFTs might emerge that are different from those in stable environments which then leads to claiming and granting based on new ILTs/IFTs.

The claiming-granting processes involved in change have a particular relevance to the development of the toxic leader-follower relationship. For example,

FIGURE 10.1 Boundary conditions for the influence of the toxic triangle during change

susceptible followers may be more likely to grant leadership to a destructive leader and claim the identity of a submissive follower as they are afraid to disagree or raise questions (conformers) or claim the identity of an accomplice because they see personal gains in it (colluders). Destructive leaders might take advantage of the context of uncertainty and claim their identity as (unquestionable) leaders; while granting followers a more passive role in order to better manage the situation into the direction they desire. Thus, the claiming and granting process during change might encourage destructive leadership processes.

Consequently, we can assume that there are implicit theories concerning what constitutes a great change leader/follower/environment which serve as benchmarks individuals use to interpret expectations towards themselves and others. Our framework is presented in Figure 10.1.

Breaking the toxic change spiral

In order to break the reinforcing link between destructive leaders, susceptible followers and conducive environments of change, organizations should signal that all leadership and followership behavior has to be grounded in the broader organizational context (Lord, Brown, Harvey, & Hall, 2001) and that certain behaviors are sanctioned while others are severely punished. That is, organizations should make existing ILTs and IFTs salient in the change process so that role claiming and granting can happen based on what is desired, not on stakeholders' assumptions.

Organizations should invest in modeling implicit theories or explicit roles related to how they expect leaders and followers to behave in a change event. Here, a strong organizational culture might be a path to help individuals endorse a leader/follower theory that is aligned with the organization's core values. Organizations should highlight the motivational rewards for engaging in the claiming and granting of positive leadership roles as well as proactive, critical and engaged follower roles during change (DeRue & Ashford, 2010). Instrumental rewards like promotions, bonuses, power and status or even higher tolerance for risk taking and creative thinking (for example by creating a problem-solving team whose goal is to put forth alternative solutions for the problems that stem out of the change process) should be clearly attached to positive identities as leaders and followers.

Organizations should also pay attention to the development of their formal and informal structures, particularly during the transitional identity stage. During a change process, individuals might find themselves in a liminal state where the old self is no longer viable and the new self is yet to emerge, often leading to the development of transitional identities (Clark, Gioia, Ketchen, & Thomas, 2010). These transitional identities are fundamental for the organization (and its members) to move forward and help shape the ILTs/IFTs linked to change processes. Because individuals tend to grant leadership roles to others in supervisory positions, the expectations associated with leadership roles within a specific social structure, specifically regarding the use of power and status, should be clear and attached to the enactment of positive behaviors. We consequently argue that implicit theories within the claiming and granting of leadership during change can serve as a boundary condition that inhibits the toxic relational process from spiraling and might even transform it into a virtuous process, which should help increase commitment to change.

In this chapter, we highlighted the relevance of the toxic triangle in change processes. We outlined how leaders, followers and context are interrelated and how implicit theories might perpetuate rather than mitigate a negative spiral of toxic change. Our discussion will hopefully contribute to change management by signaling that organizations need to assume a holistic perspective and pay attention to all three elements in an integrated fashion to create better and more sustainable change processes.

Note

1 This effect was significant only for supervisors low in self-control.

References

Armenakis, A., & Harris, S. (2002). Crafting a change message to create transformational readiness. *Journal of Organizational Change Management*, *15*, 169–183.

Armenakis, A., Harris, S., & Mossholder, K. (1993). Creating readiness for organizational change. *Human Relations*, *46*(3), 1–23.

Ashforth, B. (1994). Petty tyranny in organizations. *Human Relations*, *47*, 755–778.

By, R., Hughes, M., & Ford, J. (2016). Change leadership: Oxymoron and myths. *Journal of Change Management*, *16*, 8–17.

Chidiac, M. (2013). An organisational change approach based on Gestalt psychotherapy theory and practice. *Journal of Organizational Change Management*, *26*, 458–474.

Clark, S. M., Gioia, D. A., Ketchen, D. J., & Thomas, J. B. (2010). Transitional identity as a facilitator of organizational identity change during a merger. *Administrative Science Quarterly, 55*, 397–438.

Coch, L., & French, J. R. P., Jr. (1948). Overcoming resistance to change. *Human Relations, 1*, 512–532.

Conger, J. A., Kanungo, R. N., & Menon, J. T. (2000). Charismatic leadership and follower effects. *Journal of Organizational Behavior, 21*, 747–767.

Cunha, M. P., Neves, P., Clegg, S. R., & Rego, A. (2015). Tales of the unexpected: Discussing improvisational learning. *Management Learning, 46*, 511–529.

DeRue, D. S., & Ashford, S. J. (2010). Who will lead and who will follow? A social process of leadership identity construction in organizations. *Academy of Management Review, 35*, 627–647.

Eden, D., & Leviatan, U. (1975). Implicit leadership theory as a determinant of the factor structure underlying supervisory behavior scales. *Journal of Applied Psychology, 60*, 736–741.

Ford, J. D., Ford, L. W., & D'Amelio, A. (2008). Resistance to change: The rest of the story. *Academy of Management Journal, 33*, 362–377.

Fraher, A. L. (2016). A toxic triangle of destructive leadership at Bristol Royal Infirmary: A study of organizational Munchausen syndrome by proxy. *Leadership, 12*, 34–52.

Graetz, F. (2000). Strategic change leadership. *Management Decision, 38*, 550–562.

Herscovitch, L., & Meyer, J. (2002). Commitment to organizational change: Extension of a three-component model. *Journal of Applied Psychology, 87*, 474–487.

Hollander, E. P. (1978). *Leadership dynamics.* New York: Free Press.

House, R. J., & Howell, J. M. (1992). Personality and charismatic leadership. *The Leadership Quarterly, 3*, 81–108.

Kanter, R. M., Stein, B. A., & Jick, T. D. (1992). *The challenge of organizational change.* New York: The Free Press.

Kiewitz, C., Restubog, S. L., Zagenczyk, T. J., Scott, K. D., Garcia, P., & Tang, R. T. (2012). Sins of the parents: Self-control as a buffer between supervisors' previous experience of family undermining and subordinates' perceptions of abusive supervision. *The Leadership Quarterly, 23*, 869–882.

Kotter, J. P. (1995, 2007). Leading change: Why transformation efforts fail. *Harvard Business Review, 73*, 59–67.

Kotter, J. P., & Schlesinger, L. A. (1979, 2008). Choosing strategies for change. *Harvard Business Review, 57*, 106–114.

Levay, C. (2010). Charismatic leadership in resistance to change. *The Leadership Quarterly, 21*, 127–143.

Litwin, G. H., & Stringer, R. A. (1968). *Motivation and organizational climate.* Boston, MA: Harvard Business School Press.

Lord, R. G., Brown, D. J., Harvey, J. L., & Hall, R. J. (2001). Contextual constraints on prototype generation and their multilevel consequences for leadership perceptions. *The Leadership Quarterly, 12*, 311–338.

Lord, R. G., Foti, R. J., & De Vader, C. L. (1984). A test of leadership categorization theory: Internal stricture, information processing, and leadership perceptions. *Organizational Behavior and Human Performance, 34*, 343–378.

Lord, R. G., & Maher, K. J. (1991). *Leadership and information processing: Linking perceptions and performance.* Boston, MA: Routledge.

Luecke, R. (2003). *Managing change and transition.* Boston, MA: Harvard Business School Press.

Meindl, J. R. (1990). On leadership: An alternative to the conventional wisdom. In B. M. Staw & L. L. Cummings (Eds.), *Research in organizational behavior* (Vol. 12, pp. 159–203). Greenwich, CT: JAI Press.

Meyer, J. P., Srinivas, E. S., Lal, J. B., & Topolnytsky, L. (2007). Employee commitment and support for an organizational change: Test of the three-component model in two cultures. *Journal of Occupational and Organizational Psychology, 80*, 185–211.

Neider, L., & Schriesheim, C. (2010). *Research in management: The "Dark" side of management* (Vol. 8). Greenwich, CT: Information Age Publishing.

Neves, P. (2014). Taking it out on survivors: Submissive employees, downsizing, and abusive supervision. *Journal of Occupational and Organizational Psychology, 87*, 507–534.

Offerman, L. R., Kennedy, J. K., & Wirtz, P. W. (1994). Implicit leadership theories: Content, structure, and generalizability. *The Leadership Quarterly, 5*, 43–58.

Oreg, S. (2003). Resistance to change: Developing an individual differences measure. *Journal of Applied Psychology, 88*, 680–693.

Oreg, S. (2006). Personality, context, and resistance to organizational change. *European Journal of Work and Organizational Psychology, 15*, 73–101.

Padilla, A., Hogan, R., & Kaiser, R. B. (2007). The toxic triangle: Destructive leaders, susceptible followers, and conducive environments. *The Leadership Quarterly, 18*, 176–194.

Paulhus, D. L, & Williams, K. M. (2002). The Dark Triad of personality: Narcissism, Machiavellianism, and psychopathy. *Journal of Research in Personality, 36*, 556–563.

Powers, S., Judge, L. W., & Makela, C. (2016). An investigation of destructive leadership in a Division I intercollegiate athletic department: Follower perceptions and reactions. *International Journal of Sports Science & Coaching, 11*, 297–311.

Ritter, B. A., & Lord, R. G. (2007). The impact of previous leaders on the evaluation of new leaders: An alternative to prototype matching. *Journal of Applied Psychology, 92*, 1683–1695.

Schaubroeck, J. M., Hannah, S. T., Avolio, B. J., Kozlowski, S. W. J., Lord, R. G., Treviño, L. K., Dimotakis, N., & Peng, A. C. (2012). Embedding ethical leadership within and across organization levels. *Academy of Management Journal, 55*, 1053–1078.

Shin, J., Taylor, M., & Seo, M. (2012). Resources for change: The relationships of organizational inducements and psychological resilience to employees' attitudes and behaviors toward organizational change. *Academy of Management Journal, 55*, 727–748.

Shondrick, S. J., & Lord, R. G. (2010). Implicit leadership and followership theories: Dynamic structures for leadership perceptions, memory, and leader-follower processes. *International Review of Industrial and Organizational Psychology, 25*, 1–33.

Sy, T. (2010). What do you think of followers? Examining the content, structure, and consequences of implicit followership theories. *Organizational Behavior and Human Decision Processes, 113*, 73–84.

Szabla, D. B. (2007). A multidimensional view of resistance to organizational change: Exploring cognitive, emotional, and intentional responses to planned change across perceived change leadership strategies. *Human Resource Development Quarterly, 18*, 525–558.

Thoroughgood, C. N., Hunter, S. T., & Sawyer, K. B. (2011). Bad apples, bad barrels, and broken followers? An empirical examination of contextual influences on follower perceptions and reactions to aversive leadership. *Journal of Business Ethics, 100*, 647–672.

Thoroughgood, C. N., & Padilla, A. (2013). Destructive leadership and the Penn State scandal: A toxic triangle perspective. *Industrial and Organizational Psychology, 6*, 144–149.

Thoroughgood, C. N., Padilla, A., Hunter, S. T., & Tate, B. W. (2012). The susceptible circle: A taxonomy of followers associated with destructive leadership. *The Leadership Quarterly, 23*, 897–917.

Umphress, E. E., Bingham, J. B., & Mitchell, M. S. (2010). Unethical behavior in the name of the company: The moderating effect of organizational identification and positive reciprocity beliefs on unethical pro-organizational behavior. *Journal of Applied Psychology, 95*, 769–780.

Waldman, D. A., Ramírez, G. G., House, R. J., & Puranam, P. (2001). Does leadership matter? CEO leadership attributes and profitability under conditions of perceived environmental uncertainty. *Academy of Management Journal, 44*, 134–143.

Wohl, M. J. A., Branscombe, N. R., & Reysen, S. (2010). Perceiving your group's future to be in jeopardy: Extinction threat induces collective angst and the desire to strengthen the ingroup. *Personality and Social Psychology Bulletin, 36*, 898–910.

11

ORGANIZATIONAL CHANGE AND HEALTH

The specific role of job insecurity

Birgit Thomson and Alexandra Michel

Introduction

Organizations undergoing structural change often fail to strategically, incrementally and progressively introduce changes. Instead, management often chooses rapid, discontinuous, abrupt, drastic and short-termed restructuring transformations. Reorganizations such as downsizing, mergers and acquisitions, often include strategic short-term efficiency orientation, usually related to layoffs (Probst, 2003). Although organizational prosperity and survival doubtlessly require adaptation, changes can thwart the intended outcomes by having unintended negative impacts on employees. Indeed, an estimated 50% to 80% of restructuring measures miscarry (Balogun & Hailey, 2004; Cartwright & Schoenberg, 2006) because management fails to sufficiently consider indirect and undesirable effects on work attitudes, work behavior, well-being and health (Brown & Humphreys, 2003; Rigotti & Otto, 2012).

Even though change is stressful, change management research has rarely studied how organizational change can generate health-related outcomes (Wilson, 2010). However, a few researchers are beginning to consider the impact of change-related stressors on employee mental and physical health as well as well-being (Kieselbach et al., 2009; Michel & Gonzáles-Morales, 2013). If organizations are to be prosperous and enduring, they must recognize their moral obligations to manage restructuring soundly by promoting employee health and well-being in that process, for a workforce that is less likely to show absenteeism (Hanebuth, Meinel, & Fischer, 2006), presenteeism (Darr & Johns, 2008) or turnover (Moore, Grunberg, & Greenberg, 2006).

One of the most salient stressors – if not the most important – in organizational restructuring is *job insecurity* (JI) (De Witte, 1999; Sverke, Hellgren, & Näswall, 2002). Quantitative JI captures employee uncertainties about whether they will keep their jobs (Heaney, Israel, & House, 1994); qualitative JI depicts the value employees

Organizational change and health **143**

place on various job characteristics (De Witte, 1999; De Witte, De Cuyper, Handaja, Sverke, Näswall, & Hellgren, 2010). Most studies focus on quantitative rather than qualitative JI (De Witte et al., 2010). JI definitions include two common subjective perceptions: (1) that one might face unemployment and (2) that JI is undesirable and stressful even if it offers new chances or resources. As JI is the perceived threat of a fundamental and unfavorable encounter, it categorizes in accordance with the most prominent stress models (Karasek & Theorell, 1990; Lazarus & Folkman, 1984; Siegrist, 1996) as an important stressor.

Against this background, our objective in this chapter is to discuss the well-being and health impact of drastic organizational change using JI as a prominent example for important stressors in the course of change. First, we introduce the healthy organizational change model (HOC-M) building the theoretical background for this chapter. It considers perceived job insecurity (JI) as one of the most prominent work stressor during organizational change. Next, we present results based on a scoping review about the impact of JI on health-related outcomes. We conclude our chapter with recommendations for managers at the strategic and workplace level as well as Human Resource Management.

Change and health

In 1948, the World Health Organization (WHO) defined health as "a state of complete physical, mental and social well-being and not merely the absence of disease or infirmity". In 1984, the WHO went beyond that approach and revised the definition to identify health as a resource for living rather than a mere temporary state. Thus health was defined as:

> the extent to which an individual or group is able to realize aspirations and satisfy needs, and to change or cope with the environment. Health is a resource for everyday life, not the objective of living; it is a positive concept, emphasizing social and personal resources, as well as physical capacities.
>
> *(WHO, 1984)*

Health impact of restructuring: the healthy organizational change model

Restructuring and particularly downsizing can be stressful and thus may impact employees' mental health (Mohr, 2000; Probst, 2003), physical health (Kivimäki, Vahtera, Pentti, & Ferrie, 2000; Kivimäki et al., 2001; Kivimäki et al., 1997; Vahtera et al., 2004) and well-being (De Cuyper, De Witte, Vander Elst, & Handaja, 2010; Kivimäki, Vahtera, Elovainio, Pentti, & Virtanen, 2003; Köper, Seiler, & Beerheide, 2012). Accordingly, the HOC-M was devised to integrate stress and organizational theories and to explain why change processes can be stressful and negatively affect employees' mental and physical health and well-being (Michel & Gonzáles-Morales, 2013). The model describes factors that promote and hinder health-related outcomes in times of organizational change (Figure 11.1).

The HOC-M draws on various stress theories (Demerouti, Bakker, Nachreiner, & Schaufeli, 2001; Karasek & Theorell, 1990; Lazarus & Folkman, 1984; Siegrist, 1996; Weiss & Cropanzano, 1996), with particular focus on the well-established transactional stress theory (Lazarus & Folkman, 1984) that explains how stressors can cause adverse behavioral, affective and physical reactions. Cognitive appraisals and resulting emotions are the central mediators that cause stressors to be associated with health outcomes (Lazarus, 2006). First, individuals primarily appraise whether events or situations are challenging, threatening or irrelevant. Applying the cognitive appraisal process to the change context, individuals might appraise change as a threat to job security or psychological certainty (e.g. Ashford, 1988, Hellgren, Sverke, & Isaksson, 1999). Then they will make secondary appraisals about whether they have sufficient organizational, social and individual resources to cope (Lazarus & Folkman, 1984). For example, during organizational change, employees might estimate how much control they have in the change process (Paulsen et al., 2005) or whether they are rather subject to uncertainties. They will consider various coping options, including changing or accepting the situation, seeking more information or acting impulsively (Folkman, Lazarus, Gruen, & DeLongis, 1986).

Cognitive appraisal, coping actions and reappraisal processes will include one or more stress-related emotions, such as anxiety and fear, which then deteriorate health by weakening immune resources and thus evoking somatic changes that encourage acute or chronic illness (Lazarus & Folkman, 1984). Thus, the HOC-M suggests that individuals can appraise organizational change as a stressor which then can "influence health related outcomes" (Michel & Gonzáles-Morales, 2013, p. 71).

Moreover, based on the job-demand resources model (JDR-M, Demerouti et al., 2001), appraisal processes, resources, individual characteristics, as well as job and organization demands all determine how organizational change impacts health (Michel & Gonzáles-Morales, 2013). In line with affective events theory (AET, Weiss & Cropanzano, 1996), employees appraise whether work events are meaningful and relevant. They react accordingly depending on characteristics of the change event (i.e. type and frequency), and characteristics of the change process (i.e. participation and communication) (Michel & Gonzáles-Morales, 2013).

Finally, to provide a comprehensive framework, the HOC-M also considers social exchange (Blau, 1964; Eisenberger, Huntington, Hutchinson, & Sowa, 1986; Greenberg, 1987; Rousseau, 1989): the "voluntary action of an individual in favour of another person or an organization . . . motivated by individuals' expectations of reciprocity" (Michel & Gonzáles-Morales, 2013, p. 80, 81). For example, if employees perceive that change processes are fair and that they have organizational support, they are likely to use control-oriented coping strategies and perceive that the change will be efficacious. Thus, the HOC-M proposes that "social exchange characteristics mediate the relationship between organizational change and its appraisal" (Michel & Gonzáles-Morales, 2013, p. 80).

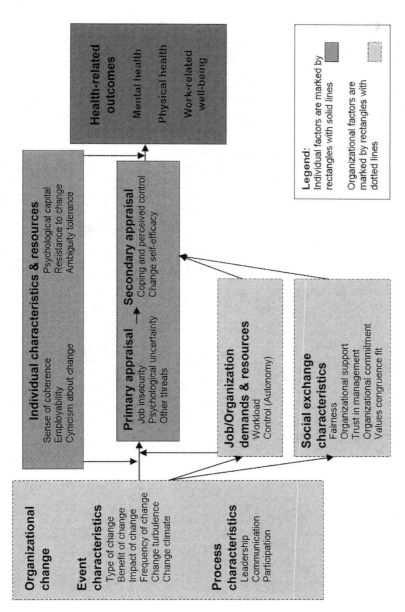

FIGURE 11.1 The health organizational change (HOC-M) model that describes promoting and hindering factors for employees' health-related outcomes in organizational change

Note: The figure of the HOC-M model was originally printed in Michel and Gonzalés-Morales (2013, p. 71).

We refer to previous publications on the HOC-M to gather detailed information about the literature background and the theoretical and empirical foundations for the model (Michel & Gonzáles-Morales, 2013). As an overall framework, HOC-M shows how organizational change involves JI, psychological uncertainty and other perceived threats in turn being related via secondary appraisals processes of coping to mental and physical health as well as well-being. Next, we specifically focus on JI and its relation to health and well-being because drastic organizational changes are in the majority of cases related to layoffs and accordingly JI (Eurofound, 2012). Hence JI has received a considerable and increasing amount of research attention in recent years (Kim & Knesebeck, 2015).

Job insecurity, health and well-being during organizational change: a systematic review

Empirical and theoretical research (Cheng & Chan, 2008; Sverke et al., 2002) indicates that JI is one of the most salient stressors during organizational change, if not the most important. In line with the HOC-M we chose JI as a prominent example in order to depict how change is related to health and well-being impact. We conducted a scoping review (k = 223) to summarize the current state of research on JI and health to provide evidence for the HOC-M, especially the proposed relation between JI and health-related outcomes.

Theory

Our review showed that most research uses theoretical approaches that are consistent with theories underlying the HOC-M. Change stressors mediate the process starting with a change decision and then affect the employees´ actual working conditions, including objective job uncertainty and JI (Keim, Landis, Pierce, & Earnest, 2014; Köper & Gerstenberg, 2016). The studies in our review referred to theories, which focus on the meaningfulness of work (Jahoda, 1982), on stress reactions (Ashford, 1988; Lazarus & Folkman, 1984; Karasek & Theorell, 1990; Siegrist, 1996) and on social exchange theories (Colquitt, 2001; Rousseau, 1989). The latent deprivation model (Jahoda, 1982) explains that work is essential to life: it satisfies basic social and economic needs. It generates income, enables social contacts and social identity, and contributes substantially to the development of individuals and their personal resources such as vocational and social skills (Rosenstiel, 2014). If individuals are at risk of losing their jobs, they can feel great fear and stress that keeps them from applying effective coping strategies that might resolve the situation (Ashford, 1988; Hartley, Jacobson, Klandermans, & Van Vuuren, 1991; Joelson & Wahlquist, 1987; Lazarus & Folkman, 1984). Like all stressors, JI is related to strain and negative health effects (Lazarus & Folkman, 1984; Siegrist, 1996). Indeed, a recent meta-analysis showed that JI is even more powerful than actual unemployment for being significantly associated with depressive symptoms (Kim & Knesebeck, 2015). The HOC-M explains why perceived JI potentially impairs health and well-being. If employees appraise organizational restructuring initiatives as a threat, perceptions of JI are likely. Although drastic change is not the only reason for perceived JI, it is the dominant one. Mohr (2000) for instance could identify JI as the strongest stressor compared to other significant change threats such as increased workload, concentration of demands or problems in work organization.

To explain restructuring impacts, the HOC-M and other scholars' research also draw on social exchange approaches (Blau, 1964; Bernhard-Oettel, De Cuyper, Schreurs, & De Witte, 2011; De Cuyper & De Witte, 2006; Rigotti, De Cuyper, De Witte, Korek, & Mohr, 2009; Vander Elst, Bosman, De Cuyper, Stouten, & De Witte, 2013; Vander Elst, De Cuyper, Baillien, Niesen, & De Witte, 2014) explaining that parties such as employers and employees have obligations to one another. Social exchange includes the mutual trust that if one party provides benefits, the other party will reciprocate in a long-term cycle (Blau, 1964). A prominent example of social exchange is the psychological contract theory explaining that negative consequences result if employers fail to adhere to their obligations and thus break or violate employees´ expectations or promises made to them (Morrison & Robinson, 1997; Robinson, 1996; Rousseau, 1989). If employees perceive that the employer has failed to honor salient contents of the psychological contract, their work attitudes, work behavior, health and well-being will be negatively affected (Coyle-Shapiro & Parzefall, 2008; Rigotti et al., 2009). Among the central contract contents is job security (Morrison & Robinson, 1997). Without it, the contract is breached or even violated, which then can have impact on emotions, well-being and health (Rigotti et al., 2009).

Method

Literature search

We conducted a systematic literature search to identify original and peer reviewed studies published in English or German. In line with the aims of a scoping review we focused our search not only on studies explicitly including JI in the change context, but also on studies including JI and health and well-being outcomes. The search was restricted to original papers, dissertations and books published between January 2000 and October 2014 featuring analyses of quantitative perceived JI and effects on mental, physical or general health. To identify studies, we used MEDLINE (via PubMed), PsychARTICLES, PSYNDEX, PsychINFO and EconLit databases using the following string: *job insecurity* OR *arbeitsplatzunsicherheit* OR *arbeitsplatzsicherheit* OR *job security* OR *employment uncertainty* OR *job uncertainty*.

Inclusion/exclusion criteria and data extraction

We included studies that referred to subjective quantitative JI, rather than, for example, unemployment rates, downsizing, contractual insecurity and part-time work. In line with the assumptions of the HOC-M, we decided to focus on JI and

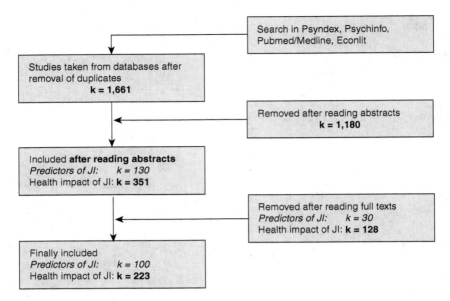

FIGURE 11.2 Flow diagram for studies included

health-related outcomes rather than on attitudinal or behavioral aspects such as task commitment, organizational commitment, organizational citizenship behavior, turnover intentions, work satisfaction, performance or organizational outcomes. In turn our results can be a comprehensive test of the proposed HOC-M assumption. Given the subjective nature of stress or perceived contract breach, objective measures for the risk of getting unemployed would not have been suitable for this purpose. We included studies from the year 2000 on, because most studies regarding the impact of JI were published after 2000. This is due to the significant increase of organizational downsizing from the 1990s on (de Witte, 1999). Two reviewers discussed and reached consensus regarding agreements about studies to be included or excluded. Figure 11.2 depicts a flow diagram explaining the study selection criteria and the corresponding steps in the selection process.

Categories of health-related outcomes

We meta-classified reported health outcomes under the categories *mental* and *physical* health largely according to the International Classification of Diseases and Related Health Problems (ICD-10) to make our results comparable with relevant national health surveys (WHO, 2011) and relevant meta-analyses (Cheng & Chan, 2008; Sverke et al., 2002). Many studies also measured unspecified self-estimated general health, including absenteeism and presenteeism, so we added this category. The health outcomes considered did not represent clinical diagnoses but were based on self-reports. Table 11.1 summarizes the health outcomes mentioned in the included studies.

Organizational change and health **149**

TABLE 11.1 Outcome variables

meta category	category	outcome examples used in included studies
mental health	psychological well-being	affective well-being, negative affective reactions, irritation, anxiety, stress, strain
	burnout/(dis-)engagement	exhaustion, lack of vigor, disengagement, need for recovery, fatigue, cynicism, depersonalization
	psychological symptoms (ICD F00–36)	psychosomatic symptoms, mental health disorders, depressive symptoms/major depression, psychological symptoms, insomnia, social phobia
physical health	cardiovascular symptoms (ICD I00–99)	coronary heart disease, cardiovascular disease, heart failure, stroke, CV mortality, myocardial infection, hypertension
	musculoskeletal symptoms (ICD M00-M99)	musculoskeletal disorders, low back pain, neck pain, shoulder pain
	endocrine, nutritional and metabolic diseases (ICD) and diseases of the digestive system (ICD K00–93)	endocrine, nutritional and metabolic diseases: obesity, diabetes, cortisol diseases of the digestive system: stomach ache, gastroenteritis
	infectious diseases (ICD A1–99 and B 1–99)	HIV, common cold, flu
	other diseases	IDC groups J, L, G, N, S, T, D
general health	self-estimated general health	physical well-being, chronical diseases, immune problems, poor work ability
	health behavior	prolonged sick leave, time to return to work, presentism, smoking, misuse of alcohol and drugs

Source: Köper & Gerstenberg, 2016, p. 454.

Results

In our review we considered 223 studies on the relationship of JI and the various health outcomes described in Table 11.1. The included studies were by majority not specifically designed to analyze JI in the context of change. Yet, in a recent meta-analysis about the determinants of JI, change could be identified as a prominent aspect causing JI (Keim, Landis, Pierce, & Earnest, 2014). In line with the HOC-M restructurings such as changes of the work organization (Armstrong-Stassen, Wagar, & Cattaneo, 2004; Bernhard & Krause, 2014; Blackmore & Kuntz, 2011), downsizings (Allen, Freeman, Russell, Reizenstein, & Rentz, 2001; Campbell-Jamison, Worrall, & Cooper, 2001; Moore et al., 2004, 2006; Murphy & Pepper, 2003), privatization (Struwig & von Scheers, 2004), outsourcing (Melvin, 2006) and mergers/ acquisitions (Collins, 2005; Van Knippenberg, & Van Leeuwen, 2001) predicted JI. Other determinants such as increase of atypical work contracts (temporary work, temporary agency work etc.) are closely related to change (Bernhard-Oettel, Rigotti, Clinton, & de Jong, 2013) as they are − comparably to downsizing or outsourcing − strategic attempts to gain more cost flexibility and productivity.

Most of the studies (135) were cross-sectional and conducted in Europe (115), followed by the United States (25), Canada (19), Australia (12) and Asia (12). Despite our wide inclusion of reviews from various types of literature, the vast majority (94%) were published in scientific journals. We included both primary and epidemiological studies resulting in a mean sample size of N = 1188. The mean age was 40 years with 50.2% female persons. As regards industry sectors or specific job groups, the samples were predominantly mixed so that specific findings for industries or jobs cannot be reported. We found more JI associations with mental (250) rather than physical (110) or general health (96). This alone is not necessarily an indicator that there are stronger links between JI and mental as opposed to physical health. As we included studies even if they measured only one of the relevant outcome criteria (see inclusion criteria) this difference might have to do with a research bias.

JI was significantly correlated with mental health (76.6 % or reported results), followed by general health (70.1%), and physical health (43.6%). The results for mental health were most consistent; JI was significantly associated with negative mental health in about 70% of the associations, and with physical health in about 43% of the associations. Likewise, the associations were strongest for mental health. We found mean correlations of about for mental and for both physical and general health.

Within the mental health category, most correlations referred to psychological and behavioral disorders (99) based on the ICD diagnosis groups F00-F99. 78 correlations referred to psychological well-being and 58 to burnout. Most correlations for physical health referred to musculoskeletal diseases (MSD) (43) and cardiovascular diseases (CVD) (20). Effect sizes were small ($r < .3$ / Cohen, 1992) but were stronger for JI and mental health as opposed to physical and general health. Table 11.2 depicts the mean correlations for JI and the various health categories, the range of correlations and the underlying number of correlations.

The studies we analyzed were of low or medium methodological quality. Only 124 of 453 associations (27%) reported Cronbach's alpha for JI and the various health measures. Often the researchers measured JI with only one item, particularly in epidemiological studies.

Organizational change and health **151**

TABLE 11.2 Mean correlations for JI and various health outcomes

Outcome variable	r_{ij}	Spread	Based on k correlations
Mental health/well-being			
overall	0.19	0.002–0.44	136
mental health impairment unspecified (captured as "mental health"	0.22	0.19–0.28	9
psychological/ affective well-being impairment	0.17	0.01–0.43	46
burnout	0.19	0.05–0.41	40
psychological and behavioral disorders (IDC)	0.20	0.002–0.44	41
Physical health			
overall	0.13	0.0033–0.32	31
General health/well-being			
overall	0.12	0.02–0.43	38
Self-estimated general health and well-being impairment	0.14	0.02–0.43	25
Negative health behavior	0.11	0.04–0.19	12

We also extracted information in terms of practical recommendations. Evidence-focused journal articles rarely considered explicit work design recommendations. Of the 223 studies included in our review, only 95 recommended work design measures. In most cases (59%), the authors gave unspecific practical recommendations, mostly focused on general stress reduction. Some recommendations corresponded with national labor market or health policies rather than with organizational issues. We found no intervention studies which specifically focused on the evaluation of work design measures mitigating the impact of JI during restructuring.

The HOC-M suggests that organizational demands and resources as well as individual resources can moderate the negative relation between JI and health-related outcomes (Michel & Gonzáles-Morales, 2013). Thus in our scoping review we also extracted information referring to moderation analysis results. Few studies included organizational demands (e.g. contract conditions/Bernhard-Oettel et al., 2013; Kirves, De Cuyper, Kinnunen, & Nätti, 2011; Mauno, Kinnunen, Mäkikangas, & Nätti, 2005; Rigotti et al., 2009). Some other studies considered organizational resources

152 Birgit Thomson and Alexandra Michel

(i.e., control, Kinnunen, Mauno & Siltaloppi, 2010; Schreurs, van Emmerik & De Witte, 2010; organizational culture, Probst & Lawler, 2006; co-worker/supervisor social support, Mohr, 2000; Plaisier et al., 2007). Results reveal that the negative relation between JI and health is stronger for employees with a permanent contract than for employees with a temporary contract (Bernhard-Oettel et al., 2013; Kirves et al., 2011; Mauno et al., 2005; Rigotti et al., 2009) as permanently employed workers expect job security as salient part of their psychological contract (Robinson & Morrison, 2000). In terms of organizational culture Probst and Lawler (2006) found that for workers in organizations characterized by individualism the association between JI and negative affective reactions was lower compared to organizations with collectivistic cultures. Social support by supervisors and colleagues can buffer the impact of JI on negative affective reactions (Mohr, 2000) and depressive disorders (Plaisier et al., 2007).

Other studies evaluated also moderating effects of individual resources, e.g. employability (Mohr, 2000); self-efficacy (Lo Presti & Nonnis, 2012) or external locus of control (Näswall, Sverke & Hellgren, 2005). In line with the HOC-M (Michel & Gonzáles-Morales, 2013) these resources buffered the negative relation between JI and health-related outcomes. The identification of these organizational factors is particularly useful with respect to designing and evaluating organizational measures that may reduce the negative impact of JI.

Discussion

For this study, we based our assumptions on the HOC-M (Michel & Gonzáles-Morales, 2013), which indicates that organizational change will be associated with unfavorable well-being and health impact. The review findings confirm the HOC-M´s theoretical assumptions, and demonstrate that change results in work stressors, such as JI (Keim et al., 2014; Köper & Gerstenberg, 2016). JI as the most detrimental stressor in change (Mohr, 2000) is consistently and significantly related to health-related outcomes. We analyzed 223 mostly cross-sectional studies published between 2000 and 2014. In line with the HOC-M the included studies on JI and health drew on various stress models (Demerouti et al., 2001; Karasek & Theorell, 1990; Lazarus & Folkman, 1984; Siegrist, 1996) and social exchange concepts, particularly the Psychological Contract Theory (Rousseau, 1989).

We categorized health outcomes as (1) mental health/mental well-being, (2) physical health and (3) unspecified general health categories. Most entries fit the mental health category, particularly appropriate to the F00-F99 ICD classification described as "mental and behavioural disorders", followed by "impairments of psychological (affective) wellbeing and burnout". Within the physical health category, JI was mostly associated with musculoskeletal disorders and cardiovascular diseases.

JI was consistently and significantly associated with all outcome categories (see Table 11.2). The associations between JI and mental health were the strongest and the most consistent compared to the other outcome categories, that is to say, physical health and general health assessments. Transactional stress theory (Lazarus &

Folkman, 1984), which is central to the HOC-M, would predict that a stressor such as JI first causes strain and then psychological impairment, while actual physical impact occurs after some time has passed (Lazarus & Folkman, 1984; Triemer & Rau, 2001).

Negative affectivity is related to exhaustion and burnout leading to increased cardiovascular risks (Appels & Schouten, 1991; Booth-Kewley & Friedman, 1987; Landsbergis et al., 2011). Consequently, as predicted by the HOC-M, JI damages physical health through stress, negative emotional reactions and mental health impairments. Other systematic reviews/meta-analyses on the various impacts of JI have confirmed our findings of stronger and more consistent associations with mental health (Cheng & Chan, 2008; Sverke et al., 2002). One meta-analysis found that studies of JI impacts on physical health had lower associations and higher variances than studies of JI impacts on mental health: the mean correlation for JI and physical health was (k = 19) and (k = 37), for mental health (Sverke et al., 2002). Similarly, another study found a mean correlation of (k = 77) for mental health and smaller effect sizes for physical health (Cheng & Chan, 2008).

The studies we analyzed had low or medium methodological quality, which was expected given that we conducted a scoping review rather than a meta-analysis in which study quality would have been an exclusion criteria. Existing meta-analyses consider and categorize a broader variety of outcomes with a focus on attitudinal and behavioral outcomes. Our purpose, however, was to find broader evidence for the health and well-being outcomes of JI as a most important change feature (see Figure 11.1). At any rate only about a third of the studies (27%) reported Cronbach's alpha for JI and the various health measures. Often the researchers measured JI with only one item, particularly in epidemiological studies. The measurement reliability increases with the number of items, so the studies often failed to capture JI with sufficient reliability. Indeed, when JI was captured with only one item, JI had a lower impact on satisfaction and performance; thus, the type of JI measurement moderates the association of JI and job satisfaction/performance (Sverke et al., 2002). However, recent research has shown that single item measures can fully capture the construct of interest and can be as reliable as multi-item measures (Bergkvist, 2015; Bergkvist & Rossiter, 2007).

Cohen (1992) categorizes effect sizes in no effect ($0 < r \le .10$), small ($.10 < r \le .30$), medium ($.30 < r \le .50$) and large ($r > .50$), implying little meaningfulness for small effects. However, although our review and others identified small effect sizes, JI is still relevant in organizational prevention measures, given its prevalence. The 2010 European Working Condition Survey (EWCS) found that 16% of workers suffer from JI (Eurofound, 2012). With effect sizes of about (Table 11.2), there would be an attributive risk for mental health impact of PAR = .09.[1] Hence, for about 9% of EWCS participants, JI caused mental health impairment. It is therefore important to identify options, which might prevent or mitigate the well-being and health impact of JI. The following section refers to this important issue.

Practical recommendations

Our scoping review went beyond simply adding to the evidence that JI has health impacts. Instead, we also derived practical recommendations for preventing or mitigating health impairments from the included studies.

To extend these practical recommendations given by the study authors, we build on the HOC-M, which suggests that organizational demands and resources as well as individual resources may moderate the association of JI and the various well-being and health outcomes.

Recommendations for managers at the strategic and the workplace level

At the strategic level managers are advised to announce upcoming restructuring carefully and transparently. They should consider in their planning the likelihood of health-related problems such as the reactions and behaviors of people who have "survived" massive organizational downsizing ("survivor syndrome", Brockner, 1988). The HOC-M considers aspects such as cynicism about change, resistance to change or ambiguity. Carefully planned and structured communications of the change vision, its objectives and the concrete restructuring measures address these moderators and help to mitigate negative health-related outcomes (Kieselbach et al., 2009). Top managers and supervisors involved in planning and implementing restructuring processes should consider the impact of their decisions and communication for work demands and individual health and well-being. This includes conducting work design measures to recognize that restructuring processes should include work control options and work latitude (Kinnunen et al., 2010; Mohr, 2000; Schreurs et al., 2010). Strategists are advised to reassess the use of atypical work contracts such as temporary work and particularly make clear that expectations for the employees in their various contract forms are transparent (Kirves et al., 2011; Rigotti et al., 2009). Employers should invest in qualification measures to improve employability (Mohr, 2000), to assure that employees have management and supervisory social support (Mohr, 2000; Plaisier et al., 2007). Union membership has also been identified as a moderator, indicating the value of an organizational culture that allows and encourages union membership (De Cuyper, Schreurs, Vander Elst, Baillien & De Witte, 2014; Dekker & Schaufeli, 1995). Hence developing or maintaining a culture of trust should be on the top- and middle-managers' agenda. In line with the HOC-M restructuring was found to be an important determinant for JI. Hence the consideration of change-related stressors as depicted by the model should be considered when planning the course of actions for the change process (Vander Elst, Van den Broeck, De Witte, & De Cuyper, 2012, Hellgren & Sverke, 2003; Mauno, De Cuyper, Tolvanen, Kinnunen, & Mäkikangas, 2014).

It is important that expectations – for instance in terms of psychological contract contents – are clear and transparent (Kinnunen et al., 2010; De Cuyper et al., 2014). Hence also at the workplace level, direct managers should assure that their communications are transparent, fair, and inclusive (Bernhard-Oettel et al., 2013; Vander Elst et al., 2012; Mauno et al., 2014), especially for vulnerable workers, such as temporary workers or those who have undergone frequent and significant restructuring before, because the latter are at higher risk of health impact (Kivimäki et al., 2003).

Recommendations for HR measures to support employees

Perceived employability (Mohr, 2000) and perceived control (Kinnunen et al., 2010; Näswall, Sverke & Hellgren, 2005) were identified as individual moderators for the association of JI and well-being as well as health outcomes. Authors of the studies included in our review recommended to improve employability (De Cuyper, Bernhard-Oettel, Berntson, De Witte, & Alarco, 2008; De Cuyper, Mäkikangas, Kinnunen, Mauno, & De Witte, 2012; Mäkikangas, De Cuyper, Mauno, & Kinnunen, 2013). This could be achieved by investments in the Human Resource Management program and structured employee qualification and career consulting in changing organizations.

The HOC-M draws predominantly on transactional stress theory (Lazarus & Folkman, 1984) and suggests that negative health-related outcomes are mediated by primary and secondary appraisal. We suggest therefore that employees should be provided with stress prevention measures, which improve both the cognitive and affective processes related to threats and uncertainty in restructuring (De Cuyper et al., 2014; Mauno et al., 2014; Michel, Stegmaier, Meiser, & Sonntag, 2009). For employees who have evident problems in adapting to their new role, new demands etc. in restructuring and show high degrees of uncertainty individual coaching is also an option suggested by the authors of studies included in our review (De Cuyper et al., 2010; Michel et al., 2009; Richter et al., 2013).

Many of these recommendations, however, require significant time, staff and monetary resources, which causes a dilemma: organizations undertake restructuring primarily to reduce costs, e.g. through downsizing or to replace fixed by flexible costs, e.g. through outsourcing. Although restructuring predicts JI (Keim et al., 2014), the general purpose of restructuring is to make structures and processes more efficient. Thus, the dominant paradigm of drastic change in an organizational crisis is to reduce personnel costs rather than enhance human resource development, and the major focus is on implementing a new structure or dealing with technical or procedural issues rather than improving HR conditions. Hence, organizations often neglect to consider individual concerns, uncertainties, fears and resistances. Even most of the change management literature focuses on strategic interests rather than the consideration of the workforce perspective (Oreg, By, & Michel, 2013). Wilson (2010, p. 283) for instance critically concludes "It is only the interest of management that seems to be represented in much of the change management literature [. . .]. There seems to be no acknowledgement of how change represents the interest of workforce."

Change often fails, mainly because management neglects to consider individual concerns (Burnes, 2011; Kotter, 2007). The most important forces generating resistance to change are fear, uncertainty, impaired health from survivor syndrome (Brockner, 1988), lack of perceived justice (Colquitt, 2001) and lack of transparency regarding the change vision, the strategic objectives and the steps of implementation (Balogun & Hailey, 2004). Inversely, the literature commonly identifies positive forces driving change. These are (1) broad acceptance of the change vision, (2) sufficient and well-structured communication regarding the urgency of change, change-related training, change objectives and the change measures, (3) employee participation, (4) change-aligned HR programs and (5) control of success as regards change measures (Kotter, 2007; Whelan-Berry & Somerville, 2010). The recommendations coming from the change literature related to planful change are consistent with the suggestions we gathered from the studies in our scoping review.

Note

1 $PAR = \dfrac{p_{pop}(R-1)}{1 + p_{pop}(R-1)}$; $OR = exp\left(\dfrac{2r\pi}{\sqrt{3(1-r^2)}}\right)$; $R = \dfrac{OR}{1 - q(1 - OR)}$ with PAR =

Population Attributive Risk; OR = odds Ratio; R = relative Risk; P_{pop} = prevalence in population; r = correlation coefficient; q = incidence in the group of non-exposed persons; conservative estimation: 0.3

References

Allen, T. D., Freeman, D. M., Russell, J. E. A., Reizenstein, R. C., & Rentz, J. O. (2001). Survivor reactions to organizational downsizing: Does time ease the pain? *Journal of Occupational and Organizational Psychology, 74*, 145–164.

Appels, A., & Schouten, E. (1991). Burnout as a risk factor for coronary heart disease. *Behavioral Medicine, 17*, 53–59. doi:10.1080/08964289.1991.9935158

Armstrong-Stassen, M., Wagar, T. H., & Cattaneo, R. J. (2004). Work-group membership (in) stability and survivors' reactions to organizational downsizing. *Journal of Applied Social Psychology, 34*, 2023–2044.

Ashford, S. J. (1988). Individual strategies for coping with stress during organizational transitions. *The Journal of Applied Behavioral Science, 24*, 19–36. doi:10.1177/0021886388241005

Balogun, J., & Hailey, V. H. (2004). *Exploring strategic change* (2nd ed.). Harlow: Pearson Education Limited.

Bergkvist, L. (2015). Appropriate use of single-item measures is here to stay. *Marketing Letters, 26*, 245–255. doi:10.1007/s11002-014-9325-y

Bergkvist, L., & Rossiter, J. R. (2007). The predictive validity of multiple-item versus single-item measures of the same constructs. *Journal of Marketing Research, 44*, 175–184. doi:http://dx.doi.org/10.1509/jmkr.44.2.175

Bernhardt, J., & Krause, A. (2014). Flexibility, performance and perceptions of job security: A comparison of East and West German employees in standard employment relationships. *Work, Employment and Society, 28*(2), 285–304.

Bernhard-Oettel, C., De Cuyper, N., Schreurs, B., & De Witte, H. (2011). Linking job insecurity to well-being and organizational attitudes in Belgian workers: The role of security expectations and fairness. *The International Journal of Human Resource Management, 22,* 1866–1886. doi:10.1080/09585192.2011.573967

Bernhard-Oettel, C., Rigotti, T., Clinton, M., & de Jong, J. (2013). Job insecurity and well-being in the temporary workforce: Testing volition and contract expectations as boundary conditions. *European Journal of Work and Organizational Psychology, 22,* 203–217.

Blackmore, C., & Kuntz, J. R. C. (2011). Antecedents of job insecurity in restructuring organizations: An empirical investigation. *New Zealand Journal of Psychology, 40,* 7–18.

Blau, P. M. (1964). *Exchange and power in social life.* New Brunswick, NJ: Transaction Publishers.

Booth-Kewley, S., & Friedman, H. S. (1987). Psychological predictors of heart disease: A quantitative review. *Psychological Bulletin, 101,* 343.

Brockner, J. (1988). The effects of work layoffs on survivors: Research, theory, and practice. *Research in Organizational Behavior, 10,* 213–255.

Brown, A. D., & Humphreys, M. (2003). Epic and tragic tales: Making sense of change. *The Journal of Applied Behavioral Science, 39,* 121–144. doi:10.1177/0021886303255557

Burnes, B. (2011). Introduction: Why does change fail, and what can we do about it? *Journal of Change Management, 11,* 445–450. doi:10.1080/14697017.2011.630507

Campbell-Jamison, F., Worrall, L., & Cooper, C. (2001). Downsizing in Britain and its effects on survivors and their organizations. *Anxiety, Stress & Coping: An International Journal, 14*(1), 35–38.

Cartwright, S., & Schoenberg, R. (2006). Thirty years of mergers and acquisitions research: Recent advances and future opportunities. *British Journal of Management, 17,* 1–5. doi:10.1111/j.1467-8551.2006.00475.x

Cheng, G. H. L., & Chan, D. K. S. (2008). Who suffers more from job insecurity? A meta-analytic review. *Applied Psychology: An International Review, 57,* 272–303. doi:10.1111/j.1464-0597.2007.00312.x

Cohen, J. (1992). A power primer. *Psychological Bulletin, 112*(1), 155–159.

Collins, G. (2005). The gendered nature of mergers. *Gender, Work and Organization, 12,* 270–290.

Colquitt, J. A. (2001). On the dimensionality of organizational justice: A construct validation of a measure. *Journal of Applied Psychology, 86,* 386. doi:10.1037//0021-9010.86.3.386

Coyle-Shapiro, J. A.-M., & Parzefall, M.-R. (2008). Psychological contracts. In J. Barling & C. L. Cooper (Eds.), *The SAGE handbook of organizational behavior* (pp. 17–34). London: SAGE Publications.

Darr, W., & Johns, G. (2008). Work strain, health, absenteeism: A meta-analysis. *Journal of Occupational Health Psychology, 13,* 293–318. doi:10.1037/a0012639

De Cuyper, N., Bernhard-Oettel, C., Berntson, E., De Witte, H., & Alarco, B. (2008). Employability and employees' well-being: Mediation by job insecurity. *Applied Psychology: An International Review, 57,* 488–509.

De Cuyper, N., & De Witte, H. (2006). The impact of job insecurity and contract type on attitudes, well-being and behavioural reports: A psychological contract perspective. *Journal of Occupational and Organizational Psychology, 79,* 395–409. doi:10.1348/096317905X53660

De Cuyper, N., De Witte, H., Vander Elst, T., & Handaja, Y. (2010). Objective threat of unemployment and situational uncertainty during a restructuring: Associations with perceived job insecurity and strain. *Journal of Business and Psychology, 25,* 75–85. doi:10.1007/s10869-009-9128-y

De Cuyper, N., Mäkikangas, A., Kinnunen, U., Mauno, S., & Witte, H. D. (2012). Cross-lagged associations between perceived external employability, job insecurity, and exhaustion: Testing gain and loss spirals according to the conservation of resources theory. *Journal of Organizational Behavior, 33,* 770–788.

De Cuyper, N., Schreurs, B., Vander Elst, T., Baillien, E., & De Witte, H. (2014). Exemplification and perceived job insecurity: Associations with self-rated performance and emotional exhaustion. *Journal of Personnel Psychology, 13*, 1–10.

Dekker, S. W., & Schaufeli, W. B. (1995). The effects of job insecurity on psychological health and withdrawal: A longitudinal study. *Australian Psychologist, 30*, 57–63. doi:10.1080/00050069508259607

Demerouti, E., Bakker, A. B., Nachreiner, F., & Schaufeli, W. B. (2001). The job demands-resources model of burnout. *Journal of Applied Psychology, 86*, 499. doi:10.1037/0021-9010.86.3.499

De Witte, H. (1999). Job insecurity and psychological well-being: Review of the literature and exploration of some unresolved issues. *European Journal of Work and Organizational Psychology, 8*, 155–177. doi:10.1080/135943299398302

De Witte, H., De Cuyper, N., Handaja, Y., Sverke, M., Näswall, K., & Hellgren, J. (2010). Associations between quantitative and qualitative job insecurity and well-being. *International Studies of Management and Organization, 40*, 40–56. doi:10.2753/imo0020-8825400103

Eisenberger, R., Huntington, R., Hutchinson, S., & Sowa, D. (1986). Perceived organizational support. *Journal of Applied Psychology, 71*, 500–507.

Eurofound. (2012). *Fifth European working conditions survey* (Publications Office of the European Union ed., pp. 1–160). Luxembourg: European Commission.

Folkman, S., Lazarus, R. S., Gruen, R. J., & DeLongis, A. (1986). Appraisal, coping, health status, and psychological symptoms. *Journal of Personality and Social Psychology, 50*, 571. doi:10.1037/0022-3514.50.3.571

Greenberg, J. (1987). A taxonomy of organizational justice theories. *Academy of Management Review, 12*, 9–22. doi:10.2307/257990

Hanebuth, D., Meinel, M., & Fischer, J. E. (2006). Health-related quality of life, psychosocial work conditions, and absenteeism in an industrial sample of blue- and white collar employees: A comparison of potential predictors. *Journal of Occupational and Environmental Medicine, 48*, 28–37. doi:10.1097/01.jom.0000195319.24750.f8

Hartley, J., Jacobson, D., Klandermans, B., & Van Vuuren, T. (1991). *Job insecurity: Coping with jobs at risk*. London: SAGE Publications.

Heaney, C. A., Israel, B. A., & House, J. S. (1994). Chronic job insecurity among automobile workers: Effects on job satisfaction and health. *Social Science & Medicine, 38*, 1431–1437.

Hellgren, J., & Sverke, M. (2003). Does job insecurity lead to impaired well-being or vice versa? Estimation of cross-lagged effects using latent variable modelling. *Journal of Organizational Behavior, 24*, 215–236.

Hellgren, J., Sverke, M., & Isaksson, K. (1999). A two-dimensional approach to job insecurity: Consequences for employee attitudes and well-being. *European Journal of Work and Organizational Psychology, 8*, 179–195. doi:10.1080/135943299398311

Jahoda, M. (1982). *Employment and unemployment: A social-psychological analysis*. Cambridge: Cambridge University Press.

Joelson, L., & Wahlquist, L. (1987). The psychological meaning of job insecurity and job loss: Results of a longitudinal study. *Social Science & Medicine, 25*, 179–182. doi:10.1016/0277-9536(87)90386-8

Karasek, R., & Theorell, T. (1990). *Healthy work: Stress, productivity, and the reconstruction of working life*. New York: Basic Books.

Keim, A. C., Landis, R. S., Pierce, C. A., & Earnest, D. R. (2014). Why do employees worry about their jobs? A meta-analytic review of predictors of job insecurity. *Journal of Occupational Health Psychology, 19*, 269–290. doi:10.1037/a0036743

Kieselbach, T., Armgarth, E., Bagnara, S., Elo, A. L., Jefferys, S., Joling, C., . . . Widerszal-Bazyl, M. (2009). *Health in restructuring: Innovative approaches and policy recommendations (HIRES)*. Muenchen, Mering: Rainer Hampp Verlag.

Kim, T. J., & Knesebeck, O. (2015). Perceived job insecurity, unemployment and depressive symptoms: A systematic review and meta-analysis of prospective observational studies. *International Archives of Occupational Environmental Health, 89*. doi:10.1007/s00420-015-1107-1

Kinnunen, U., Mauno, S., & Siltaloppi, M. (2010). Job insecurity, recovery and well-being at work: Recovery experiences as moderators. *Economic and Industrial Democracy, 31*, 179–194. doi:http://eid.sagepub.com/archive/

Kirves, K., De Cuyper, N., Kinnunen, U., & Nätti, J. (2011). Perceived job insecurity and perceived employability in relation to temporary and permanent workers' psychological symptoms: A two samples study. *International Archives of Occupational and Environmental Health, 84*, 899–909. doi:10.1007/s00420-011-0630-y

Kivimäki, M., Vahtera, J., Elovainio, M., Pentti, J., & Virtanen, M. (2003). Human costs of organizational downsizing: Comparing health trends between leavers and stayers. *American Journal of Community Psychology, 32*, 57–67. doi:10.1023/A:1025642806557

Kivimäki, M., Vahtera, J., Pentti, J., & Ferrie, J. E. (2000). Factors underlying the effect of organisational downsizing on health of employees: Longitudinal cohort study. *BMJ, 320*, 971–975. doi:10.1136/bmj.320.7240.971

Kivimäki, M., Vahtera, J., Pentti, J., Thomson, L., Griffiths, A., & Cox, T. (2001). Downsizing, changes in work, and self-rated health of employees: A 7-year 3-wave panel study. *Anxiety, Stress and Coping, 14*, 59–73. doi:10.1080/10615800108248348

Kivimäki, M., Vahtera, J., Thompson, L., Griffiths, A., Cox, T., & Pentti, J. (1997). Psychosocial factors predicting employee sickness absence during economic decline. *Journal of Applied Psychology, 82*, 858. doi:10.1037/0021-9010.82.6.858

Köper, B., & Gerstenberg, S. (2016). *Psychische Gesundheit in der Arbeitswelt – Arbeitsplatzunsicherheit (Job Insecurity)*. Dortmund: Bundesanstalt für Arbeitsschutz und Arbeitsmedizin.

Köper, B., Seiler, K., & Beerheide, E. (2012). Organisational restructuring – status of research (Stand der Forschung). *Zeitschrift für Arbeitswissenschaften, 4*, 5–13.

Kotter, J. P. (2007). Leading change. *Harvard Business Review, 85*, 96–103.

Landsbergis, P. A., Schnall, P. L., Belkic, K. L., Baker, D., Schwartz, J. E., & Pickering, T. G. (2011). Workplace and cardiovascular disease: Relevance and potential role for occupational health psychology. In J. C. Quick & L. E. Tetrick (Eds.), *Handbook of occupational health psychology* (2nd ed., pp. 243–264). Washington, DC: American Psychological Association.

Lazarus, R. S. (2006). *Stress and emotion: A new synthesis*. New York: Springer Publishing Company.

Lazarus, R. S., & Folkman, S. (1984). *Stress, appraisal, and coping* (Vol. 1). New York: Springer-Verlag.

Lo Presti, A., & Nonnis, M. (2012). Moderated effects of job insecurity on work engagement and distress. *TPM-Testing, Psychometrics, Methodology in Applied Psychology, 19*, 97–113.

Mäkikangas, A., De Cuyper, N., Mauno, S., & Kinnunen, U. (2013). A longitudinal person-centred view on perceived employability: The role of job insecurity. *European Journal of Work and Organizational Psychology, 22*, 490–503.

Mauno, S., De Cuyper, N., Tolvanen, A., Kinnunen, U., & Mäkikangas, A. (2014). Occupational well-being as a mediator between job insecurity and turnover intention: Findings at the individual and work department levels. *European Journal of Work and Organizational Psychology, 23*, 381–393.

Mauno, S., Kinnunen, U., Mäkikangas, A., & Nätti, J. (2005). Psychological consequences of fixed-term employment and perceived job insecurity among health care staff. *European Journal of Work and Organizational Psychology, 14*, 209–237.

Melvin, M. D. (2006). The effects of outsourcing on the information technology professional: A case study. *Dissertation Abstracts International, 67*, 2085.

Michel, A., & Gonzáles-Morales, M. G. (2013). Reactions to organizational change: An integrated model of health predictors, intervening variables, and outcomes. In S. Oreg, A. Michel, & R. Todnem By (Eds.), *The psychology of organizational change* (pp. 65–91). Cambridge: Cambridge University Press.

Michel, A., Stegmaier, R., Meiser, D., & Sonntag, K. (2009). Ausgebrannt und unzufrieden? Wie Change-Charakteristika und veränderungsspezifische Arbeitsplatzunsicherheit mit emotionaler Erschöpfung, Arbeitszufriedenheit und Kündigungsabsicht zusammenhängen [Burned out and dissatisfied? How change characteristics and change-specific job insecurity are related to emotional exhaustion, job satisfaction, and turnover intentions]. *Zeitschrift für Arbeits- und Organisationspsychologie, 53*, 11–21.

Mohr, G. (2000). The changing significance of different stressors after the announcement of bankruptcy: A longitudinal investigation with special emphasis on job insecurity. *Journal of Organizational Behavior, 21*, 337–359. doi:10.1002/(SICI)1099-1379(200005)21:3<337::AID-JOB18>3.0.CO;2-G

Moore, S., Grunberg, L., & Greenberg, E. (2004). Repeated downsizing contact: The effects of similar and dissimilar layoff experiences on work and well-being outcomes. *Journal of Occupational Health Psychology, 9*, 247–257.

Moore, S., Grunberg, L., & Greenberg, E. (2006). Surviving repeated waves of organizational downsizing: The recency, duration, and order effects associated with different forms of layoff contact. *Anxiety, Stress & Coping: An International Journal, 19*, 309–329.

Morrison, E. W., & Robinson, S. L. (1997). When employees feel betrayed: A model of how psychological contract violation develops. *Academy of Management Review, 22*, 226–256. doi:10.2307/259230

Murphy, L. R., & Pepper, L. D. (2003). Effects of organizational downsizing on worker stress and health in the United States. In C. L. Peterson (Ed.), *Work stress: Studies on the context, content and outcomes of stress: A book of readings* (pp. 53–71). Amityville, NY: Baywood Publishing.

Näswall, K., Sverke, M., & Hellgren, J. (2005). The moderating role of personality characteristics on the relationship between job insecurity and strain. *Work & Stress, 19*, 37–49.

Oreg, S., By, R. T., & Michel, A. (2013). Introduction. In S. Oreg, A. Michel, & R. T. By (Eds.), *The psychology of organizational change: Viewing change from the recipients' perspective* (pp. 3–14). Cambridge: Cambridge University Press.

Paulsen, N., Callan, V. J., Grice, T. A., Rooney, D., Gallois, C., Jones, E., Jimmieson, N. L., & Bordia, P. (2005). Job uncertainty and personal control during downsizing: A comparison of survivors and victims. *Human Relations, 58*, 463–496. doi:10.1177/0018726705055033

Plaisier, I., de Bruijn, J. G. M., de Graaf, R., ten Have, M., Beekman, A. T. F., & Penninx, B. W. J. H. (2007). The contribution of working conditions and social support to the onset of depressive and anxiety disorders among male and female employees. *Social Science & Medicine, 64*, 401–410. doi:10.1016/j.socscimed.2006.09.008

Probst, T. M. (2003). Exploring employee outcomes of organizational restructuring: A Solomon four-group study. *Group & Organization Management, 28*, 416–439. doi:10.1177/1059601102250825

Probst, T. M., & Lawler, J. (2006). Cultural values as moderators of employee reactions to job insecurity: The role of individualism and collectivism. *Applied Psychology: An International Review, 55*, 234–254.

Richter, A., Näswall, K., De Cuyper, N., Sverke, M., De Witte, H., & Hellgren, J. (2013). Coping with job insecurity: Exploring effects on perceived health and organizational attitudes. *The Career Development International, 18*, 484–502.

Rigotti, T., De Cuyper, N., De Witte, H., Korek, S., & Mohr, G. (2009). Employment prospects of temporary and permanent workers: Associations with well-being and work

Organizational change and health **161**

related attitudes [Beschäftigungsaussichten von Zeitarbeitern und Festangestellten: Zusammenhänge mit Wohlbefinden und arbeitsbezogenen Einstellungen]. *Psychologie des Alltagshandelns*, *2*, 22–35.

Rigotti, T., & Otto, K. (2012). Organisationaler Wandel und die Gesundheit der Beschäftigten. *Zeitschrift für Arbeitswissenschaft*, *66*, 253–267.

Robinson, S. L. (1996). Trust and breach of the psychological contract. *Administrative Science Quarterly*, *41*, 574. doi: 10.2307/2393868

Robinson, S. L., & Morrison, E. (2000). The development of psychological contract breach and violation: A longitudinal study. *Journal of Organizational Behavior*, *21*(5), 525–546.

Rosenstiel, L. v. (2014). Die Bedeutung von Arbeit. In H. Schuler (Ed.), *Lehrbuch der Personalpsychologie* (pp. 15–42). Göttingen: Hogrefe.

Rousseau, D. M. (1989). Psychological and implied contracts in organizations. *Employee Responsibilities and Rights Journal*, *2*, 121–139. doi:10.1007/BF01384942

Schreurs, B., van Emmerik, H., Notelaers, G., & De Witte, H. (2010). Job insecurity and employee health: The buffering potential of job control and job self-efficacy. *Work & Stress*, *24*, 56–72.

Siegrist, J. (1996). Adverse health effects of high-effort/low-reward conditions. *Journal of Occupational Health Psychology*, *1*, 27–41. doi:10.1037//1076-8998.1.1.27

Struwig, F. W., & van Scheers, L. (2004). The effect of privatisation on front line employees in a service organisation. *South African Journal of Economic and Management Sciences*, *N.S.*, *7*, 1–21. doi:http://sajems.org/index.php/sajems/issue/archive

Sverke, M., Hellgren, J., & Näswall, K. (2002). No security: A meta-analysis and review of job insecurity and its consequences. *Journal of Occupational Health Psychology*, *7*, 242–264. doi:10.1037/1076-8998.7.3.242

Triemer, A., & Rau, R. (2001). *Positives Arbeitserleben: Psychophysiologische Untersuchungen zum Einfluß kognitiv-emotionaler Bewertung der Arbeitssituation auf Wohlbefinden und Gesundheit*. Bremerhaven: Wirtschaftsverlag NW Verlag für neue Wissenschaft GmbH.

Vahtera, J., Kivimäki, M., Pentti, J., Linna, A., Virtanen, M., Virtanen, P., & Ferrie, J. E. (2004). Organisational downsizing, sickness absence, and mortality: 10-town prospective cohort study. *BMJ*, *328*, 555. doi:https://doi.org/10.1136/bmj.37972.496262.0D

Vander Elst, T., Bosman, J., De Cuyper, N., Stouten, J., & De Witte, H. (2013). Does positive affect buffer the associations between job insecurity and work engagement and psychological distress? A test among South African workers. *Applied Psychology: An International Review*, *62*, 558–570. doi:10.1111/j.1464-0597.2012.00499.x

Vander Elst, T., De Cuyper, N., Baillien, E., Niesen, W., & De Witte, H. (2014). Perceived control and psychological contract breach as explanations of the relationships between job insecurity, job strain and coping reactions: Towards a theoretical integration. *Stress Health*, *32*, 100–116. doi:10.1002/smi.2584

Vander Elst, T., Van den Broeck, A., De Witte, H., & De Cuyper, N. (2012). The mediating role of frustration of psychological needs in the relationship between job insecurity and work-related well-being. *Work & Stress*, *26*(3), 252–271.

Van Knippenberg, D., & Van Leeuwen, E. (2001). Organisational identity after a merger: Sense of continuity as key. *Social Identity Processes in Organizational Contexts*, 249–264.

Weiss, H. M., & Cropanzano, R. (1996). Affective events theory: A theoretical discussion of the structure, causes and consequences of affective experiences at work. In B. M. Staw & L. L. Cummings (Eds.), *Research in organizational behaviour: An annual series of analytical essays and critical reviews* (pp. 1–74). Greenwich, CT: JAI Press.

Whelan-Berry, K. S., & Somerville, K. A. (2010). Linking change drivers and the organizational change process: A review and synthesis. *Journal of Change Management*, *10*, 175–193. doi:10.1080/14697011003795651

Wilson, F. M. (2010). *Organizational behaviour and work: A critical introduction*. Oxford: Oxford University Press.

World Health Organization. (1948). Preamble of the Constitution of the World Health Organization as adopted by the International Health Conference, New York, June 19–July 22, 1946; signed on July 22, 1946 by the representatives of 61 States (Official Record of the World Health Organization, no. 2, p. 100) and entered into force on April 7, 1948. Retrieved from http://whqlib-doc.who.int/hist/official_records/constitution.pdf

World Health Organization. (2011). *Mental health atlas 2011*. Retrieved from http://apps.who.int/iris/bitstream/10665/44697/1/9799241564359_eng.pdf

World Health Organization. Regional Office for Europe. (1984). *Health promotion: A discussion document on the concept and principles: Summary report of the Working Group on Concept and Principles of Health Promotion, Copenhagen, July 9–13, 1984*. Retrieved from http://apps.who.int/iris/bitstream/10665/107835/1/E90607.pdf

12

IMPROVING OUR UNDERSTANDING OF COLLECTIVE ATTITUDES TOWARDS CHANGE FORMATION

Gavin Schwarz and Dave Bouckenooghe

In the late 1960s, Zimbardo conducted an experiment to demonstrate how situational anonymity is related to vandalism. As part of the social experiment, he parked an old car in the Bronx, removed its license plates, put its hood up, and then watched what happened. Within minutes vandals had begun randomly plundering the "abandoned" automobile, and 24 hours later virtually everything of value had been stripped by these well-groomed and seemingly upstanding passersby (Zimbardo, 2007). This episode highlights a key context to this chapter on collective change attitudes: how individual change attitudes influence others or the process of how individual change attitude transfers to the collective. In the automobile experiment, anonymous individuals came together in different ways, joining with others in vandalizing the property. Some individuals saw others and decided to participate, several called over friends, while some came to vandalize as a group. Common to all was the way that the collective process radiated from the individual. Similarly, in this chapter we observe that in organizational change, collective attitudes are formed through the dynamics between individuals. Although several researchers have focused on how change attitudes form (Oreg & Sverdlik, 2011; Rafferty, Jimmieson, & Armenakis, 2013; Vakola, Armenakis, & Oreg, 2013) they primarily focus on individual attitude formation (Bouckenooghe, 2010; see Figure 12.1, Part A). In response, we develop a more nuanced multilevel perspective centering on the emergence of collective change attitudes.

In over five decades of research into the causes and consequences of organizational change and development (Schwarz, 2012), a myriad of factors have been mapped with an emphasis on how individual attitudes to change are formed (e.g., Piderit, 2000), adapted (e.g., Rousseau & Tijoriwala, 1999) or revised (e.g., Vakola, 2014). Although this literature has improved our understanding of how attitudes can be managed, there has been little theoretical exposition of the mechanisms that underpin the process of how individual attitudes to change merge into a collective attitude (we acknowledge the vastness of the study of attitudes but refer specifically to the principles of this merge; see Figure 12.1, Part B). This omission

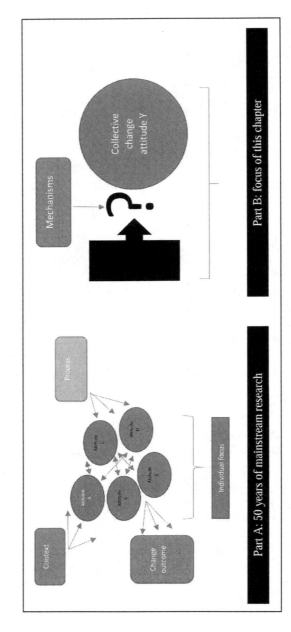

FIGURE 12.1 Framing of literature on formation of attitudes towards change

Improving our understanding **165**

is concerning given the agreed importance (Rafferty et al., 2013; Schwarz, Cummings, & Cummings, 2017) of establishing strong theoretical frameworks and the need to adopt a multilevel approach to organizational change. Developing a better understanding of this approach is key to building scholarship on change attitudes and its measurement.

In response, this chapter lays a platform for better understanding collective change attitudes by elaborating the principles of what are collective change attitudes and how these emerge from individual change attitudes. Our intention is to lay the platform for more theorizing on the process of how collective change attitudes form (for a visual representation of this theorizing, see Figures 12.2a and 12.2b). As a primary contribution, we highlight collective change attitudes and the different ways they arise, followed by an elaboration of a social network process (Barabási, 2016) explaining how collective attitudes form through the social interaction patterns between connected individuals. Establishing this collective phenomenon enables both scholar and practitioner to understand that the emergence of change attitudes is a more intricate phenomenon than simply combining or aggregating individual attitudes.

Shifting to the collective

Despite a long research tradition, there lacks detail in scholarship specific to the mechanisms underlying the movement from the individual to the group, when dealing with change attitude. Several researchers have developed aspects of this theme and consider how the dynamics between individual and contextual variables shape different change attitudes (Oreg & Sverdlik, 2011; Rafferty et al., 2013; Vakola et al., 2013). Acknowledging the importance of these perspectives, this same literature has remained silent on the transition of collective change attitudes. Defined as the amalgamation of change attitudes between individuals within a group, the collective does not process change the same way that individuals do, and instead, collective attitude is inferred from a combination of individuals.

Given established principles in literature (e.g., Michard & Bouchaud, 2005; Moussaid, Kammer, Analytis, & Neth, 2013), we argue that collective evaluation of change emerges from and is driven by the individual. Interactions *between* sets of individuals play a pivotal role in producing higher-level group attitudes. This perspective differs from more traditional consensus type theorizing on group aggregation, such as direct consensus or referent-shift consensus models (Chan, 1998), which present within-group agreement as the driver of aggregation. Core to this proposed dispersion perspective is that individuals may come together willingly to capture a collective benefit, based on the presumption that the collective good exceeds the separate gain to individuals in the group. Before delineating its underlying principles, we establish the basis of theorizing regarding the traditional consensus type perspective or sharing of attitudes toward change.

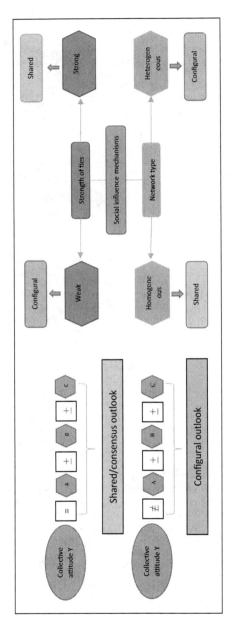

FIGURE 12.2A Collective attitude formation towards change based on social interaction between individuals

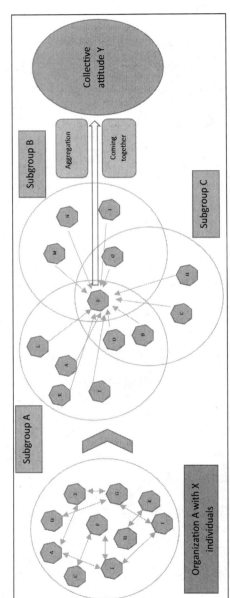

Improving our understanding **167**

Anchored in psychology research, attitude toward change is an evaluative response, suggesting that people form attitudes and then evaluate change (Lines, 2005; Petty & Wegener, 1998). That is, they do not act on change until they have decided to behave in one way or another. Accepting this conceptualization, organizational researchers have theorized organizational behavior as a manifestation of the individual, aggregating data to form a common attitude, and in doing so have given limited attention to whether distinct attributes can be ascribed to the collective when it comes to organizational change. Although we acknowledge that work on the collective phenomenon such as its reasoning, behavior and action, (e.g., Useem, 1998) is well-established in explaining consensus and disagreement, this process is under-developed in the context of change attitude.

Influenced by a growing stream of multilevel research and theorizing, it has been proposed that a work group's and an organization's change attitude emerges from the cognitions and affects of individuals that become shared through social interaction processes (e.g., Bouckenooghe, 2012). From this shared, consensus type perspective, mainstream literature has conceptualized collective attitude as the outcome of a coming together as individuals collaborate and seek out commonality or consistency with others. In this respect, scholars have argued that to theoretically justify aggregation at the group or organization level, change attitudes should be conceptualized as a collaborative state that organizational members hold in common.

Extending this outlook, we propose an alternative view that encompasses the process character of how and why collective change attitudes emerge and shift. In this way, the assumption is that collective change attitudes emerge as a reflection of a progressive adaptation of individual attitudes (rather than aggregation). This conceptualization emphasizes that differences in attitude strength (e.g., resistance and readiness to change) result in the dispersion of individual attitudes leading to a coming together, rather than treating collective attitudes towards change as having the same properties and meaning as individual change attitudes (i.e., homologous constructs). In summary, capturing this process-related character of how the dispersion of individual change attitudes form into a new collective attitude enables us to better understand how the collective responds to change. To do so, we next consider the different representations of collective attitude, followed by a brief introduction of social network theory and how it offers a conceptual platform for the mechanisms underlying this process of how collective attitude comes together.

The shared and configural nature of collective attitude

Following Weick and Roberts (1993), at the base of the formation of collective change attitudes is recognition that the collective cannot be understood without specific attention to the choices of its individual members. Central to this perspective is that individuals come together to capture a collective benefit, based on the presumption that the collective good exceeds the separate gain to individuals in the group. This coming together is forged through two properties: the shared and configural nature of adopting collective attitude.

First, and aligned with the previously mentioned mainstream approach to attitude, is a consensus type approach. This perspective relies on *shared constructs*, the characteristics that are common to individuals coming into existence when individuals form a mutual evaluation around the same views and perceptions of change. In a change context, the extent to which organizational members are ready to or have the capacity to implement a change emerges from how they share the same content and meaning associated with the change. The basic idea is that organizational change involves an individual and group sense-making process that is a product of constant human production and interaction (George & Jones, 2001). Hence, the meaning of any change event is negotiated and ultimately determined by this sharing. As McAvoy and Butler (2009) exemplify in a study of new software development, following the announcement of this change, team members responded favorably to the idea, translating to collective support for the change and smooth launch of the project. Organizational members arrive at shared beliefs and converge on a common view regarding change events by communicating with each other to make sense of their changing workplace.

This principle of sharing has resulted in the common operationalization of collective change attitudes as one of coming together: how most organizational members sharing similar attitudes have enough common ground to evolve towards a shared belief about change. Hence, collective attitudes have been operationalized as the sum of individual-level change attitudes or the outcome of within-group consensus in attitude between individuals of the collective (Chan, 1998). Underlying this shared construct perspective is the idea that members of the same group increase the likelihood that their interactions will reinforce common opinions and the development of shared collective attitudes. The greater the intensity of interdependence between groups, the stronger the identification and sharing of attitudes within the ingroup will be, whereas the hostility towards the other group will increase (Brewer, 1979).

Besides the mainstream shared attitude approach, a second way how individual change attitudes develop into a collective one is through the *configural approach*. Following this outlook, when there is no clear majority effect of in-groups, the collective attitude of the team may be different from the individual attitudes. When individuals interact with each other, over time they do not necessarily reach a consensual change attitude, even if they still come together (Olson & Zanna, 1993). This configural form of reconciliation describes the way that collective attitude emerges through a compilation process (Hofmann, 2002). With no clear homogeneity or similarity in feelings, although still coming together, the group encompasses different attitudes that contribute to the whole. A configural approach recognizes that when different organizational members vary in their initial change attitudes interaction between these individuals may lead to unique exchanges allowing for the emergence of different collective views of change. Having detailed this divergent nature of how individual attitudes can come together, we next elaborate on the mechanisms through which collective change attitudes emerge. The way collectives make sense of the change and form an attitude is a function of multiple social influence mechanisms. In what follows we draw from social network theory (Barabási, 2016; Krackhardt, 1997) and highlight how different networks and strength of ties are two key dimensions of social influence that affect the way attitudes come together (i.e., shared consensus versus configural).

Social processing: collective attitude formation

Missing in an already well-developed field is theorizing that details the character of how a collective change attitude evolves from interactions between people whether they have similar *or* different change attitudes. We propose that by recognizing attitude formation as a social response to change – part of a social system of interaction among change recipients – we can explain better how collective attitudes to change form as shared or configural constructs. Social scientists have gathered compelling evidence that attitudes spread across and between social networks of individuals, creating clusters of shared attitudes in groups or organizations (List, 2014). Yet a significant gap in change attitude research is the general failure to account for the impact of social interactions on the change process (Weiner, 2009), and more generally the impact of higher-order contextual factors on change attitude formation (Jones, Jimmieson, & Griffiths, 2005). If change attitudes are the result of cognitive and sense making processes, as both the shared and configural perspectives assert, then there is a need to account for the social processes/mechanisms that inform collective attitude formation. Drawing from Weick and Roberts (1993), meaning-making is a collective process shaped by the social context that individuals of the collective are part of. Given this framing, and its connection to emotion, actions and situation, we acknowledge Barrett's call (1995) for shifting the locus of meaning in attitude formation from the individual to the relationships between individuals. From this, and as part of an ongoing contribution to building the field, we propose a social network approach to framing the collective as a stream of research (from Barabási, 2016; Krackhardt, 1997). This response denotes the process by which individuals both synthesize and contest meanings associated with change events and their evaluation of the event. Framing collective attitude formation as a social process within social network theory, the social influence mechanisms (i.e., type of social network and strength of ties) we propose in the next section will highlight that collective attitudes do not always follow a shared/consensus approach (e.g., aggregation) but can also come together through the configural approach (see Figures 12.2a and 12.2b).

Social network theory and social influence mechanisms

Using social network theory enables us to understand the nature of interactions that form from social organization and behaviors between individuals (Krause, Croft, & James, 2007). This theory is concerned with the knowledge structures and processes that are constituted by relations between individuals, rather than by their personal attributes. Unlike attitude research focused on individuals in isolation, an individual's network position (i.e., social environment) centers social ties and context interactions, forging a collective change attitude, emerging from the resultant structured social relations. Hence, this social network underpins the structure of relationships between individual actors providing both opportunities and constraints on attitudes and their subsequent behaviors (Monge & Contractor, 2003). From this perspective, collective attitude can result from individuals holding different attitudes toward change because of the strength of social network connections. For example, an individual's network can limit their exposure to other points of view to those within their own social circle. While at other times it can expand their exposure to additional perspectives beyond this network. From this stance, all attitudes to change are social in the sense that they develop, function, and change in a reciprocal relation within a social context (Prislin & Wood, 2005).

Type of networks

An important dimension *of social influence* (and one that informs both the shared and configural nature of change attitudes) is the role that agreement (i.e., homogeneity) and disagreement (i.e., heterogeneity) play in affecting collective attitude formation. The type of social network will impact whether individuals maintain, shape or shift their change attitude to converge with the collective. In cases where individuals are part of a homogeneous network, consensus becomes the most basic outcome for members, with the collective attitude shaped by and reflective of the shared outlook. When individuals are strongly linked to a change, they are more likely to share similar experiences, and are more likely to embrace a shared collective change attitude. After all, as research on social comparison suggests, people are motivated to assess the correctness of their attitudes by comparing their attitudes to others' attitudes – especially similar others. A comparison in a homogeneous network will lead to action to reduce any discrepancies between the person and the other(s) with whom the comparison is being made, in the form of a pressure toward uniformity (Festinger, 1954). In this social environment, individuals will resolve this pressure towards uniformity by changing their attitude and moving closer to the evaluation, opinions and beliefs of the group (or conversely, removing themselves from the group). According to Wegener and Carlston (2005) the impact of social influence of homogenous networks on collective attitude formation can be explained through a need for "balance" or "congruity". Because perceived balance or congruity in attitudes feels better, people are more likely to gravitate toward agreeing with liked others or disagreeing with disliked others (Priester & Petty, 2001).

Building on the role of homogeneity on collective attitude formation, other scholars have also considered the role of disagreement in heterogeneous networks. While Marsden and Friedkin (1993) agree that attitudes can be reinforced when they match those of a comparison group, they also point out that attitude can shift continuously away from the individual as a means of resolving intra- and

Improving our understanding **171**

interpersonal conflict in a social influence context. After all, as Anderson (2008) illustrated, heterogeneous networks have a significant impact on the strength of attitudes formed at the group level, as well as the dispersion of attitudes at the individual level (reflecting the configural approach). This recognition that collective attitudes form in a social network just as much from disagreement challenges conventional views on change attitude. Specifically, the transmission of attitude to the collective via heterogeneous networks suggests that the formation of collective attitude is more unpredictable than consensus type theorizing in that it can both weaken or strengthen original beliefs, feelings and intentions towards the change.

In heterogeneous networks, instead of converging on a general attitude, exposure to multiple attitudes in the network may result in individuals resisting opposing change attitudes by formulating counter arguments held by others. This response may result in a collective change attitude that differs from others. Hence the collective change attitude formed may be less pronounced in comparison to the original attitudes held by its members (Visser & Mirabile, 2004). Besides weakening initial change attitudes heterogeneous networks can also strengthen these same attitudes, evoking a more polarized or dispersed response to change. In summary, and as illustrated in Figure 12.2b, the type of network that members of the collective are part of is an important social process mechanism that influences the way collective attitudes towards change are formed. For example, from the above theorizing we conclude that in the case of homogeneous networks, the collective attitude formed is more likely to follow the shared consensus path. In cases of heterogeneous networks, the collective attitude that is formed is more likely to follow a configural outlook.

Strength of ties

Allied to the social network impact, the strength of connections or ties among members of a network is also an important dimension in better understanding how individual attitudes transition into collective change attitudes. Both strong and weak network ties may play a role in change implementation, albeit different ones (Hansen, 1999). Strong ties, characterized by higher quantity, quality and frequency of interaction, facilitate intense and rich communication between individuals (Granovetter, 1983; Uzzi, 1996). They afford extensive interaction important for assimilating, combining and contextualizing complex knowledge associated with fundamental organizational change. Through this extensive interaction and exchange of ideas, members with strong ties are more likely to grow towards a shared collective change attitude. As Krackhardt and Stern (1988) note, successful implementation of change is a function of a collective change attitude, created by an abundance of strong ties that cut across subunit boundaries. They argue that strong interlocking ties between members of the collective will influence people's general motivations, opinions and beliefs through identities. When people identify with one another, people of the same entity are more willing to engage in cooperative and altruistic attitudes and behaviors necessary to make the change work for the organization. Put differently, strong ties ensure people will think and act in ways that are beneficial for the collective. Although strong network ties are likely to create a cohesive collective attitude, it also makes it more difficult to alter attitudes when novel, challenging ideas arise. In contrast, the power of weak ties lies in the fact that it enables exchange among a wider variety of contacts and prevents insularity through communication among groups (Hansen, 1999). In other words, through weak ties members of the collective will encounter enough diverse views that help to challenge existing beliefs and opinions, without feeling pressure to conform. Accordingly, we suggest that when members of a collective have strong network ties they are more likely to form a cohesive attitude that resembles the attitudes of the individual members (i.e., shared/consensus path). Whereas in cases of weaker network ties, the emerging collective attitude is less the result of aggregation and conformity but a coming together of diverse views, beliefs and opinions (i.e., configural path, see Figure 12.2b).

In summary, this social network based response and the mechanisms introduced (i.e., social networks and strength of ties) suggest a more dynamic, interactive account for understanding collective change attitudes. This outlook suggests that there are multiple possibilities and different paths that shape collective attitudes to emerge from the group (shared or configural), and that individuals holding different or similar attitudes still come together yet not always through a process of aggregation. Recognizing this diversity provides scope for future research on collective change attitudes.

Recommendations and implications

With this chapter, our intention was to develop a basis for more sophisticated theorizing on how collective change attitudes form. Moving away from recurrent themes in change attitude research we make several additions to organizational change literature. First, we highlight that collective attitudes are not merely a representation of when individual attitudes are shared by the group. Second, by delineating and then anchoring collective attitude formation within social network relationships, we offer organizational researchers a stepping stone that further refines our understanding of how collective change attitudes unfold from and through individual change attitudes. The implications of these additions are relevant to scholarship on collective change attitudes.

The use of social networking shows that change attitudes formed at the collective do not necessarily emerge from a linear aggregation of individual-level experiences or observations. Instead, we suggest that change attitudes can also reflect interactions between sets of individuals and produces higher-level group attitudes. This thesis offers a different way to approach the study of collective change attitude, enabling researchers to explore different ways of measuring, assessing and operationalizing collective-level representations of change attitude. Under the influence of multilevel theorizing and measurement (Kozlowski & Klein, 2000), the formulation of within-group level agreement has become a critical factor in justifying the aggregation from individual change attitudes to a collective change attitude. This mainstream consensus type approach, however, presents an important challenge for how we typically measure collective attitudes. Specifically, in justifying aggregation of individual attitudes at the collective level values of .70 have been used (e.g., for r_{wg}) as the traditional cut off point denoting high versus low values of within-group agreement (Lance, Butts, & Michels, 2006; LeBreton & Senter, 2008) – used for justifying individual attitudes as shared or not shared. Applied to a measure of collective change attitudes, proposing such a definitive boundary is tantamount to drawing a line in the sand for change researchers. Very often in studies when individual attitudes towards change at the collective level do not meet this criterion, a lack of agreement at the collective level leads to discarding this data further for multilevel analysis. Yet disagreement and further analysis of these "discarded" data may offer valuable insights of how the collective attitude is in the process of coming together.

Given our discussion and role of social context a problem with this bounded approach ("aggregation") is that it does not account for the centrality and force of unit members and their (social) influence on attitude formation. With this observation in mind, and noting the way that the process aggregates attitudes, we suggest that to establish attitude as a shared unit construct (rather than one of consensus or based on universal principles) researchers should re-evaluate having a definitive measurement criterion cut off. With a lack of robust guidelines, we suggest that organizational researchers studying change attitudes should provide evidence for aggregation using a combination of different within- and between-agreement measures (see Lebreton & Senter, 2008 for a more elaborate discussion). The basis of this suggestion is that the more (or less) these different metrics converge, the greater confidence researchers will have in treating change attitudes as a shared (or configural) construct. Also, considering Lebreton and Senter's (2008) revised standards for within-group agreement, a stricter criterion that is a minimum .90 of within-group agreement should be demonstrated before data are aggregated, because otherwise a significant but important minority group within the collective may still shape the collective attitude formation.

In conclusion, by embedding collective change attitude in shared and configural approaches, relative to social network relationships, we have offered organizational researchers an important platform to enhance our understanding of how collective change attitudes unfold. Furthermore, insights into the social network mechanisms discussed in this chapter may offer change practitioners an interesting toolkit if they want to direct the collective towards a predictable cohesive response (i.e., shared consensus attitude) or one that results from disagreement and exchange of ideas (a configural approach). For instance, a more predictable collective shared attitude will emerge when the team members are strongly connected, whereas members with weaker ties may be more useful to plant a seed in the collective mindset that challenges existing routines and beliefs. In short, we hope these recommendations, together with this theorizing, will pique continued interest to study collective change attitudes.

Reference

Anderson, M. H. (2008). Social networks and the cognitive motivation to realize network opportunities: A study of managers' information gathering behaviors. *Journal Organizational Behaviors, 29*, 51–78.

Barabási, A.-L. (2016). *Network science.* Cambridge: Cambridge University Press.

Barrett, K. C. (1995). A functionalist approach shame and guilt. In J. Tangey & K. Fisher (Eds.), *Self-conscious emotions: The psychology of shame, guilt, embarrassment, and pride* (pp. 25–63). New York: Guilford.

Bouckenooghe, D. (2010). Positioning change recipients' attitudes toward change in the organizational change literature. *Journal of Applied Behavioral Science, 46*(4), 500–531.

Bouckenooghe, D. (2012). The role of organizational politics, contextual resources, and formal communication on change recipients' commitment to change: A multilevel study. *European Journal of Work and Organizational Psychology, 21*(4), 575–602.

Brewer, M. B. (1979). In-group bias in the minimal intergroup situation: A cognitive-motivational analysis. *Psychological Bulletin, 86*(2), 307.

Chan, D. (1998). Functional relations among constructs in the same content domain at different levels of analysis: A typology of composition models. *Journal of Applied Psychology, 83*(2), 234–246.

Festinger, L. (1954). A theory of social comparison processes. *Human Relations, 7*(2), 117–140.

George, J. M., & Jones, G. R. (2001). Towards a process model of individual change in organizations. *Human Relations, 54*(4), 419–444.

Granovetter, M. (1983). The strength of weak ties: A network theory revisited. *Sociological Theory, 1*, 201–233.

Hansen, M. T. (1999). The search-transfer problem: The role of weak ties in sharing knowledge across organization subunits. *Administrative Science Quarterly, 44*(1), 82–111.

Hofmann, D. A. (2002). Issues in multilevel research: Theory development, measurement, and analysis. In S. G. Rogelberg (Ed.), *Handbook of research methods in industrial and organizational psychology* (pp. 247–274). Malden, MA: John Wiley and Sons.

Jones, R. A., Jimmieson, N. L., & Griffiths, A. (2005). The impact of organizational culture and reshaping capabilities on change implementation success: The mediating role of readiness for change. *Journal of Management Studies, 42*, 361–386.

Kozlowski, S. W., & Klein, K. J. (2000). A multilevel approach to theory and research in organizations: Contextual, temporal, and emergent processes. In K. J. Klein & S. W. Kozlowski (Eds.), *Multilevel theory, research and methods in organizations: Foundations, extensions, and new directions* (pp. 3–90). San Francisco, CA: Jossey-Bass.

Krackhardt, D. (1997). Organizational viscosity and the diffusion of controversial innovations. *Journal of Mathematical Sociology, 22*(2), 177–199.

Krackhardt, D., & Stern, R. N. (1988). Informal networks and organizational crises: An experimental simulation. *Social Psychology Quarterly,* 123–140.

Krause, J., Croft, D. P., & James, R. (2007). Social network theory in the behavioural sciences: Potential applications. *Behavioral Ecology and Sociobiology, 62*(1), 15–27.

Lance, C. E., Butts, M. M., & Michels, L. C. (2006). The sources of four commonly reported cutoff criteria what did they really say? *Organizational Research Methods, 9*(2), 202–220.

LeBreton, J. M., & Senter, J. L. (2008). Answers to 20 questions about interrater reliability and interrater agreement. *Organizational Research Methods, 11*(4), 815–852.

Lines, R. (2005). The structure and function of attitudes toward organizational change. *Human Resource Development Review, 4*(1), 8–32.

List, C. (2014). Three kinds of collective attitudes. *Erkenntnis, 79*(9), 1601–1622.

Marsden, P.V., & Friedkin, N. E. (1993). Network studies of social influence. *Sociological Methods & Research*, *22*(1), 127–151.

McAvoy, J., & Butler, T. (2009). The role of project management in ineffective decision making with agile software development projects. *European Journal of Information Systems*, *18*(4), 372–383.

Michard, Q., & Bouchaud, J.-P. (2005). Theory of collective opinion shifts: From smooth trends to abrupt swings. *The European Physical Journal B-Condensed Matter and Complex Systems*, *47*(1), 151–159.

Monge, P. R., & Contractor, N. (2003). *Theories of communication networks*. New York: Oxford University Press.

Moussaid, M., Kammer, J. E., Analytis, P. P., & Neth, H. (2013). Social influence and the collective dynamics of opinion formation. *Plos One*, *8*(11), 1–8.

Olson, J. M., & Zanna, M. P. (1993). Attitudes and attitude change. *Annual Review of Psychology*, *44*(1), 117–154.

Oreg, S., & Sverdlik, N. (2011). Ambivalence toward imposed change: The conflict between dispositional resistance to change and the orientation toward the change agent. *Journal of Applied Psychology*, *96*(2), 337.

Petty, R. F., & Wegener, D. T. (1998). Attitude change: Multiple roles for persuasion variables. In D. Gilbert, S. Fiske, & G. Lindzey (Eds.), *Handbook of social psychology* (pp. 323–390). New York: McGraw-Hill.

Piderit, S. K. (2000). Rethinking resistance and recognizing ambivalence: A multidimensional view of attitudes toward an organizational change. *Academy of Management Review*, *25*(4), 783–794.

Priester, J. R., & Petty, R. E. (2001). Extending the bases of subjective attitudinal ambivalence: Interpersonal and intrapersonal antecedents of evaluative tension. *Journal of Personality and Social Psychology*, *80*, 19–34.

Prislin, R., & Wood, W. (2005). Social influence in attitudes and attitude change. In B. T. Albarracin, B. T. Johnson, & M. P. Zanna (Eds.), *The handbook of attitudes* (pp. 672–706). Mahwah, NJ: Lawrence Erlbaum.

Rafferty, A. E., Jimmieson, N. L., & Armenakis, A. A. (2013). Change readiness: A multilevel review. *Journal of Management*, *39*(1), 110–135.

Rousseau, D. M., & Tijoriwala, S. A. (1999). What's a good reason to change? Motivated reasoning and social accounts in promoting organizational change. *Journal of Applied Psychology*, *84*(4), 514.

Schwarz, G. M. (2012). Shaking fruit out of the tree: Temporal effects and life cycle in organizational change research. *Journal of Applied Behavioral Science*, *48*(3), 342–379.

Schwarz, G. M., Cummings, C., & Cummings, T. G. (2017). Devolution of Researcher Care in Organization Studies and the Moderation of Organizational Knowledge. Academy of Management Learning & Education, 16(1), 70-83.

Useem, B. (1998). Breakdown theories of collective action. *Annual Review of Sociology*, *24*, 215–238.

Uzzi, B. (1996). The sources and consequences of embeddedness for the economic performance of organizations: The network effect. *American Sociological Review*, 674–698.

Vakola, M. (2014). What's in there for me? Individual readiness to change and the perceived impact of organizational change. *Leadership & Organization Development Journal*, *35*(3), 195–209.

Vakola, M., Armenakis, A., & Oreg, S. (2013). Reactions to organizational change from an individual-differences perspective: A review of empirical research. In S. Oreg, A. Michel, &

R. T. By (Eds.), *The psychology of organizational change: Viewing change from the employee's perspective* (pp. 95–122). Cambridge: Cambridge University Press.

Visser, P. S., & Mirabile, R. R. (2004). Attitudes in the social context: The impact of social network composition on individual-level attitude strength. *Journal of Personality and Social Psychology, 87*(6), 779–795.

Wegener, D. T., & Carlston, D. (2005). Cognitive processes in attitude formation and change. In D. Albarracin, B. T. Johnson, & M. P. Zanna (Eds.), *The handbook of attitudes* (pp. 493–542). Mahwah, NJ: Lawrence Erlbaum.

Weick, K. E., & Roberts, K. H. (1993). Collective mind in organizations: Heedful interrelating on flight decks. *Administrative Science Quarterly, 38*(3), 357–381.

Weiner, B. J. (2009). A theory of organizational readiness for change. *Implementation Science, 4*(1), 67. doi:10.1186/1748-5908-4-67

Zimbardo, P. (2007). *The Lucifer effect: Understanding how good people become evil.* New York: Random House.

INDEX

Note: Page numbers in *italic* indicate a figure and page numbers in **bold** indicate a table on the corresponding page.

ABC model 117
absenteeism 142
abusive supervision 132–134
affect 48, 54; *see also* emotions
affective events theory (AET) 144
appraisals: situation-attention-appraisal-response sequence 69, 70–71; of threat 43, 72; *see also* change appraisals
assimilation 104, 110
attentional deployment 71, 72
attitudes: collective 163–173; toward change 7, 8, 47–62, 114–115
autonomy 23, 78

bandwidth-fidelity 115
boosting hypothesis 23
boundary conditions 17, 22–23, **137**
buffer hypothesis 16, 17, 22, 23
burnout 21, 31, 36, 150, 153

career outcomes 1
CAS *see* Change Attitude Scale
CATS *see* cognitive appraisal theory of stress
CCS *see* Commitment to Change Scale
CFA *see* confirmatory factor analysis
challenge appraisals 6
change: appropriateness of 47, 54; attitudes 7, 8, 47–62, 114–115; collective attitudes toward 163–173; communication

about 19, 51, 53, 60, 86; dispositional resistance to 48, 50, 53; emotional reactions to 50; emotional responses to 48; employee involvement in 18, 51–53, 72, 81, 93–94; feelings about 67–75; frequency of 60, 131; health impacts of 142–156; measuring reactions to 114–126; participation in 51–52, 53, 72, 81; perceptions of 54, 67, 79; primary appraisal of 70; resistance to 6–8, 131, 132, 156; stress related to 22, 27, 30; support for 47; transformational 54, 58; valence of 47, 54, 58, 59; *see also* organizational change
change agents: change management by 28–29, 86, 106–107, 132; emotion contagion and 74; employees as 93; failure to consider "human factor" 78; organizational flexibility and 108–109; psychological contracts and 105, 106–107
change appraisals 9–10, 73; case study 82–87, *86*; employee outcomes and 78–87; negative 80–81; positive 6, 9, 72, 75, 80–81, 84–85; primary 70; process of 70; reappraisal 6, 71, 72, 75, 144; research on 80–81; role of 93–95; secondary 70; trust and fairness perceptions and 92–93, 96; well-being outcomes and 83–86; work engagement and 90, 93–95, 96

178 Index

Change Attitude Scale (CAS) 115
change consultation 5, 27–43; as coping resource 29–43; overview of 28–29; research on 29–43, **31**, **32**, *33*, *34*, **39**
change leadership *see* leadership
change management 7, 42; change consultation and 28–29, 43; employee perceptions of 78–79; leadership of 7–9, 85–87, 131–132; specificity for 115; toxic triangle and 132–138, **137**; *see also* change consultation
change readiness: coping resources and *49*, 60, 61; dimensions of 5, 53–54; theoretical framework for 47–48
Change Recipients' Reactions (CRRE) scale 7, 114–126; advantages of 123–124; development of 116–18; factor structure of 118–120, **119**; reliability of 120, 122–123; validity of 120, **121**, 122, 123
change-related stress 22, 27–28, 30
change self-efficacy 47
charismatic leadership 133
claiming-granting process 136–137
cognitive appraisals *3*, 6; *see also* change appraisals
cognitive appraisal theory of stress (CATS) 79–81, 144
cognitive rigidity 50
cognitive weariness 31–33, 35, **39**, *41*
collective change attitudes 163–173; formation of 169, 172–173; research on 165, 167; shared and configural nature of 167–169, 173; social network mechanisms *166*, 169–172
colluders 134, 137
Commitment to Change Scale (CCS) 120
communication: about change 19, 51, 53, 60, 86; superior-subordinate 19–20, 28–29; transparency in 155
configural approach 168–169
confirmatory factor analysis (CFA) 56
conformers 134, 136, 137
conservation of resources (COR) theory 15–17, 20–21, 35, 42, 48
control 48
convergence model 91
coping hypothesis 23
coping resources 56, 144; change readiness and *49*, 60, 61; dispositional resistance to change 48, 50, 53, 59; external 53, 59, 60, 61; generalized self-efficacy 48–49, 53, 59, 62; as predictors of change attitudes 47–62; trait positive affectivity 48, 50–51, 53, 58–59; types of 48

coping styles 20
core self-evaluations 62
CRRE *see* Change Recipients' Reactions (CRRE) scale
cultural values 134

demographics 20
discrepancy belief 47, 53–54, 60
dispositional resistance to change (DRC) 48, 50, 53, 59
distraction 71, 72
distributive justice 18
downsizing 35–41, 142, 154

EFA *see* exploratory factor analysis
emotional contagion 73
emotional reactions 6, 9, 48, 50, 67–75
emotional regulation 6, 67–68, 70–73
emotions: defined 69; negative 67–70, 72–73, 103, 115, 153; in organizational change 69–70; positive 48–52, 56, 58–61, 67, 70, 73, 103; role of 69
employee functioning 15–23
employees: attitudes toward change of 7, 8, 47–62, 114–115; autonomy of 23; change appraisals of 78–87; change perceptions of 54, 67, 79; communication with 19–20, 28–29, 51; emotional reactions to change by 67–75; health impacts of change on 142–156; impact of organizational change on 27–28, 78–87, 142–156; involvement in change process 18, 51–53, 72, 81, 93–94; measuring change reactions of 114–126; perceptions of organizational leadership of 90–97; personal resources of 5, 9, 20–22, 48, 152; psychological contracts of 102–110; redeployment of 35–41, **38**, **39**; role stressors on 27–28, 30–43; strain on 30–43; voice 109–110, **109**; well-being of 78–87
empowerment 52
exploratory factor analysis (EFA) 116
external resources 48, 53, 59–61

fairness 6, 9; change appraisals and 92–93; concept of 90; dynamics between trust and 92; employees' perceptions of 79, 84, 87, 90–97; as resource 18
followers 136
frustration 15

generalized self-efficacy (GSE) 48–49, 53, 59, 62

health impacts, of organizational change 142–156, **149**, **151**

healthy organizational change model (HOC-M) 8, 143–156, *145*

heterogeneous networks 171

high performance work practices 17–18

homogeneity 170–171

HSE Management Standards Indicator Tool 29

human resources (HR) 155–156

identity construction 136–137

ideology of hate 133

imminent threat, perception of 134

implicit followership theories (IFTs) 136, 137–138

implicit leadership theories (ILTs) 135–136, 137–138

individual-level resources 5, 9, 20–22, 48, 152

individuals: impact of organizational change on 1–4, 8–10; *see also* employees

information, about change 51, 53, 60

instability 134

internal resources 48–62

Inventory of Attitudes Toward Change (IATC) 115

job crafting 6, 10, 21–23, 90, 93–97

Job Demand-Control Model 30

job-demand resources model (JDR-M) 144

job demands 16, 78, 93–95

job demands-resources (JD-R) theory 15–17, 21–23

job insecurity 84, 86, 142–156, **151**

job resources 16, 30, 48

job satisfaction 1, 18, 21, 22

job scope 94–95

job security 147

justice: distributive 18; organizational 18; perceptions of 92; procedural 18

latent deprivation model 146

layoffs 142, 146

leader-member exchange (LMX) 20

leadership 85, 86–87; of change management 7–9, 85–87, 131–132; charismatic 133; destructive 133–138; employee perceptions of 90–97; followers and 136–137; hierarchical levels of 91, 93, 96; implicit leadership theories 135–136, 137–138; team-level resources and 19–20; transformational 19–21

meaning-making 21

mental health **149**, 150, **151**; *see also* health impacts

monitoring and blunting hypothesis 41

morale 15

narcissism 133, 134

negative emotions 6, 7, 9, 67–70, 72–73, 103, 115, 153

negative life themes 133

optimism 21

organizational change: as affective event 68–69; assessment of 4, 15; emotional reactions to 6, 9, 48, 50, 67–75; employee functioning and 15–23; failure rate 1, 2, 78; future research on 96–97; health and 142–156; heightened role demands during 27–28; holistic approach to 6, 9; impact of 1–4, *3*, 9–10, 27–28, 78–87, 142–156; leadership of 7–9, 131–132; perceptions of 79–80; psychological contracts and 102–110; resistance to 6–8, 131, 132, 156; social networks and 107–108; stress from 22, 27–28, 30; trust and fairness during 90–97; zone of negotiability during 108–110, **109**; *see also* change; change appraisals

organizational commitment 1

organizational culture 154

organizational flexibility 108–110, **109**

organizational justice 18

organizational-level resources 4, 17–19

organizational restructuring 27–43

organizational tenure 56, 58, 60

organizational trust 18–19; *see also* trust

organizational values 134

ostracism 132

perceived organizational support (POS) 19

personality traits 20

personal resources 5, 9, 20–22, 48, 152

physical health **149**, 150; *see also* health impacts

positive emotions 48–52, 56, 58–61, 67, 70, 73, 103

positive reappraisal 6, 72, 75

presenteeism 142

primary appraisal, of change 70

proactive behaviors 21–22

procedural justice 18

psychiatric morbidity 80

psychological contract (PC) theory 7, 104

180 Index

psychological contracts: breach of 103–104; changes to 104–105; defined 102; disruptions to 102, 106–110; dynamic phase model of 104, 105, 106; expectations of 154–155; obligations of 7; organizational change and 102–110; promoting functional 105
psychological needs 20
psychological resources 95

Readiness for Change Questionnaire (RCQ) 120
reappraisal 6, 71, 72, 75, 144
redeployment 35–41, **38**, **39**
resilience 18
resources: conservation of resources (COR) theory 15–17, 20–21, 35, 42, 48; coping 47–62, 144; defined 16; external 48, 53, 59, 60, 61; individual-level 5, 20–22, 48, 152; internal 48–62; job 16, 30, 48; job demands-resources (JD-R) theory 15–17, 21, 22–23; organizational-level 17–19; psychological 95; team-level 19–20
response modulation 71
response regulation 72–73
role ambiguity 5, 30, 32–33, *34*, 37, *40*, 41, *41*
role conflict 31–33, *33*, 37
role overload 30, 37
role stressors 27–28, 30–43
routine seeking 50
rumination 71, 72

SATC *see* Specific Attitude Toward Change
self-efficacy 21, 48–49, 53, 54, 58, 59, 62
self-esteem 48
shared constructs 168
short-term focus 50
situational anonymity 163
situation modification 71, 72
situation selection 71
social exchange theory 92, 144, 147
social exclusion 132
social influence 170–171
social networks 7, 9, 107–8, 169–172
social network theory 169–172

social processing 169
social supports 21–22
socioeconomic context 22–23
Specific Attitude Toward Change (SATC) 115
stress: change-related 22, 27–28, 30; cognitive appraisal theory of 79–80, 81, 144; role-related 27–28, 30–43; theories of 30, 144, 152–153, 155
superior-subordinate communication 19–20, 28–29
supervisors 91, 93; *see also* leadership
survivor syndrome 154

team change climate 20
team context 9
team-level resources 4–5, 19–20
top management 91, 93
toxic triangle 7–8, 132–138, **137**
trait positive affectivity (TPA) 48, 50–51, 53, 58–59
transactional stress theory 144, 152–153, 155
transformational change 54, 58
transformational leadership 19–21
Tripartite Attitude Model 117, 122
trust 6, 9, 78; change appraisals and 84–85, 87, 92–93; concept of 90; dynamics between fairness perceptions and 92; organizational 18–19; in organizational leadership 90–97; trickling of, between top management and supervisors 91
turnover 142

uncertainty 15, 18–19, 92
unemployment rates 22

well-being: defined 79; of employees 78–87, 142–156
work attitudes 1
work engagement 90, 93–96
work environment 27–28, 90
work intensification 28
workload 28
work practices, high performance 17–18

zone of negotiability 108–110, **109**